Power to the Players

The GameStop Phenomenon
and Why It's Only Getting Started

"Conspiracy theorists believe in a conspiracy because that is more comforting.... The truth is far more frightening. Nobody is in control."

— Alan Moore (2003)

Report: Conspiracy Theorists Now More Accurate Than Journalists

— The Babylon Bee (2021)

Rob Smat

Power to the Players

The GameStop Phenomenon
and Why It's Only Getting Started

GAUDIUM

Gaudium Publishing

Las Vegas ◊ Chicago ◊ Palm Beach

Published in the United States of America by
Histria Books
7181 N. Hualapai Way, Ste. 130-86
Las Vegas, NV 89166 U.S.A
HistriaBooks.com

Gaudium Publishing is an imprint of Histria Books. Titles published under the imprints of Histria Books are distributed worldwide.

Library of Congress Control Number: 2023938042

ISBN 978-1-59211-315-6 (hardcover)
ISBN 978-1-59211-340-8 (eBook)

Contents

For my teachers, both in the classroom and beyond.

Preface

On February 3rd, 2021, after a rollercoaster of a month spent covering r/WallStreetBets and their epic GameStop squeeze, I journaled the following: "The benefit of WSB was always its anonymity. While some users knew the identities of others, most everyone was in the dark. Any movie, TV show, or book to debut alongside this one misses out on the whole story."

After more than two years and numerous books and films about the phenomenon, those words ring truer than ever.

If you're reading this, it's for one of three reasons:

1.   You're a r/WallStreetBets or r/Superstonk ape interested in an authentic history, especially after so many attempts from the mainstream.

2.   You're interested in pop culture, finance, and/or GameStop mania.

3.   A crisis has seized financial markets, and no one seems to understand how or why.

Maybe number three hasn't happened yet. Maybe it's currently happening. Or maybe it's about to. At time of publication, no one knew what would happen because this movement was — and still is — unprecedented. And when I say unprecedented, I mean truly without precedent.

If the shit does hit the fan, analysts will ask, "How could we have seen this coming?" in the same way they did after every previous crisis. The signs were always there, just not in a way CNBC or Fox Business deemed worthy of sharing with their audiences. Instead, the collective Cassandra of traders and Redditors were called conspiracy theorists and basement dwellers, ridiculed for their hats made of tinfoil.

The implications of the GameStop phenomenon — both at its beginning in 2021 and in its dogged continuation — will be felt in markets as long as younger generations continue to replace their expiring elders. The GameStop story isn't just some stock squeeze in January 2021. It's not some guy in his basement who is not a cat. And it certainly isn't over and done with. It's just getting started.

In January 2021, after a year of lockdowns, firings, and small business failings, it didn't seem anything would draw attention to the suffering occurring in America's lower and middle classes, especially for young people.

My upbringing meant having friends spread across the socioeconomic spectrum: artists, athletes, liberal arts majors, blue-collar workers, cashiers, and med students. No matter what industry we found ourselves in during COVID, I watched as we struggled under the weight of intense pressures. While past generations had felt this due to natural forces or wartime, my generation felt it because of the actions taken by an older generation. GameStop felt like the first time we could all do something about it.

You may think you know the "GME" story by now, but I guarantee whatever you've been told, it's one of three things:

1. A story of stock prices going up and down where some people win, others lose, and it all comes to a depressing end.

2. A sterile archaeological dig performed by a bland academic who opines from a lofty ivory tower, leaving no stone unturned.

3. A third-person account with heavy reliance on interviews with five to fifteen members of an anonymous online community that numbers itself in the millions.

I'm excited to say this volume will be none of the above.

As I became enmeshed in r/WallStreetBets (WSB) in late 2020, I joined the collective hive-mind at the same moment that smear campaigns and disinformation flooded mainstream media. Covering old news, citing faulty sources, and in all honesty, failing to break through Reddit's opaque algorithm, the media had chosen to cover the Reddit vs. Wall Street story without joining the group or having any grasp of Reddit's role.

So, this book is focused on the primary source material from an amorphous yet transparent hive-mind protagonist, made possible by the first-of-its-kind social media network and technological marvel, Reddit.

I began recording WSB's every move more than a week before the media noticed what was happening. That early jump gave me access to many of the posts and comments you will read here, which no longer exist or have been totally buried. So this won't be an arm's length or narrativized history. Quite a bit occurs in real time, and almost all from primary source material.

But WSB wasn't the only party to which I'd been early. Again, months later, there was an entirely new group of Redditors that caught my attention on r/Superstonk. When that story blew up, I wasn't going to let other writers fumble it again. For all the fun of parts 1 and 2, parts 3 and 4 of this book are equally as important, if not vastly superior.

If your financial market is presently in crisis because of GameStop, part 3 proves that the Nostradamus hive-mind of r/Superstonk was there all along, futilely begging ancient Trojans to fear a monstrous wooden horse's hidden treachery.

As Mark Cuban said in his February 2nd, 2021 AMA on WSB, "It's not about being evil. It's about being lazy. [The media] write stories. They don't do much research. So you get stupid shit being stated about things they really don't understand."

This won't be a book of "stupid shit," especially since I grew up an avid Dallas Mavericks fan. This is how the GameStop movement actually happened, with as much accuracy and as little spin as possible.

I'll add a few disclaimers, though, before we begin.

I speak for myself and myself alone. I'm not FUD. I'm not a shill. And I'm certainly not the most "wrinkle-brained" ape.

In full disclosure, I hold between 10 and 99 shares of GME, what Redditors call an "XX holder." This gives me a personal connection to this saga without blinding the journalistic integrity necessary to tell its truth.

There are many mean things said about the Baby Boomer generation herein. Boomers *this* and boomers *that*. So I should note that in the same way that all gen

Z, gen X, or millennials aren't monoliths, so too, all baby boomers are not identical. The hate directed toward older generations isn't wholly deserved. There are
boomers amongst the apes, boomers rooting for the apes, and fellow gen Z's and
millennials helping the amorphous bad guys all the same.

While using a slash to signify the start of a new line is rather Shakespearean, I
frequently use it throughout when not indenting quoted information. Both Reddit
posts and tweets rely on this sort of formatting to communicate. Therefore, it's
essential to preserve it like punctuation, much like you might with "carpe diem"
poetry.

All times of day are in the Eastern Standard Time Zone unless otherwise noted.

Mentions of GameStop/GME are almost wholly used in reference to the stock
ticker, rather than the company itself. This is not a GameStop product and is not
endorsed by the company.

Much of the content herein is extremely speculative. It's the story of a movement made up of unconfirmed sources and conspiracy theories, documented not
to malign or accuse anyone, but instead so that if any or all of these theories come
to fruition, there will be "receipts."

On the topic of maligning members of this saga, if anything, the "most wanted"
list gets longer each and every day. Redditors don't point to one central villain,
rather, they continue to hunt for him, her, or it. There may be many bad actors,
or no villain at all. To that effect, this book's cover art is purely metaphorical.
Violence and harassment are never valid.

And, of course, it's not financial advice.

I just like the stock, and I hate what they've told you about it.

Part 1: Manifest Destiny

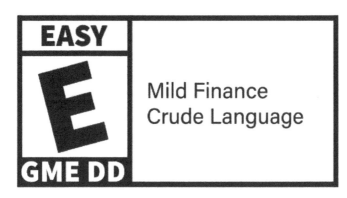

EASY

E

GME DD

Mild Finance
Crude Language

Part I: Manifest Destiny

1: Inauguration

Every four years, Americans gather around their televisions to witness a new president take office or renew his commitment to the United States. Wednesday, January 20th, 2021, was no different, as Joseph Robinette Biden took his oath of office to become our 46th commander-in-chief.

I watched the ceremony from my apartment living room. It was now about forty-four weeks since *two weeks to flatten the curve* had launched the modern pandemic era in the United States.

Surrounded by more members of the National Guard than spectators or congressmen, Biden had an audience that only the aftermath of 2020 could provide, courtesy of the capitol riots that had been borne by social sentiments on Facebook, Twitter, and Parler only two weeks prior.

"Today, we celebrate the triumph not of a candidate, but of a cause, the cause of democracy," Biden spoke, unaware that democracy was powering one of the most powerful social media engines in the history of mankind, Reddit. As his speech promised Americans security and a future amidst a global pandemic, a very different flavor of securities and futures was preparing to explode into the mainstream.

The users of r/WallStreetBets, a subreddit on the social media platform Reddit, were prepared for war with respected short seller Andrew Left — and his firm Citron Research — over a single stock ticker. On my 2012 Macbook Pro, I was refreshing web pages across Reddit throughout the afternoon, paying little attention as *Hail to the Chief* blared from the speakers of my bargain bin flatscreen.

GameStop, considered by analysts to be the dying Blockbuster of video games, had been on its last leg for over four years after a decade of industry dominance. Paying out dismal rates for used games and gaming consoles, then selling them back at little to no discount, the retail chain was bleeding as game makers moved their discs online, and gamers were fueling the transition, no longer relying on such slim margins.

Vultures were circling the dying retailer by shorting its stock, a term that had reached the mainstream thanks to Adam Mckay's *The Big Short* (2015), based on the bestseller by Michael Lewis. Even as the meteoric rise in new consoles helped rescue the company's balance sheet at the close of 2020, these short sellers were determined to see GameStop come to an end.

When WSB and Andrew Left were finished with each other, the whole world would be thoroughly re-educated on this practice of shorting, and to the benefit of anyone who still cashed *Big Short* royalty checks.

On the day of Biden's swearing-in, Andrew Left was slated to make a public presentation on his short position and calculated a GME stock price of $20. In any other moment in history, a short seller hosting a midday Twitter livestream on his bearish opinions wouldn't catapult him into immediate notoriety.

But this was no ordinary day.

From the Twitter account @CitronResearch, the firm stated in a since-deleted tweet:

"$GME still going to $20 easy but Citron does not want to go live in the middle of a historic presidential inauguration. We respect the office of presidency and ou[r] country and will not interfere with market commentary. We look forward to the livestream tom[orrow]. / Gold [sic] Bless America"

To those reading this across the financial world, glancing at their Twitter feeds as Biden laid his hand on the Bible, this was business as usual. Left was known for last-minute, loquacious, and eccentric videos on why his firm was shorting or "longing" any given stock. Freshly fifty years old and usually wearing a knit sweater over a button-down, Left had one of those faces you might be able to trust. His market advice led thousands of other traders to reconsider valuations of the companies they previously thought wise to invest in, willing to question their own judgments with Left's every tweet or retweet.

But on Reddit, a rag-tag chat room of aberrant degenerates had an entirely different reaction: they believed Left was bluffing, and they were out for blood.

And speaking of blood, Left and WSB had bad blood boiling at this juncture, thanks to not one but two prior defeats that sent WSB portfolios reeling.

WSB expected that Citron would strike, given another opportunity. Yet, to have another shot at Left so soon after their most recent beating was too good to be true. The degenerates were ready this time, and they had an even more solid case centered around GameStop, which they suspected had been as overly shorted as it was undervalued.

To the members of WSB, Left's grammatically errant livestream punt wasn't a postponement; it was a retreat by their sworn adversary.

This manic-depressive, R-rated, and wannabe-methamphetamine-fueled sub-reddit had taken its first steps in taking the almighty stock market by storm. Rather than those who owned the game and wrote the rules, WSB was a microcosm of young people with everything to gain and nothing to lose.

A time bomb had been planted at the very core of Wall Street, and years after the events of January 2021, it still ticks away.

2: The First Human Hive-Mind

June 23, 2005 | GME: $16.27

While 2020 was host to protests, insurrections, and political movements, only a select few of those efforts created what we could consider lasting generational change, and none of them utilized the brilliance of an algorithm to do it. Big money snuck into — or outright shut down — so many political movements in 2020 that I expected the same to happen with GameStop.

And that almost happened about twenty or thirty times. But an unusual blend of technology and democracy stood in the breach.

One of the greatest advantages that mankind lacks is the ability to organize in the same way that insects and flocks of birds do. I've always envied bees for this reason because they just all seem to get it. They don't get in traffic accidents or argue whether golf carts should stay on the cart path after it rains. They just get shit done for the good of the flock or colony.

Mass movements and mass hysterics are the life's study of social psychologists for this very reason, as they struggle to understand what environmental events can induce hive-mind-esque actions in mammalian species that don't possess an insect or bird's brain function.

But as of 2005, there is one place where people fly in migratory formations (digitally, at least).

Like any startup or social media company, Reddit's story started in a proverbial garage, where the site was founded on June 23, 2005, by two roommates in Massachusetts. Billed "the front page of the internet," Steve Huffman and Alexis Ohanian created Reddit after they failed to successfully start a food delivery service at a local startup incubator. Like all good entrepreneurs, the two pivoted and started from scratch. Text-based food delivery would undoubtedly have its day, but long after they had built their empire.

As Reddit's site explains, "On Reddit, there is a home for everybody and a place for everyone to dive into their interests."

Within two years, the site had taken off, and Huffman and Ohanian were able to sell it to publishing giant Condé Nast for over $10 million. They remained with the company for another few years before leaving to pursue other ventures before returning in the mid-2010s to lead the company into the present day, around when I joined in the fun.

My friend Logan recommended I get active on the site in advance of the release of my first film, *The Last Whistle*. He suggested that the site's film communities had successfully boosted the profiles of first-time filmmakers and that that algorithmic nature could help magnify awareness of the film, which had no budget for paid advertising.

In August 2019, my AMA about *The Last Whistle* would land me on r/all, the front page of Reddit, under the post, "I'm 24 and just debuted my first feature film on a budget of $100,000.... [so Ask Me Anything]," which garnered 20,000 upvotes.

Not realizing the importance of reaching r/all at the time, I stepped away from my computer midway through my AMA and walked down to the Wauwatosa Collectivo for a coffee break. When I returned, my phone had blown up with friends and acquaintances having spotted me; otherwise, I would've been none the wiser. When my 2021 Thanksgiving green bean casserole photo earned over 55,000 upvotes on r/MadeMeSmile, I was better prepared for lightning's second strike.

A site redesign in 2018 helped Reddit shed an outdated, Craigslist-style simplicity in favor of a modern social media feed, in addition to a slew of other modernizing features. This shift in the site's user interface made it easier for a newcomer like me to get the hang of things and get addicted, but not in an unhealthy way.

Reddit became the vibrant source of incredibly unique information that my mind was so hungry for, and reading the site every night helped me relax in ways that improved my mental health for months and years to come. In an age of photo apps wrecking self-image-obsessed teenagers and video sites breeding new generations of insomniacs, I expect that a social media network benefitting mental health is unique.

Nowhere else but Reddit could I find news, conspiracy theories, and Pokemon GO updates that updated on six or twelve-hour cycles. There was almost always something new, engaging, and unique happening on Reddit.

Reddit had the information I had always yearned for, a source of seemingly infinite solutions for just about any question, and with random people willing to help. When it comes to questions with complicated answers or problems with incredibly specified fixes, a simple Google search or Quora post won't always get you very far.

Even forums like those hosted by companies like Apple pale in comparison, thanks to poor site builds, outdated information, and painfully slow response times. For instance, subreddits like r/Premiere are popular for this reason amongst film editors.

Some of my most specific and helpful Reddit queries include:

December 9th, 2020: "Chuck Yeager's widow is searching for good footage of him for his upcoming end of life celebrations" — Posted to r/RBI (the Reddit Bureau of Investigation)

April 4th, 2022: "[Since] people usually grow up in places where they weren't born... who would y'all say are the celebs with El Paso origins?" — Posted to r/ElPaso

December 15th, 2021: "Kicker Kicker rankings for Week 15" — Posted to r/fantasyfootball

The Kicker Kicker ranking only had one entry, then-coach of the Jacksonville Jaguars Urban Meyer, who was on the literal heels of a report that he'd kicked the team's field goal kicker weeks prior. The "shitpost" earned me a three-day ban from r/fantasyfootball.

Some subreddits are more active, specialized, or punitive than others. Make a mistake in r/puppies, and no one will care, but say something stupid in r/politics, and you'll learn the meaning of pain as countless users pile on, protected by the veil of anonymity. And this was part of the appeal of WSB: unrivaled brutality.

Blind taste tests, blind hiring processes, and blind-anything leads one to the cream of the crop, all the way back to Abbie Conant's 1980 audition for the Munich Philharmonic Orchestra. And this is Reddit's strength: follower counts won't prevent great content from finding an audience. Anyone can post Reddit's most popular content on any day of the week.

Whereas a viral Facebook or Twitter post requires an initial follower pool to exponentially increase its popularity, viral Reddit posts all start from the same degree of anonymity, and the same chances for success or failure, no matter the user.

Reddit enlists moderators ("mods") to oversee subreddits. The best subreddits typically have the best moderation teams, who consistently curate content, and with no personal reward themselves.

No matter what subreddit you join or "lurk," Reddit does an exceptional job of not only preserving tangential commentary but also raising the profiles of the best-commented content, which is partially what makes AMAs so effective. A user might find themselves reading posts and comments both, because sometimes the latter is even funnier or more insightful than the former.

A CNBC graphic would later (struggle to) explain, "How Reddit Works: Post with more 'upvotes' featured most prominently / Most upvoted posts reach r/popular / Popular WallStreetBets posts reaching homepage."

Without "influencers," whose presences have overwhelmed other sites like Twitter or Instagram, a select few users can't dictate content to the rest of the populace. This kneecaps that ego-building facet that's made social media, politics, and just about every other public arena so insufferable and inauthentic in the years leading up to now.

For its part, Reddit does have some blemishes. For instance, the hyperpartisanship that exploded in the 2010s has infused the site, skewing even the most mundane subreddits like r/Texas much further left than the population of the state it's named after. Reddit's "News" tab, too, skews noticeably left, even more so than conservatives have accused of Facebook. Additionally, users have protested Tencent's involvement in Reddit's series D funding, described by TechCrunch as "an odd pairing between one of the architects of China's Great Firewall of censorship and one of America's most lawless free-speech forums." In 2023, Reddit would draw additional ire from their mods for changing API and third-party access policies.

Inevitably, a fringe group of gambling day traders would make their own subreddit that pushed the limits of the "virgin" sub, r/investing. Before the surge of January 2021, WSB was a subreddit just like any other, with its own lexicon, unwritten rules, and a blend of eccentric flair with calculated analysis.

The same week that Donald Trump's administration ended, and only two weeks after political divisions had come to a boiling point inside our nation's capitol, here was a hilarious, self-motivated, and entirely apolitical community that was YOLO'ing life's savings on what looked like fool's gold.

Even though I wasn't as early to the party as the more established users, I joined WSB just in time to witness the beginning of the end for Wall Street as we know it.

3: A Casino Where You Can Watch Every Hand

January 2012 | GME: $23.78

For those of us bold enough to enter a casino yet too timid to lose the pocket change we walked in with, watching others gamble takes on a pastime of its own.

Casinos have always fascinated me: you aren't allowed to snap photos of your slot machine when it makes wild noises and spits out twelve dollars, but you're encouraged to stand over a craps table loaded with tens of thousands of dollars on the line, so long as you blow on the dice when asked to.

In *Ocean's Thirteen* (2007), there's a scene where Clooney, Pitt, and the rest of their cohort tilt the tables against the house, and suddenly everyone in the casino starts to celebrate as they begin to win. Numbers displayed above each gambler's head indicated their winnings in the scene. While that experience was impossible in real life and likely against any house's rules, it was on full display every day on WSB. Online, there was nothing pejorative about lurking, and no one made you blow on their dice to do it.

Unlike the jagged peaks and valleys that WSB would exact upon markets in 2021, the subreddit had to grow steadily upward first. The subreddit's founder (and former mod), Jaime Rogozinski, is the author of a brief history titled *WallStreetBets: How Boomers Made The World's Biggest Casino For Millennials*. The book, released in early 2019, tells an entertaining story of anecdotal twists and turns as the subreddit discovered its newfound financial abilities and resolved to have fun with the powerful toys therein.

As Rogozinski notes, WSB "started... back in early 2012 as an outlet for people to share high-risk investing or trading ideas. At the time, and to this day, most investing forums online take a conservative approach and tend to focus on the market as a long-term, diversified, wealth-growing ecosystem. What I was looking for was shorter term."

It was like freshman year of college all over again. Want to start a club? All you need is four other students and a name.

Jaime couldn't find a subreddit with investing boldness, knowing that three years after the recession, bullish sentiments were back on the rise. So in the way of capitalism, and in the same way as Ohanian and Huffman, Rogozinski pivoted and started from scratch.

Membership started slowly and began to grow exponentially just before 2018, which Rogozinski correlates with the increased popularity of the trading app Robinhood. Just as young people were learning the fundamentals of market trading, their use of an app over a desktop broker permitted a more user-friendly bypass of the stalwart powers that be.

Likely, if the correlation between Robinhood members and WSB users is causal, the cycle likely flowed in both directions, whether or not millennials were introduced to the phenomenon via the trading app, Reddit, or their colleagues using either, the three factors working together became the millennial investor's toolkit.

The subreddit's description reads: "Like 4chan found a Bloomberg Terminal."

The utter entropy displayed in that simple and controlled description perfectly encapsulates WSB. Who can forget 4chan and its crucial role in radicalizing throngs of QAnon supporters? Who even knows what a Bloomberg Terminal does, besides the fact a subscription costs tens of thousands of dollars and is meant to be used exclusively by financial wizards and quants in Manhattan skyscrapers?

A number of terms emerged and rotated throughout the first decade of WSB, none so important as "Diamond Hands," or rock-hard hands that hold an asset and keep it for good. Diamond hands, for all its worth, is likely the sagest sentiment of the group, as advisors show time and time again that the more trades a user makes, the worse off their position tends to be.

Diamond hands is opposite to "Paper Hands," the punitive term for those who choose to split ways with their stock holding and selling, thereby lowering the price and sabotaging the "bulls" in favor of personal gain.

Rocket emojis were used to indicate a stock price mooning in the earliest days of the GameStop squeeze. The practice faded away after a time, but in the beginning, rocket emojis had to be used in excess if a poster had any hope of topping the WSB feed. Emoji rockets incidentally point at a 45-degree angle rightward, the same direction as a surging stock ticker.

Due Diligence is abbreviated as "DD," and the DD generated on WSB isn't what you can find in textbooks or on Investopedia for the most part. WSB DD was another significant part of the subreddit in the pre-GameStop days because the best DD's required a dynamic blend of ingenuity, gambling, and incredibly dark, sometimes sinister, comedy.

To round out the lexicon of WSB terms of late 2020 and early 2021, most of which aren't in use anymore, there's:

FD: According to WSB's own definition, "To buy an FD is to buy a weekly option that is so fucking retarded it might just work." Weeklies and even dailies became inexpensive favorites of traders looking to capitalize on market volatility with no trading commissions.

Gay Bears: In a world where stonks only go up, anyone in the opposite direction is a gay (rainbow emoji) bear, despite research showing that short selling can actually have beneficial results on accurately pricing a stock.

Tendies: On a lifehack Reddit post of yore, a user noted that their local Wendy's had a single burger for $5.99, but sold their 2 for $5 with the very same sandwich included. The post suggested that by utilizing the 2 for $5 deal, one could procure the same burger, yet save a dollar and add chicken "tendies" (i.e., chicken tenders) to the mix. So tendies, in this case, reflect a bonus on top of savings, which surprisingly describes stock market dividend/profit mindsets with brilliant simplicity.

My Wife's Boyfriend: Users will mention their wives' boyfriends frequently as benefactors of their trading wizardry as if somehow the WSB users' brilliance makes them excellent husbands and providers but terrible lovers, for which they accept help all too gladly. (Or worse, WSB members have performed so poorly in their Wall Street Bets that their wives must seek financial support from said boyfriends.)

Once you acclimate to the harsh temperature of WSB, the memes, emojis, and more displayed the pristine recklessness that resembled an entire generation coming to terms with the question, "If the deck is stacked against us, why play the game by its rules?"

The answer, according to WSB: "It's food stamps or lambos."

The YOLO thought-terminating concept that fueled harmless pre-teen fun in the early 2010s seeped into WSB in the same decade, giving the subreddit its first real taste of casino dynamics. According to Rogozinski's book, a user named u/TossOut5451 announced that they were planning to YOLO upwards of $170,000 into two separate ETFs, both pegged to the S&P 500 and both leveraged at 3x.

Akin to a big player tossing a heavy chip onto a roulette table, suddenly others wanted to join TossOut's luck, or at least feel like they could be a part of something so risky and exciting. But TossOut's bet took years to materialize. As the 2010s turned to the 2020s, traders had far less capital to work with, suppressed by pandemic lockdowns, student debt, and shrinking homeownership compared to prior generations.

To someone who only has $100 to work with, it can take multiple lucky breaks in a row to reach life-changing profits. Hence, the appeal of quick wins over longer-term YOLOs.

In 2018, u/aiandi posted, "Td ameritrade made me apply to enable options. I told them I have no experience, make less than $20K per year, and have 5 dependents. They approved options trading immediately."

Nothing reeks worse of financial collapse than reading those 29 poorly capitalized words and 1 acronym.

As January 2021 came to its close, I only had a badly dated online financial literacy course under my belt, so stocks and cryptocurrencies felt fairly advanced. But to understand this sub, I knew I had to attempt at least one option trade so I wouldn't sound ridiculous documenting so many of them here. It was hard to work up the nerve to trade my first option, unlike WSB's best and brightest. Knowing the money power involved, I feared what I didn't know.

What finally pushed me over the edge was Nancy Pelosi, or more specifically, her husband, Paul. On July 18th, 2022, Marketwatch reported, "Nancy Pelosi's husband buys millions of dollars' worth of Nvidia stock ahead of vote on chip-manufacturing bill."

Social media accounts that had popped up to track Pelosi's trades were all over the news, and it was one of the most interesting instances of political stock trading yet, and by the spouse of a lifetime public servant presently worth over $100 million.

That potential conflict of interest pissed me off enough to finally buy my first call.

Even a year after the mania of January 2021, I found similarly loose restrictions around options trading, and not with WSB's favorite trading app Robinhood, but instead with an industry leader, who approved me for level 1 options trading hours after rejecting me. (I was not given a reason for either.)

I am Schrödinger's cat of options traders: both approved and denied.

Even with marked improvements to user interface, the broker's options trading process was opaque and difficult to use. Their online options trading guides, circa July 2022, were also disorganized and referred users to the site's hard-to-find Options Trading add-on to their downloadable trading program.

Yet, the ability to trade options was monumental, even in a time of relative market stability as of mid-2022, during that summer's "bull trap." There was something different about dealing in hundreds of shares tied to contracts rather than just buying and holding. Luckily, I was only putting a handful of dollars on options that Fidelity warned had 2% probabilities. Were I to actually YOLO thousands or tens of thousands of dollars on such contracts, the addiction would be admittedly difficult to break.

My first two calls ended in total losses of $40, my third call brought me a profit of $60, and my fourth options trade returned a 3,600% profit of over a thousand dollars.

I've never felt so stupid, staring at my phone in an Aldi parking lot while my groceries melted in the trunk, struggling through the same broker menus over and over again with fifteen minutes until market close, unable to sell the option I had worked so hard to diamond hand into the money. I didn't know nearly enough about what had just happened, except that it had undoubtedly happened.

In the pursuit of further profit, masked by democratized finance, the lowest rungs of blue-collar workers, college students, and young professionals were in control of buying power far beyond their current or future means to pay such debts off, should the price not hit targets.

WSB metamorphosed from a zoo for wild trades into an incubator for collaborative and magnified trading under these new tools. But these new tools didn't suddenly appear on users' "boomer broker accounts" overnight. They came from an entirely new invention, the (now infamous) stock trading app Robinhood.

Robinhood will never not be the source of controversy, but there are some critical aspects to the app, which would later be dubbed, RobbingDaHood.

In 2013, Vladimir Tenev and Baiju Bhatt founded the app-based trading company designed to disrupt the brokerage industry. After years of building brokerage computers, they were determined to provide cost-effective trading without minimums or broker fees, and by doing so, forced the entire industry to take shape around such an idea.

For other brokers, it seemed far more important to retain retail traders with free trades than to let them go to a competitor. The Robinhood app catered almost exclusively to young people and almost undoubtedly gamified the stock market with a series of sounds, images, and easy-to-follow numbers that any slot machine architect might recognize.

But Robinhood never seemed solid to me, especially when market volatility had caused the app to pause or become inactive, and on more than one occasion.

Jacobinmag chided in 2021, "What Robinhood has accomplished thus far is not the democratization of finance, but an extreme redistribution of risk. The working class of this country will not be bailed out when the market, inevitably, crashes again. In the meantime, this Robinhood shouldn't be confused with the one who robbed the rich to serve the poor."

The instability of Silicon Valley and the gamification of financial instruments weren't invented by Robinhood, to be fair. And the latter is one of the first aspects of Robinhood that the mainstream sources get wrong. In an age where attention spans have never been more valuable to developers, everything in the life of a young person is gamified.

Do you ever have to physically drag funds from one brightly colored region to another when banking on your phone? Are credit card rewards displayed on a digital game board as you make your way from meaningless reward to meaningless reward? Does your car insurance account sound like a Nintendo console?

I can't escape the shit. It's everywhere! I don't need a Pavlovian reward for transferring twelve dollars into my checking account to keep it from overdrafting.

Robinhood pushed gamification to its limits, but young users especially have the awareness that they're stepping into a gamified space, and they never needed lawmakers to protect them from that. Robinhood's "about" section states plainly that their goal is "a more human way to learn" and to provide "truly digestible financial news."

And who can forget, Robinhood tweeted in March 2016, "Let the people trade." That of course would return to haunt them five years later.

My second hesitation with Robinhood was a fear of its ease. I never wanted my stock trading to be easy or more gamified than it already was, with red and green lines flashing everywhere. Especially when handling financial instruments that can multiply buying power, a single typo could make my wife dump me for one of those boyfriends everyone was always talking about.

In June of 2020, Forbes reported on Robinhood's darkest day: "20-year old Alex Kearns, a Robinhood customer, died by suicide and in a note to his family, cited $730,000 losses on the trading platform."

While Robinhood's motives are opaque, a culture of pushing innovation past its limits in order to gain subscribers had pervaded Silicon Valley as the region boomed. Many companies assumed the most acceptable loss leader is that which leads to a new subscriber. If something is free, then you are the product.

A lawsuit settlement at the end of 2020 cost Robinhood upwards of $65 million, an outward sign of trouble to the industry, but a financial nothingburger for a company worth over $11 billion at the time.

WSB and Robinhood were inevitable bedfellows from the start, and their connection would have spawned a series of interesting results sooner or later. But thanks to the events of the year 2020, that timeline was catalyzed.

4: Four Trillion Dollars to Flatten the Curve

March 2020 | GME: Avg. $4.00

While 2020 will extend its slimy tentacles into every facet of the following decade, the GameStop squeeze was one of 2020's most immediate descendants, but not for the reasons the experts and academics have claimed.

One of the most pervasive and infuriating stereotypes of COVID and meme mania posited that young people had too much time, too much money, and too little to do with those, so they tried to blow up the stock market for a quick buck:

"The absurdist morality tale over the unalienable right of Redditors to pump up meme stocks and punish Wall Street has obscured a more reckless impulse." — Bloomberg

"How a massive 'dumb money' movement sent GameStop's stock price soaring and cost Wall Street millions" — Toronto Star

"Men Staring at Bitcoin, GME Prices Aren't Having Enough Sex, Says NYU Prof" — Decrypt

Even as recently as September 2022, Redditors were inflamed by the final words of Netflix's trailer for their documentary, Eat The Rich: "YOLO, you know? Let's destroy the economy." The stereotype never slowed.

But let's not get ahead of ourselves.

In the final days of 2019, COVID began to spread across China. The first place I would find out about it? Reddit.

First came the lab leak theories. Then came theories about vaccine micro-chipping. Finally, the conspiracists settled for vaccine passports and their fears of The Great Reset. The subreddit r/conspiracy, in particular, held this wealth of mostly unhealthy speculation, no longer dominated by the alien and bigfoot types, which I missed dearly.

In the same way I later found WSB for its investment moonshots, I began seeking less reputable news for "informational" moonshots, if that makes any sense. I knew almost all of the theories wouldn't be true in the end, but that was for me to research and try to confirm. It had worked in my fantasy football league, so why couldn't it work for a pandemic too?

In the end, I would have an early jump on COVID before the general public realized the true danger of the disease. I was able to go to stores and get supplies before the mobs rushed the shelves, and I even came one click away from buying a pack of N-95 masks. (I didn't have $50 to gamble on PPE at the time, unfortunately.)

On February 7th, 2020, an entire month before lockdowns would start in America, a since-deleted user shared, "4Chan user finds evidence of over 13k bodies being burned in an empty field outside of Wuhan," to almost 25,000 upvotes. That post was the high watermark of speculation that had built on the subreddit since as far back as December 2019, which ran directly against mainstream media sources like the L.A. Times, whose article and since-edited headline two weeks prior would age like milk:

"Should you panic about the coronavirus from China? Experts say no."

"'Don't panic unless you're paid to panic,' said Brandon Brown, an epidemiologist at UC Riverside who has studied many deadly outbreaks…. Fortunately, the virus seems to cause only minor symptoms — such as fever and difficulty with breathing — in people who are young and healthy. Most of the 41 deaths tied to the coronavirus to date have been in people who were at least 50 years old with underlying medical problems or weakened immune systems, Chinese officials said. 'We don't have evidence yet to suggest this is any more virulent than the flu you see in the U.S. each year,' said… Dr. Michael Mina."

In truth, the severity of COVID landed somewhere between apocalyptic mass graves and the common flu, especially after the first and most potent strains ran their course. Sometimes finding the truth was a game of averages.

Despite having tracked the virus for so long on Reddit, my first view of it came from a skyscraper in downtown San Francisco, where on March 9th, 2020, I had a front-row seat as the Carnival Cruise liner, containing a COVID outbreak, arrived in Oakland harbor. The other members of my film shoot chuckled as I stopped our production in its tracks to make everyone watch.

That was also the day I discovered the dark underbelly of the COVID response and the part of COVID that I believe most influenced meme stock mania: the fleecing of the young to the benefit of the old.

I found myself next door to a neighboring company's meeting as they debated their policy prior to the stay-at-home orders. The meeting was fairly cordial as the group slow-walked a plan, one which the rapid spread of COVID would later render irrelevant.

The group, composed of middle-aged men and women, planned for the office to begin a hybrid period, where the professionals would be able to work from home, and their assistants would run their desks in person. It didn't take long for one of the executives to ask, "What about the assistants? This mean they still have to come in? Shouldn't they be able to work from home too?"

I'll never forget an executive scoffing, "Assistants don't get to stay home."

The tea leaves from that moment were clear: the working class was in for a crunch, not just in high-level meetings at e-commerce companies, grocery chains, hospitals, or the meatpacking industry, but also in the halls of Congress.

Republicans bolstered corporate interests, while Democrats protected their poorest constituents. This resulted in Pandemic Paycheck Protection "loans," cruise and airline industry bailouts, and widespread unemployment benefits on the backs of multiple Congressional acts that spent more borrowed money than the country could fathom.

So what would happen to working people wasn't clear once their $600 stimulus checks ran out. These workers were told hazard pay was a bridge too far while their unemployed peers made up to 80% of their own salaries. Instead, essential workers were greeted with balloon arches ordered from e-commerce giants and flyovers by the Thunderbirds.

HEROES WORK HERE! See them? They're the ones with the bloodshot eyes trapped behind our newly installed fiberglass barriers.

While wealth inequality had reared its ugly head for years, COVID initially allowed Americans to build savings at a rate not seen in the previous decade. But it was soon evident that this was a bait-and-switch, as the richest members of society doubled their wealth in the same time period, while inflation later ate those gains in savings for the rest.

Congress borrowed twice the country's GDP, to the tune of over six trillion dollars in just 2020 alone. With an average congressional age of around sixty years old, this meant saddling future generations with trillions in debt that most or all of these congressmen wouldn't survive to pay down.

Universities required their students to engage with their studies remotely, forcibly moving them out of their dormitories and enduring canceled graduation ceremonies. Then, in the Fall, those same students would cough up no less than 100% of their ballooning tuition for a year of virtual college.

So the short squeeze wasn't about generational divides or even grievances against billionaires. It was about having a voice. It was about agency in a world that gave young people less and less while increasingly robbing them of their futures.

When someone has agency, they don't have to carry credit card debt. When someone has agency, they can buy a home rather than rent it from a corporate landlord for a higher monthly payment than a mortgage might cost. When someone has agency, they don't feel trapped.

An Esquire article released during the events of January 2021 discussed this deftly:

"Throughout this pandemic, as the American economy contracted and hemorrhaged jobs and millions upon millions of citizens were immiserated, the… market powered upwards unabated…. The equities markets are simply detached from the actual economy and any kind of value in the real world. It's a playground for speculators, a casino that runs on… nonsense and hype. If the stock market was ever really a mechanism for companies to raise funds for expanding their operations or research and development, it ain't that anymore."

When you ensnare a young working class with loans, low wages, healthcare debt, and low homeownership, why would they work 40+ hour weeks to still lose that game? COVID made this fact all too apparent and gave young people the introspection to realize they'd been duped.

For this reason, video games had a surge in popularity for generations millennial and "Z." In a world where young people lack agency, they can always come home to a game where there are rules that each player must follow. In a game, people can live in a world where they will explore quests and side quests that increase their understanding of themselves and their purpose rather than punch the clock for the benefit of a corporate entity to keep food on the table in between periods of sleep.

Admittedly, there is a lot of truth to the mainstream case for COVID lockdowns causing meme mania. But the unemployed trader with too much money in his pocket comes up short under a microscope. It's the "what" without a "why."

Even if the demographic was accurate, why didn't the great Wall Street uprising happen during the summer of protest in 2020? Why would such a movement wait until January, when the world was reopening, and restrictions were being lifted en masse? And why wouldn't the movement wait another month for the next round of stimulus checks to arrive?

Because it wasn't about the checks. It was about power, power to the players.

5: I Like the Stock

February 2002 | GME: $9.63

GameStop was listed in its current form as GME on the New York Stock Exchange on February 13, 2002. It was owned at the time by Barnes&Noble and was soon to be its own independent company.

The video game retailer would expand into numerous other countries, spin-off brands like ThinkGeek and Cricket Wireless, and draw teenagers, children, and young adults through its front doors on a daily basis.

While frequently compared to Blockbuster and sharing some characteristics with the now-extinct rental giant, GameStop was more used car dealership than rental company.

Can't afford the new Halo at sticker price? One could grab a used disc at GameStop for a 15% discount. Want to buy a new gaming console but don't have all the money? I could sell my existing console for pennies on the dollar and cover the deficit.

Got three hours to kill at a mall filled with clothing stores and department stores that make you want to blow your eleven-year-old brains all over the sticky tile floors? Get Mom to drop you off in GameStop, and blister your grubby pre-teen fingers playing their demo console with whatever other degenerates have been dropped off for free mall daycare.

GameStop was always a place where you could find "a" video game at a price you could afford or maybe a game that you hadn't heard of before. But if you were headed to GameStop for a specific item, the chances at a sizable discount weren't always worth the gas to get you there.

GameStop knew exactly what their games were worth and that you didn't have other choices when it came to used game resellers. What was I going to do? Wait two weeks for a copy of Halo to arrive from eBay? This was long before the dawn of 2-day shipping.

A large chart of in-demand games stood over GameStop counters at one point in time, a pre-teen's first commodity market. Managers would update their asking prices for Halo 3: ODST on the whiteboard segments, and as soon as you were ready to part with that poor excuse for an expansion game, the price would magically have dropped to less than the plastic on which the disc was printed. (Guh.)

We youngsters learned supply and demand and didn't even realize it at the time. (And I still have that copy of *Halo 3: ODST* if anyone can beat GameStop's best offer.)

It's amazing now to think back on a time when discs and cartridges had the value they did at GameStop. While these products still hold value in the gaming world, especially as games get larger and hard drive space struggles to catch up, many gamers have gone disc-less.

The fact that millennials, in particular, determined GameStop was worth their investment is also mystifying to some degree. The same goes for the other stock that benefitted from meme mania — AMC Theaters. Both companies had nickeled and dimed their customers into their own free market downfalls, and in 2021 those same customers opted to pull them back from the brink.

As games moved online, the gamers grew up, and as the console release slowed, GameStop began to lose its grip on success sometime around the mid-2010s. And, considering this was the era of Robinhood's rise, it was entirely possible the boys had just found new toys.

GameStop in 2020 was a different place than ever before. I found myself in Milwaukee's Mayfair Mall on more than one occasion, still buying the occasional disc at a discount. Each time I went into the store, the number of choices continued to decline. No longer were there bins of $5 video games worth digging through. The selections on the walls were mostly for consoles I hadn't yet purchased. And the influx of collectible bobbleheads, gaming memorabilia, and overpriced accessories never appealed to me in the slightest.

As of 2022, there were still occasional miniature bargain bins, in all fairness to GameStop. In 2023, GameStop announced a return to retro consoles and games as well.

When I heard the company was considering a life insurance policy, I wasn't surprised. At the time, I probably would have compared it to Blockbuster. It was time for GameStop to transition into a digital marketplace, bring customers back to their stores for things they would go out to purchase again, and survive by means of will and determination.

GameStop had served its generational purpose. But that generation wasn't ready for that lifeblood to coagulate.

While the WSB attention circling around the GME was derived from a number of DDs, the decision to go to war over the company's stock ticker had a great deal to do with this permanence in the generational headspaces of young people.

How many Blockbusters did we have left in our lives, and what would millennials give just to see a Blockbuster back on their block again?

Whether it's the blue and yellow rental outlet, or its cousins, Borders Books, ToysRUs, CircuitCity, or RadioShack, their disappearances without so much as a headstone to mark the endorphin rush they once gave us in our young lives were now replaced by soulless mega-corporations Walmart, Amazon, and Target.

While millennials were digging GameStop's grave, failing to pass on the virtues of split-screen games to their Gen Z counterparts, the short seller presence was just as responsible. Here was a(n) (assumed) baby boomer or two, who was ready to short the last existing vestige of millennial identity, driving it into the grave even faster and profiting from its suffocation.

Having had all sorts of things taken from us up until now, it was only to be expected that that sort of confrontational approach would beget trades based on emotion rather than logic, something that WSB knew well, thanks to its years of YOLOs.

Rogozinski notes in his book, "In the end, it doesn't matter. These things are fun, the prices move up and down a lot, and the grown-ups have most likely figured it all out. Besides, just because things are complicated, doesn't mean they pose systemic risks."

So the strange attachment to GameStop, and a drive to save its existence, is very much the story of Dr. Frankenstein ("The Modern Prometheus"). Desperate to create life by any means necessary, Frankenstein makes a creature so hideous that he can't be brought to accept its existence, shunning it into an exile that haunts Frankenstein and impacts the innocent lives of those around him.

Fortunately, WSB wasn't about to reanimate a totally deceased object. Instead, they were following the winds of smarter and more storied investors like Ryan Cohen and Michael Burry. Once shorts joined those two, all the pieces were in place.

6: Long Odds and Deep Value

December 2008 | GME: Avg. $20.00

Short sellers entered the mainstream after identifying key weak points in loose lending practices ahead of 2008's financial crisis. Their shorts against mortgage-backed securities were met with laughter at the institutions granting them the loans, and their successes catapulted them into the tens and hundreds of millions of dollars in profit at the same time that people lost houses and taxpayers were forced to fund bailouts.

Dr. Michael Burry became the most iconic part of *The Big Short*'s 2015 film adaptation, portrayed by Christian Bale. With a blend of brilliance, risk, and eccentricity, Bale brought Burry to life on the big screen under the skillful direction of Adam Mckay. WSB rapidly elected Bale's Burry as one of their favorite mascots.

Margot Robie makes a cameo in *The Big Short*, where, from a bathtub, the actress makes a fairly excellent summation of Burry's short.

"Our friend, Michael Burry, found out that these mortgage bonds that were supposedly 65% AAA [rated], were actually just, mostly, full of shit. So now, he's going to short the bonds, which means to bet against. Got it? Good... Now, fuck off."

While shorting stocks and buying put options aren't quite as simple as Robie makes them seem, that's all anyone needed to know about shorts at the time. Any short stands to make 100% of their bet, but their risk of loss is technically infinite by comparison, which inverts the model typically held by "longs." And sometimes, the longs can hit back against the shorts.

Another of WSB's favorite mantras? *All shorts are just future buyers.*

But short sellers are rarely considered the good guys. In the same way that WSB hated the bears, short sellers usually get in the way of *stonks go up.*

Furthermore, fellow Big Short short-seller Ben Rickert (played by Brad Pitt) made clear the short's dilemma in the film: "If we're right, people lose homes. People lose jobs. People lose retirement savings, people lose pensions. You know what I hate about fucking banking? It reduces people to numbers. Here's a number: every 1% unemployment goes up, 40,000 people die."

Despite the debated accuracy of that statistic, this notion stands at the core of any short seller: if you're betting against something that people rely on economically, it can be morally zero-sum.

In the same year as the Great Recession's beginning, a less memorable market event laid the foundation for the very goal that WSB pursued, adding a new acronym to the subreddit's lexicon.

MOASS (The Mother of All Short Squeezes) is a reference to the 2008 short squeeze of Volkswagen, in which parent company Porsche bought back enough available shares that short sellers were potentially unable to cover their losses, and to a theoretically infinite degree. When the shorts realized they were trapped, Volkswagen's stock price surged over 1,000 euros, for a moment becoming the world's most valuable company.

Inspired by MOASS, WSB started to do the math on GameStop.

On April 19th, 2020, while you, I, and everyone else I know was scrambling from grocery store to grocery store searching for anything resembling a roll of toilet paper, user u/ShadowDude9 was buying over 400 shares of GameStop stock with the announcement, "I just bought some GME, and it just might be autistic enough to work."

ShadowDude laid out 10 reasons for his bullish bet, the ninth of which was that the amount of shorted shares outpaced the number of available shares, "meaning potential for a short squeeze." ShadowDude even added a disclaimer that "I am feeling confident about this, but I am also an autist and a retard so I wouldn't be surprised if I somehow lose all of my money."

But ShadowDude wasn't as misguided as he thought. The SEC's GameStop report, released after the sneeze, said, "When examining short interest as a percent of shares outstanding, GME is the only stock that staff observed as having short interest of more than shares outstanding in January 2021."

The case for combatting GME's shorts reappears on WSB in June 2020, when the rest of us were either enjoying a recently lifted COVID quarantine or about to find ourselves in a brand new one. u/AccioSwaggio wrote a DD titled, "A Guide to finding next potential candidate for Bankruptcy (and existing ones)."

One commenter mocked the hard work with, "Dude, you[']re posting Finviz here like 99% of the autists would ever know how to even navigate past the front splash page. Fuck that, open Robinhood, stock going up? Calls. Stock going down? Puts. Can't go tits up. Get rich."

Though Reddit makes it difficult for one user to rise above the rest, and with good reason, occasionally, there are users who are upvoted to eventual positions of power.

Keith Gill, AKA Roaring Kitty on Twitter and YouTube, and u/DeepFuck- ingValue (DFV) on Reddit, would be the individual spark to light the fire on GME. DFV's GameStop play didn't start as a short squeeze, though. Now, the GME DD suddenly had a left hook.

Before DFV, WSB did have celebrities over the years, chief among them "pharma bro" Martin Shkreli (u/martinshkreli), who was a mod for some time. But DFV would become possibly the most famous Redditor[1] in the site's history, and practically overnight.

On August 29th, 2019, u/ithrowthisoneawaylol posted, "I took a look at GameStop after reading that… Mark Cuban bought 3% of the company on the basis that their balance sheet was 'actually good' and that new disk-based consoles

---

[1] u/maxwellhill would eventually tie for this honor, assuming the user's true identity could ever be confirmed. Redditors continue to insist that this user is no other than Ghislaine Maxwell, the notorious madame who coordinated underage escorts for the notorious Jeffrey Epstein. The account went silent the day Maxwell was arrested, and has remained silent ever since.

would 'extend their life significantly.' Am I missing something here? .... Do they count all of those ps2 sleeves floating around in the ocean? Admittedly, I haven't bought a disk since Left 4 Dead came out because I'm not a retard[,] but convince me not to dump my IRA on GME leaps."

While comments to this post varied in degrees of knowledgeable information, most dabbled in bearish opinions of GameStop, just like any other rational person at this time would have agreed. But in a comment recorded to their account, no longer visible in this feed, u/DeepFuckingValue joined the thread, simply commenting: "ffs" (for fuck's sake).

What "ffs" referred to is anyone's guess, but DFV had made his quiet entry into the subreddit without pomp or circumstance and, eleven months later, would make his first YouTube video on the topic.

Before he would be anointed the messiah, DFV would first be ridiculed. In early September 2019, he made his first full post to the sub:

"Hey Burry thanks a lot for jacking up my cost basis"

"Hey Burry" of course, referred to Michael Burry, whose fund Scion Asset Management was now poised to enter an even more public gambit. While Burry was mentioned in the credits of *The Big Short* as being a new short investor in water suppliers, of all things, the motion picture failed to predict his entry into the GameStop saga, and as a "long," which would take place only three years after the film's debut.

On August 19th, 2019, Scion published a letter to GameStop management, urging them to take advantage of a low stock price that was over-leveraged by short sellers. When it came to short squeezing, Burry seems to be the first whale to have raised his hand, and far ahead of the curve:

"Given recent GameStop common stock prices under $4 per share, we must re-state that GameStop complete the remaining $237,600,000 share repurchase at once and with urgency.... The unfortunate reality is that Amazon, not GameStop, bought Twitch in 2014. Instead, in 2014, GameStop started buying wireless store assets. And in 2017, Amazon, not GameStop, bought GameSparks — while less than a year ago GameStop reversed course and sold its wireless store assets.... Notably, as of July 31st, 2019, Bloomberg reports short interest in GameStop stock at 57,226,706 shares — this is about 63% of the 90,268,940 outstanding GameStop shares at last report. We submit that when share prices are at or near all-time lows and more than 60% of the shares are shorted despite cash levels much higher than the current market capitalization, lack of faith in management's capital allocation is the default conclusion."

While this insight was all too true, especially the parts about the missed acquisitions that would have boosted GameStop's synergistic gaming profile sky high, Burry's public plea meant that others started to notice a diamond in the rough, i.e., deep value.

The consensus remained that GameStop was dead in the water, especially if they were going to ignore one of their largest shareholders' unsolicited advice. Otherwise, why would GameStop be shorted by half of its total shares? Such a number was boggling.

u/cmcewen commented on DFV's post, "DFV should sell now. 85% of wallstreet [sic] thinks they're gonna miss earnings.... Plus either way their [sic] gonna be negative earnings for [the] first time. That ship is sinking".

And cmcewen's advice won the day. While 28 upvotes on a comment doesn't necessarily make for gangbusters karma on Reddit, it's certainly enough to win the top spot on a post lacking attention and beat DFV's reply to the same post in the process, something that would happen much less frequently as time went on.

DFV retorted, "Or I could keep the position and earn a lot more money."

A user who's since deleted their account (most likely out of shame, financial regret, or both) suggested with a scoff and to a petty 13 upvotes, "Or you could lose ~50K. Jesus Christ, you people are degenerates."

From there, the comments thread only punishes DFV further. Being downvoted to zero or negatives for defending his GME position and trust in deep value, DFV's debut on WSB was a bloody one.

DFV's comments are short and to the point on this day in particular. Whereas other users might dabble across their interests on other subreddits, DFV only posts and comments within WSB. There's an undeniable bullishness to his curt confidence:

"You're imputing thoughts; I haven't taken any victory laps."

"My thesis aligns with Burry's — I recommend checking out his letter to the board."

"Why is it stupid?" (in response to u/Zer033x's "So stupid and autistic but it worked").

The cream of the crop comes toward the bottom of this post's comment feed, where u/j1187064 lambasts, "Oh, right, I forgot shit companies that are barely clinging to life always come roaring back from terrible earnings. / RemindMe! 15 months and 29 days from now to confirm this idiot lost it all / That better, bb?"

For DFV's first post to be so heavily lambasted to the point that a RemindMe! got added to the mix is just too good to be true. DFV simply replied, likely grinning at the chat room cruelties, "Yes. Thanks!"

After posting his YOLO update for November 2019, showing a return near 4x, as his $50,000 call had jumped the $200,000 mark, December brought a bad earnings call for GME, causing the stock to fall nearly 20%.

u/imin2deep was the first to ruffle DFV's feathers, with a since-deleted Dec. 10th post titled: "GME Get Fucking Serious You Austist's [sic]." Apparently removed for objections to the crude content, the results can still be found in DFV's comment history.

u/WannaBeGoodBoy and u/exidis got rolling with the following back-and-forth:

"Isn't there a guy with a bunch of call options on $GME?"

"Hi"

"not you, some guy has over $100,000 on GME calls."

"Holy shit and I thought I was dumb."

"...maybe he sold some or all, I don't know."

"Hopefully he sold."

And, of course, DFV appeared like Beetlejuice: "I haven't."

Further down a similar post titled "$GME EARNINGS THREAD" and authored by u/Not_reddits, users began to wonder where the big spender was hiding out. One of the top comments went to u/WallStreetBitch, who posted with a link back to DFV's earlier posts, "RIP that GME yolo guy."

Stepping into the line of fire, DFV told the group that he was still, in fact, holding the YOLO, meriting the reply "username checks out" amid a flurry of ridicule from the rest.

But with alarming prescience for late 2019, DFV ended the thread with his most RemindMe! — worthy moment yet, predicting with blinding accuracy that only a time traveler could pull off: "January 2021."

The GME YOLO updates picked up following DFV's entries. Despite showing a loss that landed DFV under $100,000 in December, his April 2020 GME YOLO post showed a return to plus-$200,000 territory.

The final vote of confidence in GME arrived in the early Fall of 2020 when wunderkind investor Ryan Cohen disclosed a new and major stake in GameStop, even higher than Burry's (by some users' estimates).

u/DeepFuckingValue was waiting in the wings as u/airdoon considered what the new presence of Cohen could mean for the stock, posting on September 1st:

"GME short squeeze"

"This is for all of you who think GME is the next Blockbuster because games are going digital (that's why no one buys physical gift cards anymore, right?). The same geniuses throwing money at companies with no revenue, colors, and companies whose competitors are giving out their products for free. I'm going to tell you why everyone is buying it and why u/DeepFuckingValue is going to be a multi-millionaire soon.

GME is one of the most shorted stocks: 55M of 65M shares are short, including >100% of float. Based on average volume, it would take … over 15 days for all shorts to cover. More than half the shorts entered under $7 and are now taking losses. A price spike from good news could trigger a short squeeze and force shorts to cover at higher and higher prices."

DFV replied with only a gif from the show *BILLIONS*, captioned, "That's a good point."

On November 27th, 2020, while the rest of us were beginning to develop post-Thanksgiving coughs, u/Thereian had spotted the point of intersection between DFV and the MOASS seekers: "Our beloved GameStop is perfectly set up for its short squeeze, more than ever. We've got the Cohen letters, the outstanding PS5 and Xbox sales, and of course the upcoming earnings call where they will update us on their share buyback program."

And there it was in plain sight. DFV's gospel of deep value was totally married to the short squeezers. No longer would they stand apart.

"WSB has legitimately scared the institutional investors with… shenanigans. Just look at the jokes about the CNBC rants. These people are starting to appreciate the power of the idiots on here, and it will scare them shitless when GME gets hyped again."

The shenanigans Thereian mentions are in regard to Palantir, whose stock price had risen and fallen sharply in the days prior. The catalyst? A short seller with a fund named after citrus fruit, and a rather squeezable citrus fruit at that.

7: The Bostoner's Massacres

December 2020 | GME: $14.75

When it came to GameStop short sellers, I hadn't heard of Melvin Capital or most of the other publicly (or suspected) short hedge funds.

But I had heard of Andrew Left.

My second exposure to short sellers after *The Big Short* was through Alex Gibney's Netflix documentary series *Dirty Money* (2018), a now multi-season show about white-collar fraud and more. I watch just about everything Gibney has a hand in creating, and this series was no different. Thanks to Netflix's large and young viewership, *Dirty Money* was likely the second entry in short seller lore for many others like me.

The third episode of season one is titled "Drug Short," directed by Erin Lee Carr. The episode documents pharmaceutical company Valeant's meteoric rise during the 2010s, becoming one of the country's largest pharma companies. While telling a different story to stockholders, the episode details the allegedly monopolistic strategy deployed by the company's newest executive, as they repeatedly bought smaller companies with the alleged goal of increasing prices on the drugs they now owned. As profits soared, the episode further alleges that Valeant cut research and development in favor of purchasing even more companies, further boosting their drug prices, and on and on.

While Fahmi Quadir stars, John Hempton and Andrew Left round out the cast of short seller subjects. Quadir reenacts her spyworks in the episode, riding around in blacked-out SUVs, watching employees enter and exit the office park, and using binoculars to track what is happening inside. Quadir, Left, and Hempton make unlikely bedfellows who all unite under the same cause: rooting out fraud in America's largest corporations.

In 2016, Valeant's gambit buckled, facing regulatory pressure for its role in ballooning drug prices. Massive funds that bet on the company groaned as their shares plummeted by more than half, enriching the gamble taken by the public shorts and unnamed others.

So why Andrew Left was about to step into the story of GameStop is anybody's guess.

Left's fund, Citron Research, is "Voted #1 Activist Short Seller by The Activist Investing Annual Review 2019," according to its website circa January 2021:

"With over 150 reports, Citron has amassed a track record identifying fraud and terminal business models second to none among any published source. The goal of this website is and has always been to provide truthful information in an entertaining format to the investing public."

Citron's site delineates the fund's many successes in shorting history over its 17-year history and leaves out gaps in the record that Redditors frequently sought out.

In a post from 2017, u/HellspawnedJawa shared their YOLO purchase of $1,000 in Shopify shares and $4,000 in Veritone shares, titled, 'I call this trading strategy "Shitron Research."' u/someroastedbeef opined, "invers[ing] andrew left is a legitimate strategy."

While Veritone was a good shorting opportunity, Shopify would soar more than fifteen times its average price within just a few years. That track record didn't phase Left, whose site goes on to claim, "Since 2001, more than 50 companies covered by Citron Research have become targets of regulatory interventions." The four most recent on Citron's site, as of January 2021, are as follows:

Basin Water Inc.	NASDAQ: BWTR	Apr. 7, 2008	SEC charge of accounting fraud; Chapter 11 bankruptcy declared
Arthrocare Corp.	NASDAQ: ARTC	May 2, 2008	Department of Justice charge of fraud for two former executives

| Ener1 Inc. | NASDAQ: HEV | July 16, 2008 | Chapter 11 bankruptcy declared Jan. 30, 2012 |
| Amedisys Inc. | NASDAQ: AMED | Aug. 12, 2008 | Department of Justice investigation |

Left promoted his Wikipedia profile on the site before the GameStop event. It's on this page that his short sale of China's Evergrande behemoth is mentioned. His disclosures merited severe legal backlash from Asian financial institutions, forcing him off the Hong Kong Stock Exchange for five years. Evergrande would fall victim to its business practices and later default, to Left's credit.

But like WSB's grudge against the true inequities of COVID, authors and journalists have failed to get the Citron Research chapter of this story right.

First, authors have suggested that Left's fumble was just another inevitable step in the slow march toward GameStop's pressure cooker explosion a month later. Instead, GameStop was a brick of plastic explosives in need of ignition. It was a movement that demanded a catalyst, and couldn't just be accidentally set off. While Redditors maligned hedge fund head Gabe Plotkin, he, like most in his tier of the industry, remained out of the public spotlight. Alternatively, Left seemed more than willing to engage with users directly.

Second, Spencer Jakab, in particular, posits that Andrew Left's public short of Chinese electric car maker Nio Inc. was parallel with his short against Palantir and that the combination of those two made users angry enough to finally want revenge. But this chronology also misses the mark and reflects the challenge of trying to accurately chronicle events on Reddit when writing from the distant future. Left took three distinct swipes at WSB, each bolder than the one before, and the first two potentially bringing him winnings at the group's expense.

Finally, some have suggested that Left's decision to short Nio, Palantir, and then GameStop was coincidental. But Left shorted Nio in mid-November, Palantir in late November, and GameStop in December/January. For this reason, users were convinced he was in ongoing combat with them.

There was a rhyme and reason to which stocks became "meme stocks" before and concurrent with GME. Young traders are smart enough to recognize the following pieces of deductive reasoning: tech stocks are worth more than ever, tech stocks started as small players in a big field, and tech stocks are hard to buy in wealth-creating quantities if they're still traded at such high price-to-earnings ratios.

This was the rationale behind Nio (NIO) and Palantir (PLTR). The since-suspended account u/Arkislife posted in August 2020, "NIO DD," in which they volunteered, "Some fucking kid in Nigeria or some shit built a Lamborghini out of cardboard [and] he has a more viable prototype than anything the autistic fucks at [electric car maker] NKLA have ever ventured to make. / How the fuck does NKLA have a higher market cap than NIO?"

The commenters agreed wholeheartedly. And Nio's price would double between then and early November 2020, when WSB's hype over the company was in full force, sending the price over $30.

On the morning of Friday, November 13th, 2020, Reuters and others reported, "Nio stock falls after short-seller Citron targets EV maker." With the snap of a finger, a statement from Citron's site sent the stock reeling, plunging from highs of $54.20 to as low as $40.55 that day.

WSB was introduced to Left, and they wouldn't soon forget him as they turned to Palantir Technologies (PLTR). Unlike Nio's long history as a stock exchange listing, Palantir had only debuted on the NYSE in September of 2020, with a stock price hovering around $10.

Within the same Fall 2020 period, Palantir grew in popularity amongst WSB users. While there weren't many notable PLTR YOLOs, the stock was getting chatter that couldn't be found elsewhere on the web, much of which was deemed politically incorrect due to the company's connections to Trump administration contracts. But just as WSB has no respect for political correctness, they similarly don't care for politics or any kind of ethics for that matter.

One of the earliest and most highly upvoted posts came from u/nafizzaki on November 15th, 2020, only two days after Citron socked NIO: "Load up on PLTR, big time, or you will miss it."

u/NelsonTingles agreed, "Our intel bois used Palantir on deployment to let me know there was a possible threat of taking indirect fire and VBIEDs [vehicle borne explosives], while I was taking indirect fire and VBIEDs ...PLTR to 500 [dollars]".

Only on Reddit can you get stock tips from soldiers whose lives were saved by the very technologies that a company created.

On Monday, November 16th, u/TopPackage opened the new trading week with the hubristic "PLTR is the new NIO, and Citron Proof," claiming that CEO Peter Thiel could "litigate Citron out of existence."

On November 21st, u/AlexPie2 followed up with the most convincing entry of all, titled "My PLTR DD":

"For all of you visual learners out there, think of PLTR like pregnancy. A typical human fetus at 30 weeks weighs roughly 3 pounds. At 36 weeks the fetus will grow to 6 pounds. This is 100% growth rate just like what PLTR is currently doing and will continue to do based off of my technical analysis and different lines within my chart."

u/a941guy replied, "All this talk about PLTR DD and unborn fetuses and then [he] posts TSLA positions. Retarded autist at work here. I'm in."

With one point of inflection, Palantir's stock price accelerated from $10 to almost $30 between November 10th and 24th, 2020, its first and largest jump in its short lifetime as a publicly traded company.

Whether or not that jump was solely due to WSB isn't clear, but the two correlated, meaning that even if WSB inspired market motion without providing the capital to do so, WSB was suddenly in the driver's seat, a star-maker the likes of which we hadn't seen since the days of early 80s Steven Spielberg.

Andrew Left could have acted quietly, but instead, the Citron Twitter account chose to strike at the jugular the morning of November 27th, 2020:

"What a run the past month for all. But as traders looking for short exposure, $PLTR is no longer a stock but a full casino. Does not take a ball of crystal to know this will fall back to Arda. Shorting with a $20... target."

The tweet, which garnered much attention around a Citron account with hundreds of thousands of followers, sent the price of PLTR reeling. PLTR fell a whopping 25% or more, from a high of around $29 on November 24th to a low of approximately $21 only a few days later on the 1st of December, wiping out almost half the gains that WSB had rallied around during the month previous.

Even the mainstream "full of noobs" subreddit r/stocks agreed, as seen in this post from u/hockeyfun1:

"Was wondering why my PLTR dropped and I saw Citron is at it again. / 'No longer a stock but a full casino'.... go to hell Citron. I hope they get burned bad with more people buying the dip."

Where was the 'activism' in Left's two shorts? NIO and PLTR weren't Valeant in any shape or form. There was an educated case to make that Palantir was undervalued, but that's not an activist's short, is it?

Maybe Left just couldn't resist. I don't know.

While conspiracy theorists debated Left's patterns on WSB, one thing was certain: a pattern had started to develop.

WSB was a swarming hornet's nest for the first time. In broad daylight, two impressive deep-value plays by the sub had been beaten deftly by someone with a larger following and more credence.

u/GushingGranny1 touted the battle flags with "Citron Research and Andrew Left Should Be WSB Public Enemy #1:"

"Left just launched a full scale attack on the WSB community. This morning Citron Research just committed the HIGHEST level of heresy by giving PLTR a measly $20 [price target] and stating they are now short the stock saying it is akin to a casino than a 'real company' or whatever the fuck that means.... Send this gay bear back to its fuck den. Teach him what it means to fuck with each and every one of us and our tendies."

Granny's post received 3,800 upvotes, a whopping result in the normally under-the-radar stonk casino. The comment stream filled with members bemoaning Left's lack of transparency or disclosures of personal positions beside the obvious: Left was well aware that a single tweet could move markets.

PLTR would recover slowly as users bought the ("fucking") dip, and the price leveled out once more. If Andrew Left ever came back for thirds, WSB would be ready.

8: A WSB Tea Party

December 21st, 2020 | GME: $15.80

Drag racers have more lights than average motorists.

In place of red, yellow, and green, the NHRA hosts what's known as the Christmas Tree, which hosts seven tiers of lights with four colors. From top to bottom, the lights are colorless for pre-staged and staged indicators, amber for the three countdown bulbs, green for go, and red for disqualification by a false start.

WSB wasn't waiting at a standard red light. The hive-mind was pre-staged, slowly approaching the starting line while making final deposits to their broker accounts as PLTR and NIO recovered from prior month lows.

On December 21st, the staged light appeared. Ryan Cohen's RC Ventures filed their 13D form, revealing a stake in GameStop that had increased to 9.001 million shares, a possible reference to a popular *Dragonball* meme.

The filing ignited speculation that Cohen's hostile GME takeover was now underway.

What you need to know about Cohen is what WSB knew about Cohen at the time, and that wasn't his life's story, which could take up its own chapter. Two ideas floated to the surface:

1. Cohen built Chewy, a massive e-commerce platform that disrupted an industry but had to sell before realizing his enterprise's full potential.

2. Cohen was young and wasn't born into a silver spoon family. He knew firsthand both intergenerational and working-class struggles.

Cohen and DFV shared a lot of traits in their online personae, which made them both fodder for tinfoil types. Cohen was incredibly cryptic in his public statements and kept everyone on their toes as a result, closely following his every move and trying to decipher the number 741.

u/GushingGranny1 posted just after the 13D was released,

"As we are now all aware, Papa Cohen, through RC Ventures, just increased his stake…. What's more is the statement RC issued in light of the news.

'RC Ventures intends to continue to engage in discussions with GameStop's board "regarding means to drive stockholder value, including through changes to the composition of the board and other corporate governance enhancements."

While RC Ventures "desires to come to an amicable resolution with [GameStop, it] will not hesitate to take any actions that it believes are necessary to protect the best interests of all stockholders."'

Read between the fucking lines people. Cohen is preparing his war chest to bring GME to the 21st century. A hostile takeover is imminent. Get in the GME rocket now or be left behind. / Tl;dr: Get in pussies."

Two days later, as the share price surged past $20, another fiery post splashed across WSB feeds. While it's usually sensible to follow posts with the pertinent comments, I'll instead prelude the post's top comment, courtesy of u/fatstanley14: "Holy shit I read a few paragraphs and anyone with this much enthusiasm means GME will literally NEVER go tits up."

User u/CPTHubbard, a self-ascribed "Acidhead GME investor and sometimes rant-er," was the author, and the 6,126 word manifesto would garner 1.5k upvotes, titled "GME Short Squeeze and Ryan Cohen DD for Jim Cramer, The (Man)Child Who Wandered Into the Middle of the GME-Cohen Movie."

The obsession with Cramer wasn't just CPTHubbard's. Thanks to Hollywood's need for quick market analysis cutaways in film and television since as far back as 2008, when he cameoed in Marvel's *Iron Man*, Cramer was the voice of markets to younger generations, and many didn't fully realize he was there for (mostly) entertainment purposes.

"Now Jim, from what I've been able to gather, you and your Boomer stocks and your Hot Manic Takes don't always get a lot of love around here. But that's not all your fault, Jim. The Paste-Eating Rocket Kids are often good for a solid meme (FYI: it's pronounced "Mee-Mee." Feel free to use that on air without ver-ifying). But the Rocket Kids can be a dense bunch and they're also often one click away from Total Financial Ruin (Quick shout out to SPCE: Pleas fly again).[2] So you have to dig a bit in here to separate the wheat from the chaff, as someone like you actually says in real life."

Cramer wasn't going to embrace WSB immediately and would later criticize the subreddit, but in early January, he was ambivalent on the topic and stood mostly alone in recognizing something had been brewing.

While Cramer would hedge his bets repeatedly and eventually abandon then re-adopt his millennial lost children, any Cramer boost spurned the subreddit on-ward, and let the users feel they had a foothold with someone who knew a thing or two. In a way not seen since the days of Edward R. Murrow or Walter Cronkite, a newsman's opinion on a cause brought legitimacy rather than hollow punditry.

Hubbard continues,

"Those of us who watched your teevee clips last week where you reference your interest in WSB know that you, Jim Cramer, might be one of the Olds, but that you also Think Young(TM). So we're going to do our best to help your young-thinkin' brain find the Needle In the Haystack here so you can get All Your Ducks In a Row on GME. Because we know that you're a long way from being Put Out to Pasture, and though you may be an out-of-touch millionaire prone to facile yammering, we now like you here, Jim — simply because you mentioned us and that made us blush a bit since we're needy Millennials who just want our Boomer mommies and daddies to Tell Us They're Proud of Us.

So even though the Paste-Eating Rocket Kids here are often Buying A Pig in a Poke (Christ, please do not ever say that or the kids' Mee-Mees are gonna fuck

---

[2] "Pleas fly again" is a reference to the frequent prayer muttered by WSB devotees, who most likely bought at the peak of a given stock just before it deflated. This was an apt prayer for SPCE, which is Richard Branson's Virgin Galactic.

you up), we appreciate you recognizing that, every now and then, there's something worth paying attention to over in this weird little pocket of the Interwebs.... I'll tell you one thing: the GME play is a lot more fucking fun. Life in a pandemic is boring, but here in this weird WSB place, these kids like fun."

Young people everywhere on December 23rd, 2020, were sitting around the yearly re-broadcast of *Seinfeld*'s Festivus episode, forced to discuss their dismal futures with well-endowed family members, urging them to find unpaid internships for the fields they had failed to succeed in for half a decade, use their non-existent savings to open a high yield savings account that didn't exist anymore, and to find romantic partners that could lead to marriage and cohabitation within a six to nine-month window during a pandemic.

It's no wonder that Hubbard got so many eyes on the diatribe, which went on to summate the growing mass of DD in favor of GME:

"Part 1: GME's Bonkers-Ass Short Interest.... the short interest here is batshit insane. And not just your garden variety Boomer in Rolled Up Sleeves Ranting About Buying Estee Lauder While Hitting Buttons On The Beep-Bop-Boop Machine kind of insanity. Really and truly fucking nuts....there are currently more shares short than the total number of shares outstanding. And when factoring in the institutional and insider ownership, the total short percentage of float is nearly 300%."

"Part 2**: GameStop Isn't Going Bankrupt and People Actually Want to Buy Shit There... Blockbuster was nearly $1 Billion in debt and missing debt payments left and right when it was delisted way back in 2010. That was also when there was a bit of a credit crunch, if you recall, right after that whole Housing Crash Unpleasantness that you saw coming from a mile away and from which you made hundreds of millions of dollars due to your contrarian foresight — I'm sorry, I'm clearly confusing you with Christian Bale starring as Dr. Michael Burry, weirdo head of Scion Asset Management, which also holds about 1.4M shares of GME (You really gotta start looking into this stuff, Jim. This story is made for TV, man — and you Boomers were raised by TV and you turned out TV!)."

"I think 2020 GameStop at the precipice of a new console cycle might be in a bit of a better position than, say, 2010 Blockbuster relying on the latest Adam Sandler release to lift its sagging rental numbers. But I don't know. Millions of people don't watch my show looking for Candid Analysis from me and my folksy man-of-the-people-lookin' rolled-up sleeves."

"#3… Ryan Cohen is still the single largest shareholder of GME with 9,001,000 shares in total, taking his ownership of GME above the 10% threshold from 9.98% to 12.9%. And so he apparently thinks that the floor for his investment is $16.02 per share. Is he still buying? We'll know soon. But yesterday seemed like a little taste of what it might look like if a large buyer steps in to prevent short sellers from manipulating all of my nervous little Rocket Children here and their delicate little paper hands."

Hubbard follows that with several articles touting Cohen's many successes in recent years, admitting he may have to name his own children "Ryan Fucking Cohen" after all the acclaim he's creating.

He wouldn't be alone in doing so, especially once 2021 really got going and turned to 2022.

"Part 4: A Return to Our Short-Squeeze-to-Da-Moon Discussion: Who's Side Are You Fucking On, Jim? … Those of us who truly do Think Young(TM) have a hard time understanding… at what point in your lives do you Boomers all finally come to realize that it's maybe time to stop playing the game like you have been? What point do you finally have enough where doing the right thing matters more than getting paid?"

At last, GameStop wasn't about short squeezing, wealth, or wannabe market wizards. GME was a way to strike at the hearts of the "olds" sitting on every last penny while a strong middle class shrunk rapidly for the kids and their kids if they ever had any.

Hubbard concludes, "In conclusion […] This is a shitpost and is only to be used as investment and life advice for Mr. Jim Cramer, Esq." On Festivus 2020, Hubbard managed to unite logos, ethos, and pathos in a way that anyone with time to read his entire manifesto would immediately cling to.

In the same way that Americans swapped Christmas trees for Festivus poles in the days following December 23rd, so too we return to the NHRA Christmas tree analogy. After the stage indicator lights on the NHRA tree, three amber lights illuminate, indicating countdown. The countdown process lasts for just four-tenths of a second before the green light illuminates and the race starts. For this reason, timing those tenths of a second is one of the skills that most drag racers practice.

"If one waits for green, he's late," says Autoweek.

The short squeeze countdown lights illuminated on January 11th, 2021. For those who wanted to be part of the race, this would be their final chance. They had to hit the gas now, before green appeared.

"GameStop Soars With Activist Ryan Cohen Gaining Board Seats… Company reports 4.8% rise in holiday same-store sales," announced Bloomberg.

It only took two days for the stock price to double again, reaching intraday highs of over $38 on January 13th. DFV posted to over 50k upvotes, "GME YOLO update — Jan 13 2021," showing an account value of over $5 million.

u/ameyzingg commented, "Cramer is going to go crazy when he finds out about this."

Almost two weeks after the capitol riots, the news was starting to slow down. The top story on my feed that week was by @1NewsNZ, "Australian authorities investigate the case of 'Joe the Pigeon' who could be euthanized after being deemed a biosecurity risk."

GameStop was the only show in town.

The stock's share volume on January 13th exceeded 144 million shares, meaning every available share (estimated to be around 50 million in total) was traded an average of three times in just one day. Considering many of the HODLers weren't selling yet, and others were simply transacting their shares once, the turnover behind the scenes had reached a new level. Just like GameStop's plus-100% short interest, the numbers made less sense with each passing moment.

By January 15th, Andrew Left had released a (since-deleted) video about insurance company Lemonade. He would end the clip with advice he would soon fail to follow as his gaze shifted toward GME in the fast-approaching holiday-abbreviated workweek: "Have a great weekend, and cautious investing to all."

Left didn't realize the Christmas tree lights were about to turn bright green, and he would be the one to flip that switch.

9: One if by tweet, Two if by Stream

January 19th, 2021 | GME: $41.56

In the morning of January 19th, following the closed trading day for MLK Jr. observance, a new tweet arrived from @CitronResearch, making it the account's first mention of GameStop:

"Tomorrow am at 11:30 EST Citron will livestream the 5 reasons GameStop $GME buyers at these levels are the suckers at this poker game. Stock back to $20 fast. We understand short interest better than you and will explain. Thank you to viewers for… feedback on last live tweet."

For the activist investor Left claimed to be, this stab ripped open the still-healing wounds of weeks prior.

In his deleted video about Lemonade, Left blatantly mentions that there aren't a lot of short opportunities on his radar, and in Citron's December 18th tweet, he admits, "Getting emails about shorting $VUZI…. There has to be easier pickings...still doing research. Risk/Reward easier on other high flyers."

The GME share price would fall from a $41 open (and an intraday high past $44) to as low as $36.64, which is near where the price would open the morning of the 20th. It looked like Left's NIO/PLTR playbook all over again.

Like Aesop's *The Hare and the Tortoise*, wherein the tortoise's diligence allows him to win against a lackadaisical hare, WSB members gave their opponent enough respect to necessitate an all-nighter of analysis and research on GameStop DD. This even included trying to predict how and where Left might try to dismantle their work.

On Donald Trump's final day as president, and exactly one week before Reddit would make top news around the world, the first of many DDs debuted. Just like

DFV joining the short squeeze group, conversely the squeezers had decided to discover their own deep value.

u/Temporary_Search focused on theories of market manipulation in a since-hidden post:

"So, we've all seen Citron's/Shitron's tweet about how they have big news or 5 rEaSoNs WhY you should sell GME tomorrow. I think now is the time to look closely at what they're attempting to do. I'm beginning to better understand the position of the firms like [hedge funds] are in: totally underwater and fucking drowning. / Even still as GME's stock rises, these [funds] are continuing to take short positions. Now, I am just a humble retard with a ~~cultural anthropology associates~~ worthless degree, but I can read at a 6th grade level, and I think I finally figured out what that means, 'taking shorts.' .... Holy shit. Taking out a loan and then hoping you don't have to pay back the loan isn't investing — it's fucking retarded."

You have to appreciate the creative use of strikethroughs. TemporarySearch ended with, "Disclaimer: I am not a financial advisor and have been ~~gambling on the stock market~~ wisely investing for a month."

The occasional mention of Melvin Capital would slowly increase in posts and memes, referencing the massive hedge fund currently a comfortable distance from the battlefield. Melvin had made the tactical error of disclosing their GME short in their 13F form the year prior.

Part of the ease with which shorts operate is found in the lack of regulation around the practice. For that reason, shorting is incredibly opaque. Why Melvin had chosen transparency was a result of their own hubris or something else unknown.

u/ksynodias' recap of the day's events got a handful of upvotes:

"The day started of[f] with a huge uptrend, spiking at 45.40$, and this is when Citron [lemon emoji] posted their tweet @9:58AM and the price plummeted to 36.88$ within 30 minutes.... So maybe go sign the petition to get the SEC to investigate them. / Our GME Thread was on the front of Reddit, which means a lot of retards joined us today for sure."

It wouldn't be the last time a GME thread made it to the front of Reddit. The r/all feed would soon feature daily GME updates for weeks and months to come, bringing more people into a cause that would exceed the limits of basic interest in finance.

In real time, WSB self-educated themselves on the difference between market regulations and real-world enforcement of such regulations, like some kind of android awakening to the idea it could kill its human creators. Users were also beginning to realize that they were stepping into a field full of potentially rampant manipulation, and when they dialed "911," there might not be someone on the other end of the line.

One of the most enduring SEC stereotypes stemmed from a 2010 report that the regulators had spent hours on popular pornographic websites instead of investigating financial crimes. While many petitions and reports would be fruitlessly submitted to the SEC by GameStop investors over this time and the following period, memes were another weapon requiring less turnaround time.

Redditors armed with basic video editing software and ripped scenes from movies in GIF and MP4 formats were able to create an entertaining and endearing rallying cry in a way that no Xerxes or William Wallace could have hoped to accomplish, yet with full use of the movies that portrayed those real-life warriors.

u/YoungGucci66 made a meme from an action film with the title, "How It Felt Holding $GME With All Of You Guys Today. FUCK CITRON! See You Guys @ $100".

January 20th, Inauguration Day, began with excitement as DDs were reviewed and cross-examined in preparation for Left's GME-killing speech that day. But then, red, white, and blue balls struck.

In their since-deleted tweet, @CitronResearch stated,

"$GME still going to $20 easy[,] but Citron does not want to go live in the middle of a historic presidential inauguration. We respect the office of presidency and out [sic] country and will not interfere with market commentary. We look forward to the livestream tom[orrow]. / Gold [sic] Bless America"

And the subreddit erupted.

Crowding the sub with memes of Citron running for the hills, the apes were well aware for the first time that the emperor had no clothes, and all they had to do was convince everyone else that it was the case.

While any selection of internet users will have bad apples, at no point was the WSB hive-mind in consensus to harass Left, as authors and journalists would later suggest.

A post planning retribution like the since-deleted "SHITRON RESPONSE VIDEO CASTING CALL" merited top comments with five times the number of upvotes of the original post, showing its lack of support. u/BB117 got over 5k upvotes to the post's net 900 by saying, "Don't send anything. Exactly as that one popular post said today, we should not embrace a combined identity. Especially since we are not one." u/viperswhip added, "There is a way to respond, buy more GME."

To the glee of WSB, @JimCramer would tweet that day, "Watch this incredible short squeeze the Wall Street Bets people are setting up against Citron on $GME. It's brilliant... just a classic trap to be sprung...."

On Thursday, January 21st, anticipation built to sky-high levels throughout the morning as the stock opened under $40. To WSB's shock, Citron's Twitter failed to go live with Andrew Left's much-anticipated video, instead posting the following:

"Too many people hacking Citron twitter, will record and post later today. $GME going to $20[,] buy at your own risk"

Knowing that a hacked Twitter account likely wouldn't be able to tweet about its own hacking, the curtain had been pulled back. Moreover, the hesitation just felt weak. The "boomer" insults began to flow like musket balls from a row of revolutionary minutemen, but still partly out of nervous hesitation.

If Left was able to go live and nailed the livestream, he could bankrupt these deep-value enthusiasts worse than he had on Palantir. And most wouldn't recover this time.

Two hours later, when Left did manage to make his since-deleted presentation, the results were devastating, adding insult to injury to mortal injury. His video went up on YouTube and was then shared on Twitter later in the afternoon of January 21st.

Left reached forward to tap his phone to start his stream, jostling the camera. While not out of the question for anyone live streaming, it seemed amateurish for someone advising on large market dynamics.

Left was accustomed to a certain respect from his followers. That expectation made him seem cocky, and WSB can sniff out cock from a mile away.

User @Gurgavin shared a screencap of the video, shouting "NO WAY YOU TRUSTING A GUY WHO LOOKS LIKE THIS."

Left's eyes and forehead stiffen as he looks to a prepared statement below the camera lens, opening with, "Hey, this is Andrew Left at Citron Research, giving you five reasons why GameStop is going to twenty dollars."

His professional composure delves into a smug grin as he leans forward and rattles off the initial rant, ending with, "This is a failing, mall-based retailer. So the amount of people who are so passionate about putting GameStop higher, not based on any fundamentals, it just shows the natural state of the market right now... A bunch of frogs in a pot of boiling water."

Loudly tapping the table, jostling the phone taping the recording, Left was giddy to tear into the viewers. First, he cites the excitement around the high short interest, of which he admitted to being a member:

"Your first question you have to ask yourself is, why is there a high short interest? But, moving beyond that, a stock at $40 right now has an open borrow on it... uh, and, and, it's no longer, now we're looking at a trading phenomenon.... You're not going to change this story. You're not going to change the underlying fundamentals of this company. Therefore as long as the borrow's available, and insiders are still selling, uh, and the company needs money, you won't see a squeeze from here on in."

"Number two, numbers don't lie. People lie. I know! Everyone on Twitter has never had a losing trade. Everyone on Reddit is a market genius. I hear it all the time."

For all his brashness, Left's video does utilize due diligence after the initial name-calling, comparing GME to its competition and providing some work to back up his bearishness. But his voice amplifies into the monologue's third minute, and he becomes even more unpleasant to listen to, despite some important pricing fundamentals:

"I know who's long GameStop right now! The people who are ordering pizzas to my house, just signing me up for Tindr, or doing all those, cute things, trying to hack my Twitter account."

"This is gonna be J.C. Penney...or it could be Blockbuster video.... You can get mad, you can hack my account, you can go to Twitter, you could sign-on, you could call me every name. If you want to save the company, take your energy, go out there, and actually buy something, from GameStop! Because that's the only thing that saves this."

Left signed off with the even more ironic, "Cautious investing to everyone." And the stream was over.

Potentially watching the stock price skyrocket during his stream, Left's reasons for shorting weren't bad, but his swagger was lacking, not to mention including such a notorious dare to buy something from GameStop. Apes would do just that in larger and larger numbers in months to come and across physical retail locations, e-commerce, and even non-fungible tokens.

u/bnewm462 immediately suggested, to the tune of 6,000 upvotes, "Citron is starting to look a lot less like a 'research company' and a lot more like just some guy tweeting from his apartment. / How does a company not know that the fucking presidential inauguration is happening? Putting that aside, the stream does eventually go live aaaaand... it's just some guy ranting? Was it recorded on his phone?... Is there a brick-and-mortar office building, with revenues and services, or is it literally just some guy making tweets with a lemon picture? I'm so confused right now."

The top comment stream read,

u/nailattack: "He said 'we understand short selling better than you'. I was actually hoping for some good dd and some legitimate points. Almost every single point he made only made a stronger bull case."

u/stejerd: "It was like he took the top 5 bearish comments off of stocktwits"

And a since-deleted user: "This is literally what I thought. I, the big dumb student, may have actually done far superior DD than this man."

u/haggy added, in a since-deleted post, "WSB has posted numerous higher quality DD for the bear case that provide stronger arguments and cite additional resources. Almost all of these points are handwavy and when he does cite some numbers he handpicks only a few numbers that make his cases.... Hell, I bet if someone posted a similar quality, but favorable DD for GME to WSB it would be downvoted to the pits of hell due to poor quality."

It's true. WSB, and the subreddits that followed in its wake, can be phenomenally critical of poor due diligence or DDs that aren't funny or stupid enough. Left's ramble might not have garnered a hundred upvotes, much less the thousands necessary to get real attention.

Citron GME Review 01/21/21 will go down in GME history for its confirmation of WSB's suspicions. Comments on the YouTube video were disabled; the video was later unlisted and then made totally private.

The YouTube downvotes were through the proportional roof, slanting 9-to-1 negative, back when the site still enabled them. Left quite possibly may have motivated purchases of the stock thanks to the Streisand Effect, and the internet went bananas as his video spread, repeatedly downloaded to outmaneuver his increasing privacy settings.

While the Citron video occurred too late in the trading day to make any significant waves, the stock did close higher at $43.03, which emboldened the subreddit. Finally, the notorious Citron had failed to inspire a downward plunge on a stock, despite Left's greatest effort to date, attempting a full video in place of a tweet.

This was the day I bought one share from my broker account, if only to support those with bigger pockets in their mission of squeezing a short. Just to say I had joined the cause as I began documenting it.

It wouldn't be my last time buying a stock I liked.

10: The Shot Heard 'Round r/all

January 22nd, 2021 | GME: $42.60

If Citron was shorting for a $20 target, how high would the price have to go for that to capitulate? Forty dollars? Fifty? Sixty-nine dollars and sixty-nine cents?

It's unclear, but $76.76 seemed to do the trick, which the stock reached just after noon on Friday.

Left's tweet that day read, "Citron twitter page to be back up on Monday, Twitter working through multiple hack attempts. In the meantime nothing more to be said on $GME." and included a screenshot of a letter:

"We will no longer be commenting on GameStop, not because we do not believe our investment thesis but rather the angry mob who owns this stock has spent the past 48 hours committing multiple crimes that I will be turning over to the FBI, SEC, and other governmental agencies. This is not just name-calling and hacking but includes serious crimes such as harassment of minor children. We are investors who put safety and family first and when we believe this has been compromised, it is our duty to walk away from a stock."

u/quantkim shared a screenshot of the news to a sigh of relief from the sub and over 8,000 upvotes: "CITRON SAYS NO LONGER COMMENTING ON GAMESTOP."

u/Banker47 scoffed, "He's gotta be kidding when he says he's going to try and press charges on all 2 million of us."

The underlying generational avarice reared its head further down the comment stream:

u/mythrowawaybabies: "Welcome to the future, old man."

u/pmnBattleCityDev: "It's just like the past except you don't have any money. It has been replaced by a distinct feeling that the world has passed you buy [sic]."

u/Howdoiaskformoremuny: "Are we finally eating the rich? Is this it?!"

u/LegolasofMirkwood: "Kinda tastes fruity. Almost like a lemon."

u/Jabadu posted to over 20k upvotes that evening, "Boomer Old Money has bled and will get dirty going forward. Don't be an idiot, Don't poke the beehive with tweets, phone call harassment or callouts…. Boomer old money will get dirty and ethically dubious to maintain power rather than innovate and compete. I promise you, They are already meeting with one another to figure a way to turn this forum off."

WSB mods repeatedly reiterated the consensus that harassment of any kind was counterintuitive to the subreddit's iconoclastic core. These would be the first of many public-facing statements produced in record time by the WSB mods that would keep the subreddit afloat.

Investors who had entered $GME positions as early as the $4 price point watched with wonder as the ticker climbed up to its daily high of $76.76, flipping market circuit breakers not once but twice during the volatile surge upward, something that had become a common occurrence that week, and would become even more common the following week.

Nevertheless, circuit breaker halts were never met with favorable feelings by apes. As u/Ajexa spoke so eloquently the following Tuesday, "The cunts halted GME AGAIN!"

The stock price fell back to earth after the surge to $76. Some cashed in while others held on, the rush of energy surging through the subreddit, getting the community their first true taste of communal rocket ship success.

Users who jumped onto the FOMO of profits and found themselves buying near the peak began to fear they'd damaged their finances badly. Numbers between $60 and $75 were tossed around as users asked if they had made terrible mistakes, wondering if they had joined Isaac Newton in his eponymous folly.

The rampant self-guessing wouldn't be the last instance of self-doubt. Instead, it would be the last time users felt fooled for buying at double-digit price points, a scarcity before the stock price would split over a year later.

Reddit short squeezing was built with the tools buy, upvote, meme, and get access to more cash or margin to buy again. But other tactics were going on in the realm of DDs and tips shared between traders. For instance, traders presciently suggested buyers not use margin on their accounts because it allowed their brokers to lend out their shares to shorts that could prevent MOASS.

GameStop managed to recover to $65.01 in Friday's final hours, to the great surprise of some and to the exact expectations of others. While second guessers felt the color drain from their faces, those who cashed out that day were on cloud nine. One user paid off over $20,000 in student loans in a since-deleted post. Another took time to say a since-deleted "DeepFuckingThankYou." And another could only say, "Fuck all of you, congrats."

As Rogozinski says in his book, as far back as the sub's beginnings, "People post wins and losses on a regular basis on WallStreetBets; both are equally welcomed, and both are well received." GameStop wasn't a diamond hands play yet, and the paperhands were celebrated for their gain porn.

With the closing bell impending, u/jon33km shared a screencap of a Bloomberg broadcast that displayed the headline "GAMESTOP RECORD SURGE GIVES WIN TO REDDIT ARMY IN CITRON CLASH" alongside his own congratulations: "Congrats REDDIT ARMY AKA WSB!! You took on Citron and won!"

Taking the top comment, u/Trueslyforaniceguy commented, "We are not an army / Wsb and Reddit investors, gamblers, degenerates, / We're just a small piece of a very large market taking advantage of a company turning things around, with far too low a valuation and far too many shares sold short. / The market is doing this, not people in wsb."

And thus continued the active dissociation with central identity, as the alleged "kids" were smart enough to know what was and wasn't legal in the world of stock trading, having read up on the topic as recently as 24 hours prior or having recently re-watched *The Wolf of Wall Street* (2013).

Whether it was financial regulators or Silicon Valley companies, WSB would soon find itself in a struggle not to be totally wiped off the face of the internet. In a failsafe still reverberant months later, in the event their means of communication were ruined, users would retreat to the comments section of the Youtube sensation Gangnam Style (and after that, Wu Tang Clan's C.R.E.A.M.).

As the sun set on the East coast and would soon make its way below the Pacific Ocean too, u/DeepFuckingValue posted "GME YOLO update — Jan 22 2021," which earned him a staggering 95,000 upvotes. His account now stood at over $11 million, almost half of which was the result of call options that would expire three months later.

u/TRUMP420KUSH_ told jealous commenters on the post, "There are PLENTY of these opportunities to come in the future, just pay attention, be patient and be even more retarded".

And TrumpKush would be right.

I spent that night documenting everything that had occurred that week, much of which helped fill in the gaps when I would revisit the book for publishing. The info only filled a few chapters' worth at the time and, laughably, included a final line about how the aspirational $420.69 share price would never stop being the lofty, albeit unlikely, goal.

With only a couple hours of sleep, I woke up the next morning for a call with Jaime Rogozinski. I had emailed him after having read his book, not yet knowing he had been ousted by the group in the year prior. While my conversation with Rogozinski lasted less than a half hour and was off the record, there wasn't anything terribly notable about what he had to say. It reflected much of the statements that he'd later make to the media before taking his own movie deal. But talking to Jaime brought me a sense that I was early to this story, which, admittedly, I thought had reached its peak.

Because Reddit's algorithm relies on a refresh rate of 6-12 hours, something from last week, much less a year prior, wouldn't be known or easy to find for a relative newcomer like me. This is part of the reason mods use pinned posts, automod posts, and page wikis to maintain subreddit throughlines. A sub's history lives and dies by the choices its mods make, unless you're someone who's been there from the start.

So while I wasn't aware of the Rogozinski controversy at this stage, it would be reiterated by the o.g.'s later, like this post by a deleted user:

"WSB_GOD (Jaime) is back at CNN and Bloomberg.... I don`t want this sub to be known as Jaime[']s sub. / Thank you for coming to my TED talk."

It was nice to have a weekend to recap everything that had occurred with Citron, as I tweeted the week after, "Very excited to say that I started writing the definitive @wsbmod $GME book on Friday night and won't have to sift through thousands of reddit comments weeks from now."

Digital champagne flowed that weekend. It was the purest form of celebration that WSB would ever see before diamond handing made gain porn passé, and the mainstream, bots, and FUD initiated the forum "slide," a term referring to a collective shift away from a forum's original purpose.

u/Robertf1032010 took home almost 9k upvotes with his post, "A hedge fund manager[']s perspective on GME":

"I am a hedge fund manager.... Why would a value focused fund manager buy a stock that based on classic fundamental value analysis appears significantly overvalued?... This extreme short against a small common float, made more extreme no-doubt by naked shorting, could end very poorly for those short."

The attention of financial experts was there, and WSB wasn't even aware of it. They had already made a new enemy, already scrambling to contain the Trojan Horse that was Left's potential closing of his short.

u/Double_Anybody commented, "A lot of words here, some of them big words. So due to this reason I will be yoloing my life savings into GME calls."

The mods of WSB made careful efforts to re-establish a public front to meet the newfound attention they faced while similarly addressing the sub as a group. In their first post on Saturday, u/MIA4real released "Disgraceful & false media narrative about GME":

"The shit-tier level of journalism covering the GME saga has been a fucking disgrace. Half of it is plain financial illiteracy, and the other half is inter-generational bashing and fear-mongering. You think it's been bad thus far? The squeeze hasn't even really set off yet, can you imagine what happens next week when the stock hits the low triple digits? Eventually to 420.69? End game of 1000$+? Lets recap what has happened so far:

False media narrative #1: Recent rise of GME is due to sHorT sQuoZe!!!1! [sic] / Reality: GME is an undervalued company & a turnaround story.... / False media narrative #2: Rabid retail investors are victimizing the poor short sellers / Reality: Short sellers have been conducting [alleged] illegal [alleged] naked short selling to drive a company employing tens of thousands to bankruptcy.

Bloomberg blithly [sic] characterizes reddit as an 'angry mob' out to attack poor little Citron. Bullshit, an angry mob is what stormed DC on Jan 6th, not a bunch of random individuals that left internet comments you didn't agree with on your youtube video…. We, the retail investors, didn't do shit other than invest into a company that deserves a second chance. The shorts put themselves into a precarious situation through their own greed and illegal naked short selling. The media wants to punch down on the 'easy' target: Reddit and WSB. Reddit is scary to boomers who can barely navigate the reddit UI, let alone get an erection. They prefer facebook, where fake news can be piped directly into their senile brains…. We can and should push back, not by some centralized WSB twitter handle, but by what we do best: acting as individual retail investors who advocate for the truth on our soapboxes of choice."

u/Gammathetagal added in the comments, "[Wall Street] are destroyers of middle and lower class investors ['] hard earned money. They destroy companies. Then cry when retail investors beat them at their own game using their rules. Cry me a river you trust fund losers."

Then u/bawse1 followed up on Sunday morning with the second mod update, receiving over 30k upvotes, titled "How'd you guys manage to win so big it made these old guys drown in their tears?"

"There[']s 2 million of you. [T]hat is so crazy yet amazing when you think about it.

If you haven't noticed, all eyes are on r/wallstreetbets right now and a certain narrative is being pushed around to make it seem as if this community is disorderly and reckless. What I think is happening is that you guys are making such an impact that these fat cats are worried that they have to get up and put in work to earn a living."

"People like to talk shit about you when you're a winner, it just comes with the territory. The way a winner responds is by keeping your head up high and en-joy[ing] living rent-free inside the minds of those who doubted you. They'll stare you down as you walk by them with a smile as wide as the sky. You don't even notice them because you're too busy basking in all the glorious tendies you've made. They hate that you played by the rules and still won."

"Your time is now. / On behalf of the Mod team, / Make that money and be the change you want to see."

I knew I had just watched a movie play out in real life, and it was one of the most exciting moments to witness, even though I only held one share and wasn't a contributor or poster to the sub (laughably, because I was too afraid of the SEC at the time).

I was a part of something, and I was "doing my part!" which later became one of the sub's most popular memes, originating from *Starship Troopers* (1997).

Despite the claims of gammas, deltas, and technical analysis sources of coming tendies smattering the subreddit, no degenerate could expect what came next. Although one user, u/brbcripwalking, was feeling the opposite, posting, "A bear's guide to Maruchan Ramen Flavors."

"As we go into tech earnings, some of you bears will be homeless or in prison soon. Here is a ranking guide to the different flavors of ramen to keep you until the next round of commissary or eviction notice comes in."

Roasted Chicken topped the list.

Part 2: Revolution

INTERMEDIATE

I

GME DD

Intense Finance
Simulated Gambling

"Why can I Cashapp someone for feet pics in seconds, but it takes TWO WHOLE DAYS for shares to be delivered from the DTCC? Why do they also get to choose what the deposit requirements are? Something needs to change."
— WSB Mods State of the Union, February 2021

11: A New Breed at Breed's Hill

January 25th, 2021 | GME: $96.73

Monday didn't begin with GME's price plunging back to earth, as many might have expected. Instead, Monday began with a bullish meme of a spaceship named GME descending to a refueling station, captioned "To the moon!"

While some expected the boost to occur as shorts bought back shares to exit their positions, evidence of that was scarce, not because it wasn't the truth, but because transparency on shorted stock moves is opaque at best and relies on reporting that occurs bi-monthly.

It's also worth noting that the SEC found the following in their GameStop report, released months later: "Whether driven by a desire to squeeze short sellers and thus to profit from the resultant rise in price, or by belief in the fundamentals of GameStop, it was the positive sentiment, not the buying-to-cover, that sustained the weeks-long price appreciation of GameStop stock."

There was undoubtedly FOMO occurring over the weekend as word spread of Friday's exploits and user counts inflated on WSB. The pent-up excitement spread like wildfire and brought an exponentially higher series of buyers alongside the original group, knocking the stock's price up to new highs of $121 only an hour into the trading day.

At 11am, Jim Cramer officially recognized the phenomenon live on CNBC, to the glee of traders: "It's the 'wallstreetbets' people. And they have ganged up, arguably allowed by free speech purposes, to center on a few stocks…. [and] mechanics of the market are breaking down."

At that moment, the Dow Jones Industrial Average had reached the end of a 300-plus point drop, which began at market open. Cramer continued his media rounds, discussing the phenomenon with better attention than others dared.

Monday's stock price peaked at $159.18, made all too obvious when u/DavyJ posted their purchase of 50 shares with the header, "Can I get a flair for buying GME at the literal top ($155.29)?" Flairs were tightly guarded in this age of Reddit trading, but Davy was awarded *CEO of Buy High Sell Low* to their credit (which they still displayed two years later).

u/Monstermart: "Classic GameStop. Buy at full price, return for a fraction of what you paid."

u/bnard101: "Much like with trading games in, you only lose if you sell!"

Mods were forced to lock the pinned post "Daily Discussion Thread for January 25, 2021" after over 50k comments (not upvotes, mind you), caused "performance issues," per u/OPINION_IS_UNPOPULAR.

"Can I get a thumbs up for people that bought GME at top today?" asked u/dtman85 to almost 2,000 upvotes. But the energy was only getting going, as u/YouWantSumFuck99 bellowed, "I get that some of you have never had gains so high (shit, I haven't — I could've had a heart attack because of premarket gains) but the fact of the matter is, if you HOLD now, you will BENEFIT later…. Go take a walk. Pet a dog. Cook some food. For fucks sake, go do something other than stress about shit you can't change… staring at your phone."

Another top comment on the Daily Discussion thread echoed the flood of media FUD on its way: "Aw man, I can't believe after that terrible day where WSB lost it all, GME is *checks notes* only up 18% in a single day" (u/draconic86).

Transitioning from casual amusement to mild perturbation, Monday's media was forced to report on what was developing within WSB, but the story remained relatively ignored. Eyes began to turn to CNBC, though, as that network seemed to give a platform to a few more unhappy experts than the rest.

On another slow news day, in the weeks between insurrections and impeachments, it's best to broadcast whatever stories will get ratings.

In order to divert user load from the Daily Discussion thread and also allow discussion of other stonks on that post, the WSB mods created GME-specific pinned discussion posts titled "GME Megathread." The day's second edition of this thread appeared in the afternoon.

u/perennialpurist received acclaim for their opinion of the "boomer fucks on CNBC" in this thread, commenting, "...they're blaming everything on WSB. One of the fund managers even tried to imply that maybe there are foreign powers involved here. Like yeah ok you old boomer fuck, if North Korea or Iran wanted to hurt America, they'd start buying fucking GameStop shares, because that'd show us. Jesus motherfucking Christ." to which u/browndogmn replied, "Need a meme of the ayatollah buying (GME)."

The only text in the header of GME Megathred Part 2 reads like an annoyed parent slamming the door on a child's playroom: "Keep all $GME discussion and memes in here. No market manipulation."

But the mods weren't in control now, not that they ever had been. No "one" was in control. WSB all was, collectively, as individuals.

The first human hive-mind.

TIME Magazine, arguably the most reputable journalistic source to comment on WSB to date, ended the trading day with an article titled, "So, Uh, What's Up With GameStop's Stock?: People claim to be making thousands on the 'meme stock.' But it's got to blow up eventually, right?"

Out of touch, spineless, and at arm's length from taking a side, TIME wouldn't be the last mainstream outlet to fumble the story in its earliest days.

There were millions of new members on WSB, yet somehow not one was a member of the media. The term "meme stock" was regurgitated as many times as our corporate giants of consolidated media could reprint each other's source material. The term never caught on within the group until long after the insult stopped stinging.

Blackberry, Nokia, AMC, and Palantir are meme stocks. GameStop was a meme stock.

Was.

The reporters missed the essence of the newest GameStop surge and, frankly, that of the previous week. WSB conversations on GME had targeted the basic math of a short squeeze. When it came to the availability of shares in the marketplace, two-and-two did not equal four for the shorts. The hive-mind had established the fundamentals that DFV had first proposed, which helped them win against Citron. Now, the movement transcended to the next logical step, a la Andrew Yang's 2020 presidential campaign slogan: MATH.

MATH was what kept me in the squeeze in January 2021, in the stock's plunge that followed, and the peaks and valleys after that. MATH made sense: if everyone buys and enough people HODL, it's game over. MATH equaled MOASS.

Shortly before the TIME article, a different kind of math was threatening hedge fund Melvin Capital, whose GameStop bet would be a mortal wound to the entire fund, compounded with other investments as a bear market struck in the following year.

Juliet Chung reported that day for the Wall Street Journal, "Citadel, Point72 to Invest $2.75 Billion Into Melvin Capital Management."

"The injection of cash has the effect of reducing Melvin's reliance on borrowed money and, thus, the likelihood of margin calls from Melvin's prime brokers, some of the people familiar with Melvin said."

The article estimated Melvin's losses had jumped as high as 30% after posting annual returns in that ballpark. All this from a short bet that previously represented a small piece of their aggressive portfolio.

Suddenly, and without expecting such success so quickly, WSB had pierced the armor of a massive fund to the point that they had to be (allegedly) rescued by not one but two bigger fish.

Those two bigger fish were "whales." Steve Cohen, executive at Point72, owner of the New York Mets and Gabe Plotkin's former boss, was called elitist for tweeting that trading was "a tough game." Citadel LLC, under the leadership of billionaire CEO Kenneth Griffin, who also had former ties to Plotkin, was the other half of the Melvin Capital investment package.

As Robinhood's largest source of payment for order flow[3] processing, Citadel[4] would also draw the ire of those spurned by Robinhood days later. For this reason and others, Griffin would draw the most attention from Redditors after Melvin Capital had been overtaken.

Forbes ranks Griffin around 50th[5] in their 2022 wealth indices, with a net worth of around $27 billion. They also peg his "philanthropy score" at 3, estimating he's donated a little over one billion dollars to charitable causes.

Two of the world's largest investors had now tied their funds to the fate of Melvin Capital. It was clear that, as the WSJ noted, the (apparent) rescue was one which allowed Melvin to maintain their positions. It didn't seem to be a capitulation. Not yet.

Long before Iron Man would do battle with Thanos, his nemesis Whiplash warned in *Iron Man 2*, "If you can make a god bleed, people will cease to believe in him." So too, u/quantkim commented that evening, "Mf (motherfucker) is bleeding," with regard to their post sharing the WSJ's report.

u/yabadabadane: "The first domino has fallen."

u/landmanpgh: "The article might as well have said they just sent WSB a check for $2.75 billion and WSB replied, 'It's gonna be a lot more than that.'"

---

[3] Payment for order flow, or PFOF, is defined by Investopedia as "a form of compensation, usually in terms of fractions of a penny per share, that a brokerage firm receives for directing orders for trade execution to a particular market maker or exchange."

[4] Citadel is commonly conflated by Redditors, and refers to either Citadel Securities, the market maker, or Citadel LLC, the hedge fund. Griffin owned 80% of the former and 85% of the latter as of 2022. Financial regulators maintain there is no conflict of interest for a hedge fund and market maker to be largely owned by the same person.

[5] At time of publication, Griffin's Forbes rank had improved to 35th, adding another $7-8 billion to his worth. In that same span, his Forbes "philanthropy score" had fallen two points.

Resurgent calls for diamond hands amplified as WSB memes tapered off in favor of complex financial analyses and conspiracy theories. A speculative DD with 10k upvotes was posted by u/Blizzgrarg: "Today was a coordinated attack by institutions against the longs. Here's how it played out."

"1. The beginning of the day was intentional. They let fomo run GME all the way into the sky with almost no resistance whatsoever.

2. However, at around 10-10:30 AM EST, something odd happened. The brokers suddenly jacked up their margin requirements for GME. My portfolio previously had a lot of buying power, which suddenly disappeared.

3. We were intentionally allowed to break 150 (which is the highest option strike available) in order to make everyone fomo even harder. Then, the dump came, and it was vicious. At the same time, [the MSM] started an hour-long segment bashing GME nonstop....

4. As a result, everyone who chased in on margin got fucked. Even my sizeable [sic] portfolio was margin called. Fortunately, while I'm retarded, I'm not the most retarded and was not all in GME and was using only a little margin...

5. The cascading effect let us fill the gap completely and even a little past.... Going forward, stop buying GME on heavy margin. Use cash accounts if possible. Don't let yourself be set up as a domino piece for the shorts to knock over into everyone else."

"Don't buy on margin! Do I have to come over with my belt?" u/PunkNDisorderlyGamer threatened. "Yes Daddy," u/Daybyhour69er accepted.

u/Paige_Maddison commented on one of Robinhood's most freeing aspects, which had now become one of its most entrapping: "When you sign up for a RH account it's an instant account which IS A MARGIN account. / So I was never trading on a cash account to begin with[,] it looks like. Because you have to contact them to downgrade. What a shady shit ass thing to do. / So I'll have to wait until it clears or deposit more money in I guess."

To be fair, Robinhood's instant trading abilities put its useability ahead of other brokers, who would require money to settle in an account prior to trading. In

Silicon Valley, a two-day wait could mean losing customers right off the bat. Robinhood had been brilliantly seizing on younger generations' desire for imme-diacy.

u/FatAspirations would similarly dominate the evening of January 25th with "GME EndGame part 3: A new opponent enters the ring," which received over 30k upvotes, vaulting it to the r/all page alongside a handful of other GME con-tent. u/South_ParkRepublican commented, "EVERYBODY READ THIS, THIS POST IS A LIGHT IN THE DARKNESS," to Fat's credit.

"There were two halts in the day on Friday: First, when GME was up 69% (heh heh), and then a few minutes later when it kept climbing after the first halt was relaxed. Note that at the time of the first halt, the bid-ask spread was $10 on the underlying[,] a huge signal that there just were not enough shares to buy.

However, after the second halt, something strange happened. Whereas a few minutes prior, there were no sellers willing to sell their shares below $75, within 15 minutes after the halt there were sellers at 70, 65, 60, and 56. Where did these sellers come from?"

FatAspirations cited the NYSE members list, asking if there could be conflicts of interest in market makers that had connections to hedge funds.

u/dark_bravery noted, "14% [rise in] after hours [trading]. our euro-peons and asians are bidding it up so our [stock] index is matching. / i'm tempted to go all in tomorrow morning. market price."

u/Creative_alternative asked, "Do we collectively have 2.75 billion dollars floating around if they do double down?"

12: A Treaty of Amity and Commerce

January 26th, 2021 | GME: $88.56

I'll never forget what happened the afternoon of Tuesday the 26th. With the trading day at an end, I closed my computer to take a well-deserved break before the evening DD appeared.

But then, a Twitter notification popped up on my screen. My wife asked, "What?" having seen my jaw hit the floor.

"Elon Musk tweeted," I told her.

My wife patiently nodded, sighed, and returned to the other room of our one-bedroom apartment, reconciling herself with the fact we wouldn't make it to Target as planned. Not that we needed to. I don't think I'd eaten a meal since Friday, totally swept up in the madness.

Ten hours earlier, just before market open, u/Seventytwo129 posted a CNBC interview screencap with a quote from Ihor Dusaniwsky, a "predictive analytics" director, who's one of the top short-selling experts in the industry:

"4.2 BILLION lost on shorts and they're doubling down?? He called this the first line of troops going down in a rain of musket fire only to be replaced by another line. More shorts = MORE [rocket ships to the moon]."

"Sounds like a good old fashion retard-off," u/avantartist joked, to which OP replied, "They merely adopted the autism. I was born with it. Vaccinated by it."

u/ChodeFungus would catch the future as it played out, citing a reference to Revolutionary War soldiers in the screen-capped article, "We need real **Musk**et fire." u/placebotwo confirmed, "Fuck man, if Elon got in on this shit, hooooooly fuck."

The DDs of the previous night and financial wizardry wouldn't compare to the growing storm on Twitter, which was rapidly becoming Reddit's left hook in the full-blown war, featuring a younger and even more vibrant crowd of YOLO'ers ready to toss their measly life savings into the pot, hating their money just as much as their Reddit compatriots.

Chamath Palihapitiya, a then-candidate for California governor, part-owner of the Golden State Warriors, and an overall disruptor who repeatedly steps into the spotlight, announced, "Tell me what to buy tomorrow and if you convince me I'll throw a few 100 k's at it to start. / Ride or die." To which Reddit founder Alexis Ohanian replied, "LOL it's gonna be $GME and I'm here for it."

"Fuuuuuuuuccckkkkk!!!!!" Chamath replied.

Opening at $88.56, Tuesday's stock price didn't experience the volatility of the previous days, all three of which featured midday or mid-morning spikes, followed by dips that inched higher by end of day. Tuesday was a slow, steady, and menacing climb.

This wasn't the expectation of most users in the comments section of "The GME Thread Part 1 for January 26, 2021" (preemptively named because that day would require not two but three GME-specific threads on a load of nearly 300,000 comments). A since-deleted user rallied, "GET RID OF YOUR FUCKING STOP LOSSES, OR WE WILL NEVER REACH VALHALLA. / GME $200 EOD (end of day). GME $1000 EOW (end of week)."

They also added, "Robinhood makes most of it's [sic] money selling information on customer orders. It sells a lot of this information to Citadel LLC."

While fraught with statistical inaccuracies, baseless allegations, and unconfirmed rumors, Redditors began to question how these apparent market connections could help or harm their efforts.

Users who had begged for other holders to have diamond hands on Tuesday, speculating wildly that the short had not yet been "squoze" and that holding the GME price at $115 could effectively do so, were ecstatic as the price climbed.

u/can't_read_this added to megathread part 1, "I work 7 days a week 12 hour days guys[,] I'm tired. I'm tired of being a schmuck watching these hedge fund assholes run us over for years. / I don't care how much I spend, I needed this as a wake up call that I haven't been living. / God I love this company / POWER TO THE FUCKING PLAYERS".

u/hallidev, to a criminally low 166 upvotes, took their diary of the day in true wartime fashion, including, "9:30 AM-12:30 PM / I fear I have asked too much of my men. They have already proved their worth to me a thousand times over and then a thousand again, but still I ask them to push.... Privately, I despair for the men of the 159th Weaponized Autists that were left stranded and wanting for reinforcements in yesterday's fighting. Every ounce of my strength is now focused on their safe return."

On megathread part 2, u/firedude222 dared fellow apes, "One upvote and I drop another 5k into this," a comment that received over 2,000 upvotes, thus forcing firedude to do just that.

The stock closed at what was nearly its highest amount for the day, $147.98, another jump of nearly 100%, and without the roller-coaster ups and downs that previously scared off paper hands.

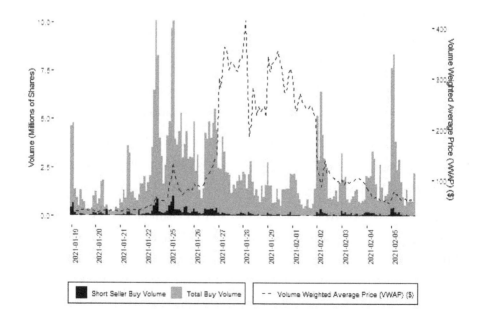

While traders didn't have the information at the time, hindsight provides us with a small look at what was happening to short positions at this point, via the chart that the SEC included with their GameStop report.

On January 26th, the SEC found a majority of buy volume was not generated by shorts buying shares in order to close positions; rather, it was predominantly retail doing so. After three consecutive days of short sellers exiting positions, as seen by the short bars, Tuesday would be the last moments shorts would choose to exit positions in meaningful numbers. Now it truly would be a fight to the bitter end.

u/benaffleks was the first of many more who would realize something even bigger was about to play out with "This is personal. For all of us." Their post would take 24,000 upvotes and also land on r/all:

"This is a big moment. A tug of war between tradition and the future. / Hedge fund managers live in the past, and continue to look down upon the retail investors. They truly believe that we, the average retail investors, don't know anything about finances or the market... and we're just gambling our money away."

"Remember that scene from the Sopranos, where Tony's wife calls to buy 5000 shares of Webonics, after she was manipulated emotionally to so? Institutions and hedge funds want us to be stuck in that world. / They're scared of the future."

"Fuck them all. This affects every single one of you, whether or not you're holding $GME."

This was something all of us had felt and seen in older generations: our parents, friends, and/or grandparents given poor financial advice by professionals only hoping to maintain their own funds' profits.

GME moved into after-hours trading,[6] where tickers still update, and buyers and sellers can still exchange. Retail traders can now participate too, though it's

---

[6] Per Investopedia, "The NYSE opened up to after-hours trading in June 1991, allowing institutional investors to trade until 5:15 p.m. for the first time." Once these trading hours were extended, the floodgates were opened, and now pre-market and after hours trading

considered less liquid and more volatile. Today's after-hours session would see in-credible volatility.

Eight minutes after market close, Musk granted GameStop this Midas's touch with a single word in a single tweet:

"Gamestonk!!"

In the same way that battles with short sellers made Elon Musk and his Tesla "cult" famous, the WSB members knew America's mad scientist had his eye on things, as he usually does when he isn't restoring human spaceflight to the country.

Musk was no friend of the SEC, who had confronted him repeatedly over his use of Twitter affecting prices of his own company and others. Earlier in 2020, he tweeted, "Tesla stock price is too high imo," which drove market leaders insane.

In addition to disruptive business models, Musk was also Wall Street's most famous source of chaos prior to the rise of WSB. In game theory, an irrational opponent is one of the most dangerous because you don't know what their next move might be. Even Investopedia has an entry on game theory: "The paradox of rationality is the observation, in game theory and experimental economics, that players who make irrational or naïve choices often receive better payoffs."

As Heath Ledger's Joker asked in 2008's *Dark Knight*, "Do I really look like a guy with a plan? You know what I am? I'm a dog chasing cars. I wouldn't know what to do with one if I caught it! You know, I just… do things."

Musk likely was aware that turning his followers' attention toward GameStop would hurt his own net worth, which had jostled back and forth with Jeff Bezos for first place, but Musk had a long history fighting Tesla shorters, and this seemed to be his chance to strike back, net worth be damned.

In the "GME Thread Part 3 for January 26, 2020 [sic]," the post was edited to include "BREAKING: Elon Musk just tweeted us" with a hyperlink to the tweet.

---

extends the trading day from as early as 4 a.m. to as late as 8 p.m. EST, with a healthy dose of futures trading in between.

u/manufacture_reborn commented, "I suddenly have strong opinions about the capital gains tax," as the after-hours price not just climbed, but erupted past $200.

The GameStop squeeze had entered its own endgame, and the largest short sellers were very likely upside-down.

u/GlideOutside laid out an interesting theory to 25,000 upvotes as night fell on the 26th:

"Curious why Papa Elon is shilling $GME? [I believe] it's because Melvin Capital shorted $TSLA for years and bragged about it."

"From Bloomberg: Plotkin described Melvin as 'a very human-intensive place. We have a lot of analysts, we require a lot out of them.' The team has modeled more than 500 companies in 'significant detail,' while a data science group reads into trends. He added that the firm has an 'intense focus' on the short side, with about 70% of profits in Melvin's first year coming from bearish bets. Plotkin expressed skepticism about mall real estate investment trusts, as well as electric-car maker Tesla Inc."

u/mavyapsy replied, "Imagine spending all that time and money 'modelling [sic] a lot of companies in significant detail'... Only to be bankrupted by a bunch of illiterate retards trading on their iPhones with cracked screens bought by their wife's boyfriend."

WSB was now three days ahead of the mainstream narrative. DFV posted his YOLO update in the same minute that Musk tweeted, so his net worth of $22 million had only grown in the minutes and hours that followed.

Now three full days ahead of the mainstream narrative, WSB began to calculate its own endgame, knowing that no larger force than the world's first or second richest man would be coming to their rescue.

Barron's would report that the once-hero of GME was souring on his recent riches, worth incredible sums: "'Big Short' Investor Who Once Touted GameStop Calls Rally 'Unnatural, Insane, and Dangerous.'" Forbes would speculate, "Perhaps, Burry is trying to put a lid on the Pandora's Box he helped open. Or he may be suffering from a bit of FOMO, or fear of missing out. The 3.4 million shares Burry purchased for about $15 million would be worth over $1 billion at current prices."

If there was a day for FOMO though, it would be Wednesday, January 27th.

13: The Guns, They've Stopped

January 27th, 2021 | GME: $354.83

Before the infamous trench run, Luke Skywalker and the Rebel starfighters in *Star Wars'* climactic battle suffered initial casualties at the hands of defensive turbolaser towers spread across the surface of the Death Star.

When the towers stopped firing, a moment of relief was tinged with dread. The Empire was shifting its defense tactics. Only moments later, Darth Vader's Tie Fighter Advanced appeared and began methodically picking off fighters one-by-one.

The evil Empire's defensive measures had grown as desperate as they were lethal.

An hour before market open on January 27th, New York Times reporter and CNBC co-host Andrew Ross Sorkin opened a new hour of *Squawk Box* with the following:

"We have some breaking news right now on what has turned into the soap opera and saga of the markets right now, and that is the story of GameStop.... Melvin Capital is now out of the stock. They got out of the stock, from what I understand, yesterday afternoon. I just got off the telephone with Gabriel Plotkin, who runs that firm. They have taken a rather huge loss."

Sorkin speaks directly to camera during the report, as a GameStop ticker soon appears to his side with pre-market numbers bouncing between $340 and $350. He stumbles over a few words and repeats some portions, too, as he likely tries to stretch thirty seconds of content over the two-minute segment.

It wasn't clear whether Plotkin had exited the short before or after Musk's tweet, but what was apparent was that he waited to share the news with the public.

While Sorkin's report isn't out of the ordinary, besides its extraordinary content, there is an interesting moment before the end. Just before the two-minute mark, Sorkin half grins and looks into the camera, suggesting, "To some degree, they [on Reddit] might be able to argue now that they succeeded. If this was really about vanquishing, if you will, Wall Street, or vanquishing, a hedge fund manager in this case, they [Melvin] did take a loss."

All the resistance to retail traders having no power or being too stupid to topple a hedge fund had instantly evaporated. The mass media that echoed the report all seemed to say the same thing.

It's over. You all won. And it's time to go home.

Jim Cramer would say the same two days later, also on CNBC: "Take the home run. Don't go for the grand slam. Take the home run. You've already won. You've won the game. You're done."

The guns, they've stopped.

All this on its own didn't make me suspicious. What did though, was the boosted post of Sorkin's report from the CNBC Twitter account, also seen by most members of the subreddit. While most users assumed the obvious, that CNBC wished to gain new viewers with this advertisement, others were understandably suspicious. I personally don't recall any other sponsored posts by CNBC in this timeframe, for instance. Why would CNBC sponsor an ad announcing that the short position had folded?

WSB hypothesized that Plotkin was bluffing. Everyone and their wives' boyfriends logged on to demand *pics, or it didn't happen*, and blast u/Yupthehoop to 50k upvotes with:

"DONT FALL FOR THE FAKE BS REPORT BY CNBC: / Melvin capital have not closed their positions!! The volume is too low for it to be even possible. The short interest has not changed! / The squeeze has not been squoze."

To which u/alwaysamorfati replied, "Still believe they closed GME shorts per the CNBC story?" attaching a link to a same-day post by Reuters, "Evotec shares rise amid speculation Melvin Capital closing short positions," which included the line, "Melvin Capital, founded in 2014 by Gabriel Plotkin, said it does not comment on positions and trading."

These were all stabs in the dark, and were not supported by sources or data. Reliable data was hard, if not impossible, to come by. The official story, despite traders' highly upvoted suspicions at the time, is what Plotkin shared with Sorkin this day.

With an opening price of $354.83, it wasn't just a struggle for gain porn. There would be no soft landing to bring the story to an end. Something would have to give, especially as short positions remained untenable.

If the events of the coming 24 hours were simply a series of simultaneous technical glitches, obscure market regulations taking effect, and convenient accidents, it was a collectively remarkable stroke of luck for those giants who were short GameStop.

The first exhibit of unusual activity struck only thirty minutes into the trading day on Wednesday: most of the major brokerages began reporting outages, even including my broker (who I had chosen over Robinhood for this very reason).

u/blooddrunk420 commented at 11 a.m., "Every fucking trading app is down."

u/emilstyle91 alleged to over 10k upvotes, "They are jamming brokers and traders accounts all over the world…. Etoro is down. Fidelity down. Schawb down. IB[KR] down. / They are trying everything they can to get those stocks down. They don[']t even let you buy or sell anymore. Something must change. I say that wall street has to fail as a whole. Bunch of scumbags. / They really deserve to lose every single penny. / We stand together. To the moon and valhalla fuck those bastards [rocket emojis]."

The mass outage couldn't be easily explained because even in moments of intense market turmoil like the COVID market crash, the non-Robinhood brokers had been stable. It couldn't be explained by trading volume either, which was around half that of the three days prior.

The only explanation was, according to WSB, this was an all-out war.

The one site still working, of course, was Reddit, where for the first time, the banner image of WSB had been changed by the mods and was now a rainbow-colored phallic silhouette producing a beige splatter, with the subreddit's name in bold lettering.

After volatility at the opening bell that dropped the price near $250, the stock went on a two-hour tear, tackling new highs with every step.

No precise target. Just up.

The day's high watermark landed at $380, preceded by a top of Reddit post from u/FlexinZack:

"FOR ALL THE BIG FUCKING HEDGE FUNDS MONITORING US, THIS IS A MESSAGE FROM US TO YOU, WE FUCKING OWN YOU NOW, FUCK. YOU…. THIS IS GONNA GO DOWN IN HISTORY."

WE LIKE THE STOCK was now flooding the stream, courtesy of Cramer, who'd made another TV appearance and rambled, "We like the stock, we like the stock, we like the stock!" in reference to why he thought traders were buying en masse. Moreover, the carefree aspect of "we like the stock" meant protection from market manipulation.

Can you punish a group of young people who simply buy something they like, even if it is considered worthless? I was under the impression that capitalism heavily relied on young people buying worthless junk, but I digress.

The YOLOs were beginning to peak too. There was no end in sight for how high the price could go.

u/hamidabuddy claimed, "YOLO'd my mom's retirement account. Let's get her a yacht to retire on… mama didn't raise no paper handed bitch," showing the user had made gains of more than $220,000 on an original position of $200,000, purely based on the morning's sharp rise at open. (For good measure, the user chimed back in that they'd pocketed $70,000 when they paper hand— I mean, exited their position.)

Posts cheering on the previously unimaginable $420.69 price point were suddenly outdone, as $1,000 was on the table, harkening back to the days of Porsche's

MOASS. The DD was proving to be more sound with each passing hour that the stock surged to the moon.

u/-gestern-'s suggestion flew atop "The GME Thread, Part 2" within the opening hour:

"VW squeeze ended bc fund managers were crying on the phone to Porsche until the agreed to bailed them out and sell…. There's no Porsche to save these criminal fucks. / We're the fucking Porsche now. Hold. The. Line."

The subreddit had realized that the true victory wouldn't be in the immediate gains seen the Friday previous when Citron capitulated. Even if the price stuck around in the $200s without MOASS, they could still win the standoff, according to u/username—_—, commenting on one of the Melvin doubter's posts:

"Every day those short shares are on the market, they pay interest based on that day's closing price…. So they could try and play a game of chicken and see if we blink first. or just admit defeat and close it early."

Not only was Reddit providing the rest of us with a real-time market education in the palm of our hand, but the Reddit algorithm was actively pushing the most critical information to the top of increasingly crowded feeds. As a result, the democratization of thought was surging and actively self-corrected when misinformation or disinformation arose.

The highest quality posts were rising to the top, rather than the most controversial, as you might find on another social media site's feed, i.e. during election seasons.

But this ease of use wouldn't go unchallenged. New accounts began to flood the daily discussion page of WSB, one, for instance, belonging to an account named u/xXSmokey_BluntzXx (a username that only a bot trying to replicate a 2000s Xbox Live profile might come up with): "Make sure to hit NOK too! sub 6 dollars as of 11:08 am EST. 100 by the end of the day! Use the profits to b[u]y more GME. LOL."

For the first time, Reddit's unforgiving spool of inside references and lexicography worked even more heavily in the sub's favor, allowing WSB to weed out newcomers with shocking alacrity. But, unlike in later months, many of these bots were potentially created by groups pumping the stock, as Reuters reported a month later, "Bots hyped up GameStop on major social media platforms, analysis finds."

Regardless, it was noise that threatened to scramble the hive-mind's hyper-efficient groupthink.

Days later, facing further bot assaults amongst an incredible volume of content surging through the subreddit, u/random_boss would nail Wednesday's sentiment: "The biggest tip off to me of these accounts were that no matter how many times they repeated [']autist and retard,['] they only ever sounded like they were cosplaying as real posters."

u/Tiiimmmaayy's bemoaned, "I used to have to sift through shitposts promoting penny stocks to find good DD, but now you're telling me I have to sift through shitposts from hedge funds?? Who am I supposed to believe now??"

Of all the new "weapons" deployed on Wednesday, one wasn't used as effectively as it could have been: the number 420.69.

Once a meme, and now somehow, some way, an actual reality, hitting $420.69 on Wednesday would have instilled a true sense of success in the group and, more importantly, triggered a widely common sell order, which would have relieved pressure innately and without need for trading restrictions.

If some villain was pulling strings, they didn't think to try that, and they wouldn't have the chance, as u/MasterofRivendell echoed what others were now realizing: "KILL YOUR MOTHERFUCKING $420.69 SELL ORDERS."

A screencap of @J_ManPrime21's tweet topped the rising posts: "The speed in which Congress will probably pass legislation to prevent something like this GameStop thing from happening again will show you the difference between 'immediate' for Wall St and 'immediate' for people waiting on those... [stimulus] checks."

This was yet another source of proof against the narrative that stimulus checks had caused meme stock mania: we hadn't received them yet.

Multiple users began to show gain porn with explanations for what the winnings would be used for: surgeries, putting food on the table, and much more.

Look at me. I am the stimulus now.

Elon Musk, whose every public action is tracked with a microscope, was seen liking a tweet from the WSB fan account @WSBChairman, which would quickly go on to give the Twitter demographic a rallying figure, despite the account's lack of association with the mod team.

Yet this was the essence of WSB, which allowed the fan account to survive and thrive: if a central body was controlling the narrative, then they were conducting market manipulation. The mods of WSB toed the line again here, allowing accounts like Chairman to persist and, in doing so, rallying troops on other platforms to the cause.

While the Chairman could have quickly spiraled out of control or given in to greed, instead, the account became an anonymous extension of the amorphous WSB tidal wave, encircling the Wall Street front lines with every passing moment, tweeting to 150,000 likes: "If they take down WallStreetBets, they better take down every single Wall Street hedge fund that has been endlessly using gangster tactics to make a quick buck."

While "gangster tactics" were never specified by the Chairman, one of WSB's biggest annoyances was how massive funds could utilize mainstream media to push companies in which they were heavily invested, or worse, "short and distort" companies that they had shorted.

At noon, shares fell from a $375 wall down to $315, causing users to speculate in the 2.1 edition of the GME discussion thread, created due to even more intense server overloads.

u/BlaCkPeZuS asked, "The fuck happened. Another attack?"

u/JWBottomtooth: "It dropped at exactly 12:00:02, so definitely a coordinated dump."

u/Wonspur: "Using lunch to do it cause everyone will be checking the stock then. Would be a smart move but we are all retarded here".

In that same moment, as prices plummeted, users with TD Ameritrade accounts began to share the same polite alert inside a green box, which read,

"In the interest of mitigating risk for our company and clients, we have put in place several restrictions on some transactions in $GME, $AMC and other securities. We made these decisions out of an abundance of caution amid unprecedented market conditions and other factors."

This was something out of left field for a legacy broker like TDA. And while most remember the Robinhood actions that would arrive the next day, they forget that so many other trading platforms were going haywire and/or restricting trading, and long before the climax.

14: The Tendie Rockets' Red Glare

4:00 p.m. | Jan. 27th, 2021 | GME: $347

A since-deleted post by u/BoringBusinessClass ascended the ranks of the sub just as power hour kicked off, titled "[I] read a New York Times article saying the SEC is reviewing this sub and...SEC PLS READ".

The body text only contained four sentences: "To the SEC retards in this sub: go fuck yourself. Why don't you start investigating why companies can shut down trading so their hedge fund buddies don't lose money. But when people lose money it's completely ok. Eat a dick."

The Times had, in fact, included such a statement from the Securities and Exchange Commission: "On Wednesday, the S.E.C. said in a statement it was 'actively monitoring the ongoing market volatility.' Lawyers say platforms like Wall Street Bets are incredibly difficult to police, and it is not clear that there have been any violations of securities law."

While the SEC continued to be the brunt of jokes referencing their aforementioned NSFW scandal, there were a series of legitimate concerns mounting in the afternoon hours of Wednesday, January 27th.

In June 2020, only six months prior, Reddit famously banned over 2,000 subreddits, of which r/The_Donald was the most well-known. r/The_Donald had hosted not only an AMA with then-presidential candidate Donald Trump, but also hosted Reddit's most concentrated force of Trump devotees, even topping subs like r/conservative and r/Republican.

The Verge opined, "It marks a major reversal for a company whose commitment to free expression has historically been so strong that it once allowed users to distribute stolen nude photos freely on the site."

While the purge of June 2020 was put into effect after numerous warnings about hate speech and more, it meant that there was a fine line to walk in Reddit's modern ecosystem, and WSB could easily land itself in hot water.

If WSB went down, it would be over. Or at least, once Gangnam Style's comments section stopped operating as the failsafe.

While my effort documenting each blow of the fight up until the current moment had been progressing at a good pace, I knew that it could all disappear as soon as that evening and might stay that way. That's when my work went into overdrive.

Among many calls for self-regulation, u/360T-Posed's since-deleted post suggested,

"PETITION FOR THE MODS TO BLACKLIST THE WORDS 'P*MP AND D*MP. 'WE ARE NOT FELONS, WE JUST LIKE THE GAMESTONK."

"IF THE SEC DECIDES TO INVESTIGATE US (which at this point is likely) I DON[']T WANT THIS SUB TO GET TAKEN DOWN. / WE DON[']T DO ANYTHING ILLEGAL IN THIS SUB, WE JUST 'LIKE THE STOCK.' WE ARE... SIMPLY SQUEEZING OUR GLORIOUS BUTTCHEEKS UNTIL WE REACH THE MOON."

As the lunch hour neared its end, and GameSpot's Twitter announced, "The White House is now monitoring GameStop's stock market situation," the fourth discussion post was already getting posted as the third had been locked at 80,000 comments.

WSB mods claimed, "Reddit's Engineering team has asked us to rotate threads more frequently because [of] our load destroying their backend."

Just after 3:15pm, The Guardian finally landed a blow for the WSB soldiers in the battle for the MSM, becoming an early source to do so as most continued to remain neutral, uninvolved, or like CNBC, stubbornly antagonistic. "GameStop's Dizzying Share Price is Game Over for the Short-Sellers," their headline read.

Cheering on the Redditors didn't mean intermixing an equal dose of skepticism, though: "After a few more rounds of excitement, expect the game to stop in the traditional way: the late-comers to the party, and those staying until the end, will learn the hard way that a paper profit is not the same as cash."

Finally, at 4:00pm, with one more small boost, the stock held nearly where it had opened, despite what was interpreted as a vicious slew of salvos launched across news media, brokerages, and social media.

Reflected in the cardiac-like beats and bounces of a stock ticker, a generation had gone to war against a giant and, like Rocky Balboa, managed to go the distance as GME Thread 3.14 kicked off to cheers:

u/goooodie: "GREATEST WEALTH TRANSFER IN HISTORY! DON[']T WORRY MELVIN[,] IT WILL TRICKLE UP."

u/huynhorlose: "Why is CNBC freaking out even more today? Why are brokers restricting trading? Why is every 3rd comment a bot? Why [are hedge funds] lying about closing all of their shorts? / Because the squeeze has yet to come."

u/Salted_Pringles: "i'm too retarded to understand scare tactics but good luck [diamond hands]."

Even Citron Research tweeted, brave enough to strike at the GME crowd again.

"The [White House] should have more pressing issues than to investigate stock forums on Reddit. We are a nation based on free speech and capitalism. Citron has fought globally for 20 years for that right and no one trading phenomenon should eliminate it. *Our first political tweet ever."

But the executive branch wasn't the only part of the U.S. government monitoring things. Rep. Alexandria Ocasio-Cortez tweeted to 750k likes, "Gotta admit it's really something to see Wall Streeters with a long history of treating our economy as a casino complain about a message board of posters also treating the market as a casino."

I began to wonder what WSB meant that the mainstream wasn't afraid to embrace its political incorrectness, especially in an age of cancel culture. But, then again, there may have been a differentiation between hate speech and *the penis game* at this juncture.

The sticks and stones moment would eventually dissolve, but on this afternoon at least, cancel culture looked the other direction in the face of overwhelming public support. For half a week in January 2021, partisan America was able to stomach sticks and stones in favor of us versus them.

Whether or not my own measly GameStop share would bounce to the $1,000 and $10,000 estimates the bulls were championing wasn't of interest to me, so much as the unavoidable collision that now seemed set for Friday, which users expected to be hedgies' last chance to cover their shorts before paying interest.

But an hour after close, when u/DailyStonks commented, "We single handly have fucked the market lmao," the market was in the process of fucking back.

u/OPINION_IS_UNPOPULAR would pin a since-deleted post around 6pm: "Wallstreetbets Discord Server Hijacked":

"At this time, we believe someone within Discord has hijacked our server and pointed it to another server not related to us. / The situation is still evolving and we apologize for the outage. As new information becomes available, we will update this thread."

When u/livingunique replied, "We aren't a discord and we aren't a subreddit. / We are individual investors who all like the same stock," they were half right. Wall Street Bets ceased to be a Discord that very night when the server was banned, not for fears of financial fraud, but for "continuing to allow hateful and discriminatory content after repeated warnings."

According to Discord, that is.

At 6:30 p.m., I'd typed, copied, pasted, and screen-capped the final bits of primary source material from WSB. Less than a half hour later, Reddit went dark, and not solely as a result of server load. A ban hammer could land at any moment.

In reality, Reddit was working tirelessly with the mods of WSB to ensure they didn't end up like Discord. Reddit's commitment to free speech eventually shone that evening for all to see.

The mods shared in a since-deleted post, which was intermittently visible, as the site struggled on and off: "We are experiencing technical difficulties based on unprecedented scale as a result of the newfound interest in WSB. We are unable to ensure Reddit's content policy and the WSB rules are enforceable without a technology platform that can support automation of this enforcement. WSB will be back."

The stock dropped under $300 in after-hours trading for the first time since beating that mark the previous day, and there was no communication from either Discord or Reddit as to when either would be back online. With the site down, I made that my moment to make that trip to Target.

I was starting to actually lose weight after a full week of intense focus on the stonk and needed food. It wasn't like Elon could tweet for the first time all over again, though future Twitter CEO Musk did fancy his first follow-up tweet to gamestonk: "Even Discord has gone corpo … ".

Michael Burry tweeted for the first time since trying to leave the site for the now-deceased Parler, his account screen name Cassandra, and his bio reading, "Twitter Abandonee & Amateur Dissident":

"#wallstreetbets is down? Not the way to deal with this. How about not allowing naked shorting, not allowing [shorts at] 150% of outstanding shares? Putting issue-specific notional limits on option open interest? Real reforms… ? You can't just delete/cancel investors."

It took less than a half hour for the subreddit to resume, but in a far more bubble-wrapped environment, now bursting at the seams with nearly 4 million members. It's unclear what caused the coincidental outages during the day, but a few things were discussed heavily upon WSB's resumption as resolve returned.

First, the rapid decline of Discord and heroics by Reddit were unnerving for users of both programs, especially since both happened virtually at once. That could have been the end for the investors, erased faster than a Thanos snap.

Second, the price crash during extended trading occurred at higher volumes than retail traders could produce when so many were locked out of extended trading hours.

u/bcjh summed things up perfectly in their since-deleted post: "We live in a world that is fucked with disease and crime and if I want to crack open a cold one with the boys when I get off work, I will. And if I want to get on a big internet message board and talk about stocks with my boys (and wife's boyfriends), I WILL."

u/fatboat_munchkinz stepped in with another popular post: "I am part of WSB and I am a part of today and I want you to know... the fact that I am part of WSB tonight actually brought me to tears.... I am not a big fish but i have seen (over and over again) how big money squeezes the little people way too much. And believe me I've seen some fucked up heart breaking shit.... I want all these dinosaurs to suffer... Gay emotional rant over."

@wsbmod on Twitter retweeted a post from @balajis, endorsing the claim that "1) Reddit did not shut down r/wallstreetbets / 2) The mods shut it down bc they were overwhelmed / 3) It's now back, for now at least."

Reddit brought down a short seller first. Then, they brought down a hedge fund. Then, that hedge fund potentially compromised a much larger fund that had taken them over. Was the contagion still spreading?

If there's one piece of good news, it's that a slew of news outlets finally picked up on the truth about WSB as Wednesday night stretched into Thursday morning, with Morningstar publishing the commentary titled "Crowd-sourcing a short squeeze," which finally recognized that GME wasn't doubling in value every day because it was a MeME sTOnK or a pump-and-dump.

But it wasn't an article from the late hours of January 27th that would get WSB talking. It was one from July 2020 by Fortune magazine: "Robinhood makes millions selling your stock trades ... is that so wrong?"

"A recent SEC filing, first cited by The Block, reveals Citadel Securities and a handful of other firms paid Robinhood nearly $100 million in the first quarter of

2020 alone. These payments are the company's primary revenue stream — far outstripping what it earns from its premium service, Robinhood Gold, or from the interest it makes on cash balances in customer accounts."

Traders the following morning, whether or not they had read this resurfaced article, would continue to extrapolate and theorize about all the possible connections at play.

With the benefit of authors with more immediate book deals and better legal teams, I find it worthwhile to here quote two other GameStop writers on this topic:

First, Ben Mezrich's narrativized account, *The Antisocial Network*, speculates on Citadel's role in the phenomenon by (ever so cautiously) pointing out, "Citadel, who, by coincidence, handled most of Robinhood's trades, and by coincidence, provided the lion's share of Robinhood's profits through its payment for order flow mechanism, now had a financial stake in Melvin Capital, most associated with [GameStop] shorts. And, had just helped lift… Melvin out of its precarious financial situation via a 2.75 billion dollar infusion of cash, along with Steve Cohen."

Second, in Spencer Jakab's journalistic rendition, *The Revolution That Wasn't*, Jakab pedantically suggests — in comparison to retail traders acting in the open, "Since the passage of modern security laws in the 1930's, it has been illegal to collude and buy up a stock to manipulate its price…. If it became known that three hedge fund managers had agreed behind closed doors to target a fourth fund… then they would soon be getting a visit from the SEC."

Redditors counted no fewer than three such managers that had the ability to have a closed-door meeting or two. But these were COVID times. No three people would dare gather behind closed doors, at least not without opening some windows first. Right?

(These hedge funds, and trading apps, and others all vehemently denied any collusion, and at time of publication, Redditors continue to search for a smoking gun.)

u/kmadnow screencapped a tweet with the headline "Nasdaq CEO Suggests Halt to Trading to Allow Big Investors to 'Recalibrate Their Positions' to Combat Reddit Users" and had the top comment:

"How is this even legal. [sic] It shouldn't be legal to even think like this."

u/El_Cid_Democrata: "You are not rich. They don't give a fuck about you."

It was beginning to feel like a game of Dungeons and Dragons, where the player outsmarts the Dungeonmaster and, rather than being rewarded for their ingenuity, was about to be nerfed for it.

In the same way CPTHubbard rallied the troops weeks prior, it was now u/ssauronn's turn to march in front of the battle lines and rally the troops. Whether sauron knew it or not, WSB's darkest hour was on the horizon, not in a collision expected to come Friday, but instead a day sooner.

Because the post wasn't stonk related, at least not directly, the first line in the body reads, "Mods do not delete, this is important to me, please read," and the mods not only understood but pinned the post for all to read, leading to another huge surge of upvotes just short of 150,000.

"I was in my early teens during the '08 crisis. I vividly remember the enormous repercussions that the reckless actions by those on Wall Street had in my personal life, and the lives of those close to me. I was fortunate — my parents were prudent and a little paranoid, and they had some food storage saved up. When that crisis hit our family, we were able to keep our little house, but we lived off of pancake mix, and powdered milk, and beans and rice for a year. Ever since then, my parents have kept a food storage, and they keep it updated and fresh.

Those close to me, my friends and extended family, were not nearly as fortunate.... Do you know what tomato soup made out of school cafeteria ketchup packets taste like? My friends got to find out. Almost a year after the crisis' low, my dad had stabilized our income stream and to help out others, he was hiring my friends' dads for odd house work.... They had the mindfulness and compassion to help out those who absolutely needed it.

To Melvin Capital: you stand for everything that I hated during that time."

"To CNBC… Your staple audience will soon become too old to care, and the millions of us, not just at WSB but every person affected by the '08 crash that's now paying attention to GME, are going to remember."

"To the boomers, and/or people close to that age, just now paying attention to these 'millennial blog posts'…. We're not asking you to risk your 401k or retirement fund on a single GME bet. We're just asking you to be understanding, supportive, and to not support the people that caused so much suffering a decade ago.

To WSB: you all are amazing. I imagine that I'm not the only one that this is personal for. I've read myself so many posts on what you guys went through during the '08 crash. Whether you're here for the gains, to stick it to the man as I am, or just to be part of a potentially market changing movement — thank you…. I love you all."

The 2008 stories that flooded this post's comment stream were too many to count. I, too, began to remember the terrible stock advice from "experts" that ruined so many that trusted them. I remember the niceties that we all had to cut back on. And I remembered no one really went to jail, and the world moved on.

u/DeepFuckingValue's position had increased to $47.9 million, and his update that night garnered a whopping, totally unheard of, 215,000 upvotes.

15: Bagging the Fox

January 28th, 2021 | GME: $265.00

Reporters that had feasted on racially tinged, politically motivated, and populist fodder in the era of Donald Trump suddenly found themselves starved with Joe Biden in office. u/lodge28 opened Thursday morning by sharing, "The Financial Times are attempting to link WSB with the alt-right. Do not let the mainstream media villainise our community and push this narrative."

They posted a screencap from the FT, which read: "It would be tempting to dismiss the [so-called] Reddit bros — some of the alt-right supporters — as 'dumb money' and their frenzied buying as a Ponzi scheme."

The moment of congratulating WSB on their short squeeze had evaporated as if it was all just an opposite day, and the prank was over. The "guns" were no longer stopped.

Two hours later, lodge28 followed up with, "In just 2hrs, WSB have forced the Financial Times to adjust their article accusing our community of being linked to the alt-right. Hold the MSM to account and be excellent to each other."

u/grebfar: "Not bad, but it would have been better not to write that alt-right rubbish in the first place."

The chat room of almost completely anonymous users did not have diversity stats on hand, nor did it discriminate between identities when admitting new members. In the later days of r/Superstonk, more women and international retail members than ever before would join the ranks and identify themselves as such to further discourage such stereotypes.

Pre-market trading on Thursday, January 28th, featured a few more articles and mentions of support from prominent celebrities, especially Mark Cuban's tweet of the night previous:

"I got to say I LOVE LOVE what is going on with #wallstreetbets. All of those years of High Frequency Traders front running retail traders, now speed and density of information and retail trading is giving the little guy an edge. Even my 11 y[ea]r old traded w[ith] them and made $."

Cuban would say on *Squawk Box* that morning, after additionally tweeting support for u/ssauronn's post from the previous night, "These are the rules that we [the market] have set. When you have given rules, you have to be willing to accept the behaviors that those rules enable."

But today wasn't Wall Street's day to follow rules. It was their day to re-write them.

u/ParrotMafia, referencing bearish early-hours trading, noticed, "GME fell from 508 to 249."

u/UnderstandingIll1227 hit back, "Market ain't open yet homeslice, get your diamond hands now."

Diamond hands wouldn't be enough to counter what came next. The death blow landed on CNBC minutes before market open: "Robinhood restricts trading in GameStop, other names involved in frenzy."

In (since-edited) blog posts, Robinhood announced to its customers, "We continuously monitor the markets and make changes where necessary. In light of recent volatility, we are restricting transactions for certain securities to position closing only, including $AAL, $AMC, $BB, $BBBY, $CTRM, $EXPR, $GME, $KOSS, $NAKD, $NOK, $SNDL, $TR and $TRVG. We also raised margin requirements for certain securities."

u/Bundaga shared the unfortunate news in a post that nabbed 130k+ upvotes despite being deleted by mods within the hour for breaking the new rule against witch hunts: "Robinhood will not let new options or shares be bought apparently. This is… manipulation lol".

u/Arachnatron replied with the widespread sentiment of the day, "Fuck it, I'm holding." And u/DarknessIsAlliSee begged, "This is illegal, right?"

The answer to the legality of this event, later dubbed "the turning off of the buy button," would be the source of class action lawsuits and investigations. At time of publishing, Robinhood has been forced by a court to confront market manipulation charges, but most charges against the company have failed to hold up.

u/ty_jax hit the nail on the head: "Fuck robinhood, considering the ridiculous…. How manipulative is this?"

u/Pope_Smoke speculated, "Free fucking market my ass."

Tyler Winklevoss of The Social Network fame tweeted, "I'm assuming that the next time a hedge fund starts to make too much money shorting and destroying a business, that they will be de-platformed from their Blo[o]mberg terminal and throttled by their prime broker in the name of orderly markets and consumer protection."

Winklevoss would later allege, "Robinhood was never what it pretended to be. It built its business on selling Wall Street Bets order flow to the hedge fund Citadel. In the moment of truth, we learned which customer it cares about the most."

With seconds ticking down to market open like some kind of fuse, Cuban popped off one more speculative tweet: "So are @robinhoodapp and @IBKR ending trading in #wallstreetbets stocks because they are losing their ass on these trades? Or maybe they don[']t have the cash to enable the trades at this scale? Anyone have any insight on their economics?"

Eventually, traders would learn more about what had occurred that morning at Robinhood. Today, it would only be hard feelings and wild guesses, with a few *trust me bro's* to boot.

The opening bell rang like a trumpeter forcing teenagers armed with rifles out of a trench and into a direct artillery barrage. The soldiers shouted as they sprinted into the throng of waiting bayonets and machine guns, drawing sabers themselves, eager for hand-to-hand combat with the market giants desperate to keep them at arm's length.

Directions for filing SEC violation complaints flowed as trading opened, in addition to added complaints directed at FINRA and Robinhood themselves, making copy/paste text available for other users to do the same. But calls for lawyers, SEC investigations into Robinhood, and even bad app store reviews were met with the repeated plea to BUY GME.

All of those legal efforts would take time and energy and only end in extended settlements (as valuable as $1.63 to $4.00 each, according to Cuban's February AMA). A dollar spent on GME today meant a dollar used with maximum power to inflict damage.

u/joeykomari was one of many inviting users to their non-Robinhood brokerages: "YOU CAN STILL BUY GME & BB on WeBull, eTrade, fidelity, and others, post your platform of choice and keep those [diamond hands] strong!"

But users were hard-pressed to find another brokerage in the insanely short time between Robinhood announcing buy restrictions and the buying opportunities that were so crucial due to the settlement time and transfer of funds usually required for a new broker account.

Within the first ten minutes of open, GME skyrocketed to $350, then $375 at 9:45 a.m., and a $404 high by 9:50 a.m. WSB members feared a $420 pre-market price might be as close as WSB got to the yearned-for $420.69 price point.

While the surge roared, an article from The Guardian held at the top of the Apple Stocks news feed laughably read, "GameStop shares likely to fall after reports of Robinhood app ban." The surge continued, hitting $415 at 9:55 a.m.

Finally, at 9:57 a.m. EST, history was made: $420.69.

Screenshots flooded the subreddit, showing the marker that many thought laughable only days before now suddenly coming to fruition. The market could have pushed the price to this selling point days earlier, but it was now too late.

With one minute to go before 10 a.m., only a half hour into trading, the stock surged to $483.00, even as that Guardian headline remained on screen, aging like milk on a hot summer day.

The surge peaked as stock traders loaded onto GME, visibly using their gains in the now-dipping NOK, BB, and others to pile on. AMC remained the only gains survivor at a cheaper price for those who still couldn't fractionally trade.

But as Reddit pummeled their adversaries in relentless hand-to-hand combat, they failed to turn their gaze away from the struggle. Had the soldiers done so, they might have noticed the enemy's rear lines had retreated prematurely, establishing a position on higher ground and loading their cannons with scattershot aimed at friend and foe alike.

Robinhood's share purchase halt took its toll just then, preventing users from purchasing shares, exercising margin, or buying options. In these moments, once the buy side had been removed, the stock price lost upward momentum.

If a stock's ticker is determined by the price that buyers are willing to pay for it, and the buyers willing to pay $420.69 are kneecapped, even diamond hands can't prevent the inevitable wave of sell orders, stop losses, and paper hands.

An immediate selloff pushed prices back to the $400 mark, despite continued calls to hold from WSB. Then GME and AMC both received circuit breaker halts (the third of the day for GME) at 10:03 a.m. and 10:04 a.m., respectively.

Fidelity and Revolut were said to be down at this time. My own account was confirmed inaccessible at this moment. It was eerily similar to the mass outage reported near noon the day before, where multiple non-Robinhood brokers experienced outages with incredible synchrony.

While these outages were temporary, other non-Robinhood brokerages also restricted trading around this time, a fact that many sources and members of the public outright forgot.

On r/stocks of all places, u/CriticDanger posted some 48 hours later, "Weekend GME Thread + Homework for all: Let's stop using brokerages that halted trading." While Robinhood topped this list as a "Horrible" broker, it was one of many that ranged from horrible to neutral. Only a handful of brokers at the bottom of the list were determined to be "good" for not restricting trading.

Other trading restrictions existed, for instance those stemming from Apex Clearing, which held control over more than one brokerage. @M1Finance tweeted, "Our clearing firm, Apex Clearing, is not allowing purchases.... We sincerely apologize for this inconvenience. This was not our decision."

When the weekend homework had ended, the thread stood at 35,000 upvotes and listed three horrible brokers, nine bad brokers, and six neutral. The biggest players most accused in this anecdote-fueled post included E-trade, Webull, and TD Ameritrade.

There would be another GME circuit breaker flipped at 10:40 a.m., having fallen another hundred dollars to $297.00. Reddit would momentarily crash minutes later, with the landing page appearing, "Our CDN was unable to reach our servers." The circuit breaker lifted just before 11:00 a.m., only to trigger yet again after a fall to $264.01, just as Reddit came back online. By 11:00 a.m., the price was down to $237, over 50% from the high just an hour before, and triggering another halt.

"IF YOU SELL NOW YOU'RE GIVING IN TO THE SUITS" — u/Jazzy-Walker

"Hedge Funds' Last Ditch Effort!!! HOLD" — u/Routine_Huckleberry5

u/caliptastree bemoaned, "It[']s amazing that the founders of Robinhood made Robinhood after seeing what happened during OccupyWallstreet. / Now during the biggest moment against Wallstreet, they completely caved / Fuck Robinhood."

As GME halted once again at 11:08 a.m. EST, now under $170, WSB went into crisis mode. Surrounded by the disembodied limbs of so many allies and enemies alike that no one could tell the difference between friend and foe, the cannon fire was so dense that a retreat was useless next to simply taking cover behind what pile of bodies one could find, choking in the growing cloud of smoke and gunpowder. Fifteen minutes and two trading halts later, GME was worth $126.01.

In the running chat, u/SaintHakop asserted, "THERE ARE NO SELLERS!!!"

u/maxnconnor: "How are they making the stock go down if nobody is selling?"

u/Graysteve: "Mass shorting I would think but I don't know."

u/tressan: "They took away the buy resistance by stopping the majority of buyers from being able to."

u/Cameron653: "Manipulation like this makes me sick. Going from 400 to 175 in a matter of minutes? Fucking bullshit!"

u/Extericore added, "Remember! Volkswagen dipped from 400 before taking off too."

u/mazarax projected a previously ludicrous target price, which would remain the most bullish projection to date: "...Thesis: GME follows the VW example, and will briefly (probably only for minutes) be worth more than the world's most valuable corp (hint: makes i phones.) / So, for a $2.3T market cap, using 70M shares, we require a share price of: $32,857."

u/OPXur smirked, "Sorry but I might take profits at $29,875."

As if it was a sign that the stock had indeed reached its lowest points, two of the most comical members of the past decade surfaced — rapper Ja Rule and presidential debate questioner Ken Bone — both unflappably showed their support for the horribly wounded remnants of the Reddit army in this hour, adding insult to injury.

When the stock unlocked, it bounced at long last, up to $150, its daily low standing at $112.25, a crazed height one week before, and today a jaw-dropping low.

The moment trading apps were accessible again, reinforcements arrived, too late to save those who had lost their lives, but with a heroism that would force back any hopes of Wall Street overrunning the entire WSB camp.

By 11:45 a.m., after a circuit breaker triggered at 11:36 a.m., the stock was back to $250. After two days of steady gains, the rollercoaster was back, and to the chagrin of anyone with a prepared script on the bubble bursting. The stock would pause yet again at 12:01 p.m., 12:11 p.m., and 12:38 p.m., with no end in sight to the volatility.

As the halts slowed the day's action, a steady trickle of remarkable price points began to flow from that morning during the halt at the $483 peak.

u/VerySlump wrangled almost 70k upvotes with "30 Seconds From Triggering Market Nuclear Bomb," a DD that included unverified but tantalizing information on the events of 10:00am that morning. VerySlump alleged a slew of market manipulations that the user worked valiantly to connect on their conspiracy corkboard, chief among them: ask prices soared in the second before crashing, revealing that the MOASS might have been about to spring as planned.

u/ReapingTurtle shared GME "ask" prices reportedly at $2,000 just before the decline triggered, with the header "2k IS THE TRUE ASKING PRICE. DO NOT SELL."

u/zshub reported their fractional share had been purchased for $2,605 per share, and u/aggieboy12 reported almost $1,000 in a similar story.

Users then shared the first class action lawsuit against Robinhood, filed by Brendon Nelson in New York, alleging, "Robinhood purposefully, willfully, and knowingly removing the stock 'GME' from its trading platform in the midst of an unprecedented stock rise thereby deprived retail investors of the ability to invest in the open-market and manipulating the open-market."

The most exciting price points were now in the rearview mirror, whether or not we all knew it at the time.

16: Winter Camp at Valley Forge

4:00 p.m. | Jan. 28th | GME: $193.60

A broken clock being "right twice a day" is an adage that won't survive another generation, not because of the lack of analog clocks, but because clocks are so energy efficient that they don't run out of battery as often as they used to. While the saying still has some weight to it, this day would mark a broken media's second moment of accuracy.

Esquire published, "Robinhood Is a Bouncer Who Works for the Guys Who Own the Club: The GameStop fiasco proves this isn't about 'democratizing' finance. It's a casino, and you're not invited to play."

"Robinhood is, as of Thursday morning, a stock-trading app in which you are not allowed to buy stocks. Well, certain stocks — the ones that some rich and powerful people bet against…. The math isn't complicated here…. These supposedly savvy market players — including Gabe Plotkin, the hedge-fund wunderkind who manages Melvin Capital, which got absolutely hosed — took a big bet and lost. They knew the rules and the risk, and rather than accept the outcome, the financial bigwigs are pulling strings to change those rules and avoid the consequences of their own actions."

After a calmer afternoon following the bloody morning, and with a share price hovering in the low to mid-200s, GameStop closed just under $200.

As I flipped through the news that afternoon, whether it was Fox, Bloomberg, or others, it was blatantly obvious that even their most educated guests were still behind the curve or well ahead of it.

Some paraphrased statements, oft-repeated, which I picked up from various broadcasts that afternoon included,

We're due for an overcorrection, and these retail traders are going to lose everything when it's over.

There's a short squeeze they've identified, and there's infinite room for the stock to grow, but they're poor and will be forced to sell out.

Next week, you'll see, GameStop will be back to seventeen dollars... GameStop will fall back to single digits...

As had been the case until now, these news experts were one of three sorts:

1. Television anchors with broadcast journalism degrees and little to no financial knowledge beyond what their staff typed into their teleprompters.

2. Experts on finance, who knew little to nothing about an irrational player in game theory.

3. Anti-meme stock mania market devotees.

One of the day's more tantalizing interviews appeared when u/Kessarean posted a screencap of their TV with the allegation "Live on CNBC [a broker's executive]... admits halting trading to 'Protect ourselves.'"

In the following months, as GameStop's price continued to undergo further movement, it was impossible to escape articles begging you to forget GameStop. Not even cryptocurrency had suffered such attacks in its early days. It may have scared off the average trader, like my great uncles and aunts, but the apparent so-called 'fear, uncertainty, and doubt' or FUD campaigns only further endeared HODL'ers to their stonk.

Like a successful long-term portfolio, the news media might have done better just leaving GameStop alone if they really wanted to win. Personally, each time I saw an article bashing GameStop in this phase and the months that followed, it made me wonder why the media was so bothered by its survival. This also was fuel to the fire of the GME Streisand effect.

u/weddingraheadache posted on Wednesday, "Hedge Funds Watching Us.... Why are you surprised?"

"Andrew, Gabe, you have to understand that you started this. WSB has loved its $GME calls and shares since November/December. Many of us are gamers, so when we heard our spot was having a hard time, we bought some shares to show our support. This had nothing to do with you — many of us didn't even know you existed.... We were happy that $GME picked up a little (to $20 then $30). / And then you guys had to go and short $GME."

"So don't take it personally. Yes, it sucks to lose billions when many wsb folks are cheering their unexpected gains — gains that will help them pay off their student loans, buy their first house or car, help their aging and ailing relatives put food on the table, or cover healthcare costs incurred during the pandemic. It's not about you."

While Paul Gosar advocated for the Justice Department to root out brokerage collusion, there were dissenters like u/Only-Tells-The-Truth, who foresaw the coming storm: "I used to work @ Merrill. Here's what likely happened today with Robinhood and what it means for short-squeezing investors":

"The clearing house is the intermediary between the counter-parties. Because they stand between sellers & buyers, they have very defined levels of risk, risk management and regulation to be in front of. The clearing house is who gives you the 'title' for your shares, the folks who make it official.... So, they call up the risk department... and tell em to stop fucking selling GME unless they want to post a huge amount of dough, there simply isn't enough float, the SEC told the clearing house they're on their own and who tf is gonna take the blame/liability if there's a massive scale, contagious 'failure to deliver' ordeal?"

The NYT would later give more advocacy to this fact, suggesting that Robinhood simply couldn't meet regulatory standards that it was held to: "The D.T.C.C. notified its member firms that the total cushion, which was then $26 billion, needed to grow to $33.5 billion — within hours. Because Robinhood customers were responsible for so much trading, Robinhood was responsible for footing a significant portion of the bill. The D.T.C.C.'s demand is not negotiable."

But even this article's private equity source would end the article with, "There's something about this that says somebody is really scared about what's going on." And later articles from other sources about the seemingly watertight explanation of the clearinghouse regulations would mention that those negotiations are opaque at best.

Hopefully, these negotiations weren't so opaque that it led to more than two parties meeting behind closed doors, because according to Spencer Jakab that could be illegal, and the SEC might take action!

The analysis of what really happened that day would continue to be debated long after GME's price point had re-stabilized, and no one would find out this evening, tomorrow, or even in the week to come. While WSB was bullish that short shares remained in small numbers, the moves that occurred Thursday could have provided the self-preservative cushion that a short seller needed to survive, and for a much longer term than WSB knew, whether they had instigated the actions or not.

For WSB, it was back to a focus on the war rather than a tribunal.

u/ONE_GUY_ONE_JAR topped the sub with 75,000 upvotes as a late convert: "I just bought $5,000 in $GME. I would not have done this if the brokerages didn't try to manipulate the market…. I don't think of my purchase as an investment, but as putting my own skin in the game as a [']fuck you['] against a rigged system."

u/ehdrewy was prepared for the final match that would signify Wall Street hadn't managed to rescue themselves, rallying for "D Day…in 8 hours" in a mod-removed post that took 19k upvotes:

"Over 76 years ago, Americans, brits, and a few filthy canadians stormed the beaches of Normandy while facing insurmountable odds and they won. In the same way we must storm the metaphorical beaches of wall street and crush this fucking squeeze. We have to win. The entire free investing world is counting on us."

The day's record-breaking seventh GME discussion thread would be closed, and while mods noted that they were keeping threads lower than the usual 100,000 comment limit, each still ranged between that height and 50,000 in number.

The gladiators were now offering spectators their timeless salute, *morituri te salutamus.*

17: The Event Horizon

January 29th, 2021 | GME: $379.71

When a supermassive star breaks down in our universe, its intense heat, pressure, and density create a black hole. Throughout the bodies of such interstellar phenomena, there exist a series of ever more intense regions of gravitational pull that exercise themselves on any object unlucky enough to find themselves drawn in.

The first layer of a black hole is called the event horizon and denotes an invisible barrier at which light can no longer escape the black hole's gravity. While all light is affected by gravity, thanks to Einstein's special theory of relativity, only black holes have gravity dense enough to ensnare a photon. And if photons are unable to escape, nothing larger or more massive has any hope.

The curious thing about a black hole's event horizon, though, is that according to theoretical physicists, should your spaceship ever be unwise in its interstellar explorations and happen to trip the boundary of the event horizon, it wouldn't be known by your crew for some time. The surrounding world would continue to look the same as it did when you were floating freely in outer space.

You would be dead, with no hope for escape, and not even know it had happened.

Friday opened with traders nervously waiting to see if GME would rise, fall, or hold steady. The only activity that would mark a decided loss would be a mass selloff. And most forgot or were ill-informed about this phase of the fight: the squeeze was not squoze when the buy button was turned off. The war still raged.

In a sign of wild market volatility, headlines from the new day flashed on my screen:

CNN: "Dogecoin soars 370% as Reddit group works to send the cryptocurrency 'to the moon.'"

WSJ: "Robinhood Raises $1 Billion to Meet Cash Needs."

WSJ: "Coinbase Crypto Exchange Frozen as Bitcoin Jumps."

A tweet from Citron went out at 8:56 a.m., with Andrew Left waving the white flag (again), stating: "Citron Research discontinues short selling research After 20 years of publishing[:] Citron will no longer publish 'short reports'. We will focus on giving long side multibagger opportunities for individual investors."

(One year later, the following was pinned atop Citron's account: "Citron was not going to write just another short report unless we found a co[mpany] that we believed was harming the system, unprofitable...and whose headwinds were only getting stronger.... we found that in agilon health.")

In the video posted to his account, Left added, "Hopefully we can put our experience to add some sanity and most of all, some kindness back in this market."

Citron's final resignation was already old news, barely deserving of the press it received. Instead, users braced for an end to the historic week with posts like u/aBetterNation's "Just YOLO'd 200k on GME PREMARKET" and u/whagar-man123's "YOLO'D $275K YESTERDAY BEFORE CLOSE. WSB, I STAND WITH YOU."

u/Space-peanut shared, "I saw hedge funders literally drinking champagne as they looked down on the Occupy Wall Street protestors. I will never forget that. / This is all the money I have and I'd rather lose it all than give them what they need to destroy me. Taking money from me won't hurt me, because i don't value it at all. I'll burn it all down just to spite them."

Friday's opening bell blasted up to pre-market trading levels around $413.98, then fell to $354 at its first circuit breaker halt, under three minutes into the trading day. The stock roller-coastered around the $340 mark thereafter.

Cramer's tune changed when he joined CNBC this morning. Calling from a hospital bed, he dodged questions about the existing short float as COVID vaccine news struggled for the spotlight on the screen's lower third: "I'm saying the government has to step in… to prevent panic," he stammered.

The stock market hadn't crashed, but Cramer possibly might have, broken by the very children who had grown up under his influence. As @stackingsatz would tweet (and then delete), "[I'm watching] Jim Cramer trying to stay relevant[,] calling from a hospital bed, asking for Governments to step in on a free market."

But DFV was about to be unmasked, for those who didn't already realize he was Youtube's RoaringKitty. The true identity of u/DeepFuckingValue broke to the Wall Street Journal, confirmed to be Keith Gill, a Massachusetts father and employee of MassMutual: "Trader known as DeepF—ingValue on the WallStreetBets forum helped turn the investing world upside down. 'I didn't expect this.'"

The moment was monumental for WSB. Except for those who had been there for a few weeks, the sub mostly knew the faceless and effectively silent user DFV, who was now unmasked on their screens.

"He said he didn't set out to draw the attention of Congress, the Federal Reserve, hedge funds, the media, trading platforms and hundreds of thousands of investors. / 'This story is so much bigger than me,' Mr. Gill told The Wall Street Journal in his first interview since the unboxing this week of a volatile new stock-market game. 'I support these retail investors, their ability to make a statement.'"

"'He always liked money,' said Elaine Gill, his mother. As a child, she said, 'he would get money from those scratch tickets that people didn't know they'd won. People would throw them on the ground.... A lot of times there was still money on them.'"

The DFV fandom only surged from there. No matter what happened or when DFV decided to sell, his demigod status was etched in stone.

The fan fiction also began in earnest that day, as in this passage from u/mabel-lemae that appeared in "GME What About Second Breakfast Club Megathread": "The year is 2085. I lay on my death bed as my seven great grandchildren, Game, Berry, Deep, Stop, Black, Mars, and Value, visit me one last time. They ask to see how much my 7 GME shares are worth, for the millionth time. I show them. $42,000,000,000.69.... I am gifting them a share each. My only request, never fucking sell. u/Deepfuckingvalue, the motherfucking king of all kings, is long gone. Not dead, but traveling universe to universe bringing millions out of poverty and unifying everything in existence…. As my body weakens, I order my wife's ex[-]boyfriend butler to bring me my whiskey one last time. After downing the bottle, I close my eyes and smile. I build up the little strength I have left and utter my final words. / 'Get fuckin rekt Melvin.'"

Holding impressively steady throughout the trading day on the backs of another million new WSB members, GME suffered a drop into the 1:00 p.m. hour, down to $275, which was bought back up with almost instantaneous furor, sending it back to $300+.

Around this time, u/Tonninc found a job posting for "Federal Affairs Manager, Robinhood" to "[potentially] navigate their impending congressional hearings."

The steady stock decline bottomed out at 2:30 p.m., at which point an hour's worth of gains was erased in the half hour left before the final 60 minutes of trading. When the final seconds ticked down to a $328 close, the day, and the week at large, were won. WSB had Rocky'd their 15 rounds and were battered and bloodied, shouting for ADRIENNE! as the end credits rolled.

Friday's afternoon punditry wasn't much better off than the day before, but it certainly was entertaining. Charles Payne shouting down the other talking head while joining Cavuto, for instance, "Who cares about your thesis?! Who cares about your thesis? Who are you?!…Who the hell is anybody out there to say you should stop being able to own GameStop at a certain price?"

One day shy of the eighth birthday of r/wallstreetbets, Saturday, January 30th was a day for celebration. After an absolute blitz of a week, I was able to take some time off too. My wife and I went to a nicer Italian restaurant, even though we both knew we'd be ordering pizza and a bottle of the house red.

As we sat down, every table was abuzz with what GameStop meant for people in this middle-class neighborhood, seemingly thrilled with this chat room's ability to effect such change. The GME squeeze had permeated the general public at long last. And while some evil empire hadn't been toppled, it had been subdued at its own expense rather than the opposite that typically ruled these peoples' lives.

Now 7 million in number, WSB called for charity in their time off. Spurred by the notion that earnings would increase GameStop's long-term valuations, users were buying gift cards and memberships en masse. Then, as in the case of u/Thomaswms01, they would donate the merchandise to children's hospitals, autism nonprofits, and much more.

The conspiracy theories would once again surge, now with a pause to analyze the market moves that had snapped open and shut in the previous week. u/johnnydaggers suggested an even more cataclysmic theory on what was happening behind the scenes:

"We probably own way more of GME than we think and that is freaking out Wall Street because it could prove they've been up to some extremely illegal shit and the whole system could implode as a result."

18: The Singularity

When misleading and outright false media narratives surfaced the week prior, it was to be expected. Information had been flying faster than reporters could keep up, and reporters so adept at Twitter were forced into an entirely new social media space.

But Monday morning, after a quiet weekend where journalists mostly tried to realign their stories behind real-life traders' ups and downs, a story swept the media, which, whether by manipulation or simply out of luck to the shorts, dealt a wounding blow to GME's surviving reinforcements.

In the early hours of Monday, February 1st, 2021, the entire media wasn't concerned about GameStop or AMC, nor were they particularly focused on a massive earnings week ahead. Instead, CNBC and many others were crowded around the blazing bonfire of a new meme, like moths led to flame.

Silver.

Out of all those early moments in the GameStop saga, many of which would seem tinfoil hat-worthy, this was one of the coincidences I couldn't ignore then or now. To the present day, I'll never forget how angry I was seeing this story break and then seeing it flood the general public afterward. It was so far off the mark.

Silver?

Of all the non-GME stocks, the early DDs, and on and on, there certainly were some opinions on $AG (First Majestic Silver Co.), but not nearly enough to where this surge was a homegrown WSB topic.

And for a media that took so long to grasp that GME was the core of the WSB play, rather than just throwing their hands up and blabbing *meme stock*, suddenly they were hyperfocused on the new alleged WSB favorite.

CNBC went live with the chyron, "THE SILVER SQUEEZE: REDDIT TRADERS BOOST SPOT SILVER," as if they knew nothing about the real-life inspiration for the ill-fated J.R. Ewing.[7]

While the memes on the page had become increasingly complex, a simple meme that looked like those of the late 2000s appeared from u/Ordinary-Fox9986 to the tune of 75k upvotes: Admiral Ackbar shouting, "IT'S A TRAP" and the caption, "The aggressive media campaign to promote silver (worldwide at the same time)."

It didn't take a complex series of Lord of the Rings battle scenes to clarify this. Reddit was not a unified entity, but there were easy corollaries between the week's popular insights and how the subreddit supported stock. Silver was not one of them, as u/SonofRaymond would say to the imaginary hedge fund guys watching, "You can't buy us with a bag of silver like Judas."

u/MajorKeyBro: "Complete lies. Stay away from silver right now."

u/SpaceBollz: "I'm on CNBC and Bloomberg they're both claiming silver is the new stock we're all chasing, there were a few posts about it here last night apparently, maybe one silver post for every 20 GME posts. / Diversion tactic[?]"

u/spoobydoo hit the nail on the head, though: "It[']s insane how this lie popped up simultaneously across ALL financial media last night. / Every. Single. Outlet repeated this…. / Either they didn't bother to check if it[']s true and just parroted what some shill was saying or… they are all in it together — as conspiratorial as that sounds, I can't think of any other explanation."

The silver surge, whether purposeful or lucky, was perfect for shorts because, despite the knowledge held by the millions on the subreddit, no one would listen

---

[7] To 80,000 upvotes, u/MarioBuzo provided DD that morning into the history of the Hunt Brothers of the late 1970's, titled, "There is no silver short squeeze happening. NONE. NEVER…. The Hunts had gambled that silver was undervalued, but they failed because they had made the price of silver too attractive for its own good." And the media would be none the wiser.

to their protestations. WSB wasn't an entity that could correct the story either; previously MOASS's biggest asset and now its Achilles heel.

Herefore, if a news outlet was to say WSB's new stock was silver, or Nokia, or Circuit City for that matter, who's to say it wasn't? Silver might as well be as ridiculous a short-term, WSB-style investment as the others. Who's to say who the media thinks likes the stock, anyway?

They'll probably tell you the same as the WSB folks: it's not financial advice, just entertainment.

No longer were the everyman Twitter personalities or primetime TV hosts rushing to WSB's defense as they had after the buy button got turned off. On Monday, they'd washed their hands of it. Maybe Friday's 600-point market drop scared Chris Cuomo straight. Maybe Cramer narrowly avoided having a pillow pressed over his face in his hospital bed. Or, maybe it was just the more likely end of a weekly news cycle.

Whatever it was, the story was over, kneecapped by 8% gains in the value of silver. Whoop de fucking doo.

GME opened Monday with a 10% plunge, which failed to drive a material selloff, returning to an even day within ten minutes of market open. Another selloff triggered after the opening recovery, pulling GME to its lowest price at the 10:00 a.m. mark, around $267, followed by another drop to $215, just as the WSB population reached 8 million degenerates.

u/nat20sfail replied to u/Shrevel's viral post, "DO NOT sell GME at low volume dips," with "Listen, the short% may have decreased from 60 to 50, IF [someone] isn't fraudulently claiming short covers. That's STILL HIGHER THAN VOLKSWAGEN'S. They are trying to scare boomers off and BUYS are needed to halt the momentum!"

It was refreshing to hear the fundamentals of the MOASS math again, which had been buried in the minutiae of alleged market manipulation most of the prior week. But I could feel a shift: the math wasn't making as much sense as it had during the ascent.

Not discounting the deep value and nostalgic aspects, what interested me most about the GME short squeeze was the unbelievable short interest, and that's also what kept me HODL'ing my single share throughout the ups and downs of the week prior.

But now it had been a week, the volume of shares traded exceeded the available float by leaps and bounds, and there was no sign that a shortage of shares was on the horizon. While *mama certainly did not raise a paperhanded bitch*, I can't ignore DD that fails to live up to projections.

u/SomethingDoDivine commented with large caps and emojis on GME Megathread Part 2, way back on Tuesday, Jan. 26th: "There is literally no way for shorts to exit their costly positions without paying us, as long as we HOLD…. Whether it happens today in a giant spike, or in small steps over the next couple months, the shorts WILL pay out."

And we had all believed it true.

Power hour was anything but for the stock, normally untouched in that phase, and now dipping from $240 to the day's low of $212. While not a significant or meaningful change, it was undoubtedly a demoralizing one for anyone watching the larger graph, down from the day's open at $316.

u/-NinjaBoss was downvoted negative 32 for commenting on "GME Discussion Thread for February 1, 2021 — Part 3" with some truth: "We're getting our asses beat at the moment… ".

u/Is-Anything_Real: "DFV WHERE ARE YOU."

He was still here, now with $35.7 million, diamond handing with still inflating fame. Two days later, DFV would post, "GME YOLO update — Feb 3[,] 2021 — heads up gonna back off the daily updates for now," returning Gill's updates to those based around price swings.

Now losing the war, and with reinforcements used up, this would be WSB's prime moment for desperately needed DDs on outstanding shorts and illegal activity evidence, hoping to reassure users that the stock would only fall as low as

Reddit would allow and the peaks and valleys of the day weren't actually their doing.

But the moving goalposts, discussing complex details like Fails to Delivery and T+2 Delivery Rules, were getting too complicated for the members of r/all to grasp, should a DD even reach the front page as they had previously.

While no manmade object has tumbled into a black hole, and our first image of a black hole only occurred later in 2021, scientists have determined that at the deepest point within a black hole is a "singularity," far below our earlier discussed event horizon. The singularity is where an object suffers complete molecular breakdown, followed by the honest-to-god scientific term "spaghettification." Then, and only then, would an object finally be at the hole's deepest point.

While the total crush is widely accepted as the prevailing theory, still a subsection of even more theoretical physicists argues that the singularity is a wormhole, which transfers surviving matter into an entirely new universe, dimension, or both.

While astrophysicists won't soon be able to test whether a black hole's singularity leads to horrendous destruction or an unfathomable new existence, WSB was about to find out, having undeniably slipped below that event horizon sometime the previous Thursday.

19: Hanging Separately and Together

February 2nd, 2021 | GME: $140

Tuesday, February 2nd, opened with an AMA hosted by WSB favorite Mark Cuban, posted directly to the sub. As mod u/turdled commented and pinned, "This is legit. Mark decided to start the AMA earlier."

Amongst other things, the Q&A session gave users support to rally around, and in hindsight, many of Cuban's predictions came true. While apes begged for their confirmation bias to be, well, confirmed, Cuban remained at surface level and wasn't talking about Wednesday, the week to come, or even the rest of 2021. He talked about fundamentals.

Questions about naked shorts, counterfeit shares, and more went ignored or outright dismissed by Cuban as these bullish buzzwords began to lose their luster. To his credit, Cuban was there to talk about the shortcomings of the SEC and a bright future for retail investors long afterward. Once the buy button turned off, that was traders' best bet in the near term, even if it seemed like there was still hope for a rebound.

Cuban's most quoted answer would gain 16,000 upvotes and numerous re-postings over the coming months: "Best thing you can do is hold on to the stock and do business with GameStop. If everyone goes to their website and buys from them that is going to help the company which will help the stock which will help everyone here. / If you still believe in the reason you bought the stock, and that hasn[']t changed, why sell?"

GME opened at $140.76 after a dismal after-hours and pre-market performance. With a momentary bounce up to $158, the price was down to $102 minutes later. Another bounce kept the ticker alive for a moment before it fell yet again to a daily low of a crushing $74.22.

I couldn't help but feel sadness alongside other apes from the start, not to mention the updated short interest numbers. S3 quoted director Ihor Dusaniwsky in a tweet: "Over the last week, the number of GME shares shorted has decreased by -37.24 million shares, worth $8.4 billion, a decrease of -59%."

This seemed to mean shorts had covered almost half of outstanding positions. This report alone seemed to suggest that the previously +100% short measures no longer indicated some kind of inescapable MOASS opportunity.

u/dezure posted "Why GME is still in the game to trigger MOASS," asking this very question, but only to 8,000 upvotes.

"SI% numbers are very conflicting. Especially the numbers that came around 30-50%. It was then later mentioned by someone in S3 that a different calculation was used. If you convert to the old calculation, you still get over 100% SI%. Why are they trying to change it all of a sudden?"

This accused shift in short interest calculations would be a sticking point for Redditors for months to come. Why change the calculation unless something is broken? And why not be fully transparent about those calculations if so?

The short interest percentages never quite would make sense. Even when users claimed Bed, Bath, and Beyond's short interest exceeded 100% in mid-2022, prompting its short squeeze, the math was no longer solid enough to confirm MOASS was possible there either. The retailer closed its doors for good in June of 2023.

One of the most important parts of writing this book was getting this story right, and calling WSB "gamblers who lost it all in a bubble pop" is a myopic lie. While some were and still are degenerate gamblers, the WSB of January 2021 was not that of Rogozinski's oft-cited manuscript, and they were not losers as stocks increasingly flashed red. They simply believed in the reason they'd invested in the first place, just as Mark Cuban had advised that morning, their diamond hands never harder.

If anything, WSB was a totally free entity, made of members who had toppled the golden calf of money. They stared financial death in the face, and while most fled, the remainder only laughed.

"WE CAN STAY RETARDED LONGER THAN YOU CAN STAY SOLVENT" became the next, and likely final, rallying cry of the squeeze. Now, markets were an episode of *Whose Line Is It Anyway?* where the prices were made up and the losses didn't matter.

Tuesday, Feb. 2nd, GameStop closed at $90.21, down $134.79 from open. Despite a midday rally, the overall picture was a resounding beating as Reddit went dark again just after the 4 p.m. hour.

When the site returned, the overnight GME chat thread, "GME overnight Pajama party megathread 9000," hosted a number of users sharing kind sentiments as they prepared for final losses again the following morning:

u/never-sleeps: "So far it looks like I'm going to have one of two outcomes: 1: Gonna be divorced and broke / 2: Gonna be divorced and rich."

u/WolfOfNallStreet: "'Hey I bought these GameStop shares a few days ago for $480, but they don't seem to be working, can I return them?' / GameStop employee: 'I can give you $80 for them.'"

This ended one of the most exciting weeks Reddit had ever seen. And it was particularly rewarding after a year of feeling insignificant against the tide of pandemic policies that helped only the fringes of society. Suddenly this global community sprung up with a working person's effort never seen before and actually made a difference on the scale of a political movement.

As Benjamin Franklin said almost three hundred years prior, "We must all hang together, or surely, we shall hang separately." And in the early morning hours, WSB was giddy to be hanging together at Pajama Party 9000.

Most of those posting and commenting were returning to where they started, some parting with as much as a $150,000 paper profit at the stock's peak, having held valiantly.

For all it was worth, that stock ticker wasn't slowing down on Thursday, before the buy button was turned off. I have no doubt in my mind that that was the MOASS, and it would have been glorious.

The week's end would bring the stock back to pre-Citron levels, held now by the truest of believers, some of whom were nursing losses over 80%.

(Since-deleted) user u/InfiniteAccuracy, echoed one last time, "If the SEC is still here: Fuck you."

Infinite accuracy, indeed.

20: State of the Union

It was fitting that a story that started on Inauguration Day should end with a state of the union address, but this speech wouldn't be delivered by the president. It came courtesy of WSB mods u/only1parkjisung, u/zjz, and u/wallstreetboyfriend in the evening of February 2nd, 2021, and has since been deleted:

"WALLSTREETBETS STATE OF THE UNION"

"Could you imagine two weeks ago a crusade was brewing, that several million traders would soon band together to fire one, big, shot, across the bow of some [of] the most powerful entities in the world. How could you have? And yet here we stand in the early acts of an epic, with Hollywood fighting to tell a story that has barely begun.

Community.

Wallstreetbets has not and will never be just one individual, rather a collective of ideals and goals greater than the sum of its parts. Reddit is the soapbox that allows these diverse individuals to amplify messages that resonate with them with their votes. That does not mean this is political — Wallstreetbets has never and will never be political.

The financial system has always been shrouded in mystery and complexity, on purpose, to keep the golden goose beneficiaries entrenched. We've especially seen it in action the last few weeks, where fairness and the now apparently idealistic thoughts of a level playing field have gone out the window as traders' control of their own investments was wrested from them. We see the users, we see the quality of the content, and we're here to evangelize on your behalf. The struggle will be long and arduous. But we're in it if you're in it with us. Let's get it done[,] you amazing degenerates."

"We don't need to occupy anything, this subreddit and communities like it are soon to be the (half ton) gorilla in the room and we're just not quite sure how to stand yet. Retail money has always loomed large, it's just never had so much information and made most of its own decisions before. It was (mis)lead by hack analysts and at best had to huddle in index funds for safety.

When we come together on platforms like this with similar goals, similar tools, and similar data, we become a force that can, even without any centralization, coordination, or deep pockets, easily destroy well-funded opponents and cause them to have to break the rules just to stay alive. Random people that have never spoken before buying GME for reasons ranging from 'haha brrr' to 30 page writeups can cause spikes that can nearly bankrupt the kind of people that aren't used to being the ones on the losing end."

"I've been here since the sub was <2000 members. It really didn't hit me on how crazy everything was getting until I checked Twitter last week.

Regardless of our personal political views, let's marvel at the fact that Ted Cruz, AOC, Trump Jr, Chamath, Musk, Cuban, and countless others from various backgrounds and viewpoints agree so strongly on a single topic. We've had everything from fractional share owners to multi-millionaires band together because they like a stock. We've been in the news cycles nonstop, and there's even tendies commercials.

Memes aside, things have been shitty for individual traders. Recent events have highlighted how skewed the game has been towards institutional traders. Whether or not there was any intentional wrongdoing, the inherent biases for a hedge fund being [allegedly] bailed out by another hedge fund and ALSO [potentially] being a major contributor to a large portion of a brokerage's earnings is kinda fucked up. While I'm not smart enough to say whether the game is 100% rigged, it certainly doesn't look good. The US government breaks up monopolies for this very reason, don't they?"

"There's an opportunity in front of us — We have a chance to make a difference and maybe level the playing field. There are government hearings on Feb 18th, and we have politicians from ALL sides offering to look into what happened. We even have billionaires like Mark Cuban and the Winklevoss Twins speaking out against this unfairness. Regardless of what happens, I'm just thankful that I got to be here from the start. Our jungle may be bigger, but it's been the same bananas the whole time.

So what now? We have an opportunity to change the game. We need to move away from a system with power in the hands of the few to one where power is in the hands of the many. The alternative is that we stay where we are now, where the fate of retail traders is at the whim of archaic institutions. Where they can arbitrarily halt stocks and shackle the free market…. Something needs to change, and I'm certain we're not limited by the technology. We're limited by the people."

To the chagrin of many WSB users, Jaime Rogozinski would open February 4th with the Wall Street Journal's announcement that he'd sold his rights to embattled producer Brett Ratner's RatPac Dune, the third WSB film now rocketing into production.

"I won. They can pretend to have this battle," he told the Journal.

At the time of publishing, there had been no additional news on the film's progress.

The Price of Money

There aren't lambos and private islands at the end of this segment because this experiment wasn't just about getting rich; it was about getting out of the rat race. For all intents and purposes, the movement resembled James O'Kane's *The Crooked Ladder* more than Jordan Belfort's *Wolf of Wall Street*.

Despite the losses, annoyances, and volatility, why were you on Wall Street so enraged when the tables had tilted against you?

When young people stopped going to movies, you thought it good, for it meant our money would be spent on tech and home entertainment.

When we stopped worshiping God, you thought it good, for it meant our tithes could go toward cruises, airlines, and casinos.

When we stopped respecting our elders, you thought it good, for it meant our wages might be spent in apparel, retail, and automotive.

When we stopped getting married, you thought it good, for it meant our savings might be spent on real estate.

When we stopped buying a home, you thought it good, for it meant our equity could be diluted into ongoing rental.

When we stopped having children, you thought it good, for it meant our childcare could be used to buy higher-margin pet products.

When we stopped respecting savings, you thought it good, for it meant our lack of funds would force us into revolving debt.

With no house, no family, no assets, no savings, no healthcare, no religion, and no upward mobility, we stopped respecting our money. And you thought that bad because, with no respect for money, we no longer had to play your game by its rules.

We had our own game, and one that we could actually win.

Part 3: A Republic, if you can Keep It

ADVANCED

A

GME DD

Theoretical Finance
Graphic Loss Porn
Multinational Fraud*

*Alleged

"What [I] love about this… is that if you pick your spots right and work as a group, you can hit again and again."
-u/mcuban AMA, February 2021

21: When I was a Young Boy in Bulgaria

February 18th, 2021 | GME: $48.49

If this was a movie, it would be over by now.

Most books and movies on the topic end at this moment, or shortly thereafter.

Either the players succeeded against all odds and made one final surge, or the villains emerged triumphant. In real life, neither happened. This wasn't a movie with a clean three-act structure, and real life is always stranger than fiction.

As u/FrenchTickler so elegantly stated in September of 2021, "Fuck that Ben Mezrich guy, writing a book and making a movie about GameStop while its not even over yet.... They really want to write history before it even happens, fuck these guys! MOASS is imminent!"

Their words, not mine.

January 2021 quickly became referred to as "the sneeze" rather than the squeeze, and what occurred after that sneeze was a slow burn compared to the utter chaos before. All the while, the remaining followers of the GameStop saga — and countless newcomers in that span — would redefine what it meant to be a player. Now the game required discipline, intelligence, and an even more resolute hive-mind behind the controller.

Before the congressional fireworks came Reddit's first public entry into the action; in between the WSB State of the Union and the *Game Stopped* congressional hearing was the 2021 Super Bowl on February 7th.

Reddit sponsored a surprise ad that night with the following message, formatted like a Reddit post, which the company initiated less than one week before the big game, and which only ran for a total of five seconds: "Wow, this actually worked."

"If you're reading this, it means our bet paid off…. One thing we learned from our communities last week is that underdogs can accomplish just about anything when they come together around a common idea…. Powerful things happen when people rally around something they really care about. And there's a place for that. It's called Reddit."

The ad was number two on Google's top 5 most searched ads from the night, a momentous accomplishment on what can be assumed to be a comparatively small ad spend. It showed the site's leadership's commitment to the social change their product had finally inspired, and on the global stage.

Reddit's second opportunity to speak about the site's success came ten days later.

On February 18th, both the once anonymous traders and formerly once-anonymous executives were put on display live for the first time, participating in "Game Stopped? Who Wins and Loses When Short Sellers, Social Media, and Retail Investors Collide," a nearly six-hour congressional hearing held by the U.S. House Financial Services Committee.

CEO and co-founder of Reddit, Steve Huffman, would join Robinhood's Vlad Tenev, Citadel's Ken Griffin, Melvin's Gabe Plotkin, and "retail investor" Keith Gill on the digital stage.

House and Senate committees go back to the founding of the United States. They are a convenient way for Congress to hear testimony regarding potential legislation and conduct investigations on a selective basis, i.e., without each of the 435 house members needing to be present.

And, of course, in the age of modern media, House and Senate committees have also become a way for representatives of both parties to make a splash, typically at the expense of those speaking before them. For this reason, many appointments to committees are made for reasons of political ascendancy and not expertise. When average people hear about committee hearings, it's due to viral lines of inquiry by Alexandria Ocasio-Cortez, Jim Jordan, and Katie Porter.

The House's Financial Services Committee traces its roots back almost two hundred years. Its members at the time included well-known politicians like chairwoman Maxine Waters, ranking member Patrick McHenry, and three of the six "squad" members, Rashida Talib, Ayanna Pressley, and Ocasio-Cortez.

Committee investigations also go back all the way to 1792, when the House appointed a special committee (a temporary sibling of the permanent standing committees like Financial Services) to investigate failures at the Battle of Wabash, in which six hundred soldiers were killed. As we have seen in 2022's January 6th special committee, the committee may also make criminal referrals to the Department of Justice.

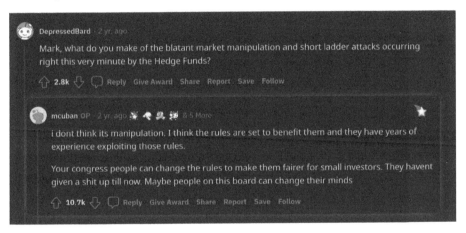

Mark Cuban AMA, Feb. 2nd, 2021

The *Game Stopped* investigation was expected to be nothing if not entertaining. The members of WSB hoped for a grilling of their sworn enemies before their elected representatives, many of whom had witnessed the events of the weeks prior and voiced their concerns on social media. The committee could at least establish legislative processes to combat naked shorting, future broker interference, and opaque short reporting standards.

However, the five-plus hours of testimony could only be compared to a boxer consistently swinging, unable to land a punch. Therefore, it's not worth rehashing the beat-by-beat from that afternoon.

Keith Gill had a few minutes to share why GameStop had excellent fundamentals and managed to add in an "I like the stock," sending Reddit into a brief tizzy. Republicans focused on social media's threat to market stability. Democrats pushed for a financial markets transaction tax. And all the rest of us lost faith in our elected officials, what faith we had left, at least.

Just past the five-hour mark, when Alexandria Ocasio-Cortez pressed most directly for testimony on Melvin Capital's shorting practices, especially asking about naked shorting, chairwoman Maxine Waters suffered technical difficulties that disrupted the line of questioning. Those tech issues endured until the congresswoman's time had expired, and Gabe Plotkin never had to speak on the matter as a result.

Though Ocasio-Cortez was among the first to notice what had occurred on the day the buy button turned off, tweeting to Elon Musk's agreement, "This is unacceptable. / We now need to know more about @RobinhoodApp's decision to block retail investors from purchasing stock while hedge funds are freely able to trade the stock as they see fit," by the day of this hearing, her "squad" seemed more focused on taxes than forcing Tenev or Griffin to divulge information under oath.

Had I expected fireworks, I might have been severely disappointed and frustrated, as many others were. But I had seen plenty that past month. No flaccid congressional hearing would change what had occurred, even under the best of circumstances.

Caleb Silver, editor-in-chief of Investopedia, summed it up best during that evening's episode of CNBC's *Worldwide Exchange*: "What we learned is that our regulators and politicians on this... committee don't really understand how markets work that well. There was so much explaining that needed to happen and there were so many people that had the wrong perception of what was actually happening between Robinhood, its customers, its market makers, and the short sellers that [they] needed a re-education.... We're not gonna see much out of this... but it was very entertaining."

After so much saber-rattling about defending constituents, the committee was easily misdirected by technical difficulties, fear of retail traders, and atrocious dysfunction. If Reddit was truly a hive-mind with lightning-fast efficiency, the House Financial Services Committee was the exact opposite.

Despite these shortcomings and the grueling hours we all had wasted watching the hearing, there were select longer-term benefits. While traders came up short this day, meme lords did not, and some terms would remain ingrained in the Reddit lexicon to date, including but not limited to:

When I was a young boy in Bulgaria — Made popular by Robinhood CEO Vlad Tenev and mentioned numerous times throughout the hearing, including his opening statement, Tenev seemed to open every response by going back decades to his childhood in Bulgaria. The repeated use of this line made him an easy target for annoyed viewers, who saw it as an easy way to stall until his time would expire, and it now stands as a reply where someone wishes to avoid the question.

One of the finest investors of his generation — Of all the unique video setups for the hearing, Gabe Plotkin's was by far the most fascinating: a totally cleaned-out office sat behind him, except for a motionless printer. It reeked of collapse. But that strange sight didn't stop Ken Griffin from stating why Citadel had taken on Melvin Capital, and Gabe with it: Gabe was apparently one of the finest investors of his generation.

Beyond the memes, a deeper investigation did occur by the committee, and they managed to hold future hearings and uncover documents and communications that were previously hidden from public view. This would be the second benefit of the hearing, albeit one that went unrealized for more than a year.

On page 48 of the June 2022 report titled "GAME STOPPED: How the Meme Stock Market Event Exposed Troubling Business Practices, Inadequate Risk Management, and the Need for Legislative and Regulatory Reform", there was a Jan. 27th, 2021 line of messaging between Robinhood's c-suite members.

In these messages, Tenev suggests, "Maybe this would be a good time for me to chat with Ken griffin [sic]." On the previous page, the committee adds, "Robinhood and Citadel Securities engaged in 'blunt' negotiations the night before the trading restrictions to lower the PFOF rates Robinhood was charging Citadel Securities."

Tenev and Griffin denied accusations of wrongdoing throughout the hearing. Redditors were left asking questions in that informational vacuum. The most cited question came from Rep. Juan Vargas: "Did you talk to them (Robinhood) about… restricting… buying in GameStop?" To which Ken Griffin answered, "Let me be perfectly clear. Absolutely not."

Both the committee's final report and a separate class action lawsuit uncovered internal communications between Robinhood and Citadel, a fact that Redditors thought conflicted with Griffin's denial. However, there's ample room for Griffin to still be telling the truth in this case, something which he maintains. A number of accusatory hashtags sprouted from such Redditor theories, which trend on social media from time to time.

(Don't get me started on the skywriters.)

As to the rest of the *Game Stopped* report, u/Rainbowphoebe said it best: "Promise kept. We've done nothing as promised."

For all the hobnobbing of the virtual hearing, Steve Huffman's opening statement was incredibly forthcoming: "At Reddit, our first duty in these situations is to our communities, and our role in this moment was to keep WallStreetBets online. Working around the clock, we scaled our infrastructure and made technology changes to help this community withstand the onslaught of traffic, and we acted as diplomats to help resolve conflict within WallStreetBets' leadership."

"WallStreetBets may look sophomoric or chaotic from the outside, but the fact that we are here today means they've managed to raise important issues about fairness and opportunity in our financial system. I'm proud they used Reddit to do so."

When the virtual hearing ended in the early evening of February 18th, GME's stock price had fallen as the day's excitement fizzled out. It now held slightly above $40.

The next day, the stock would fall to its lowest point in weeks, and a low point that would not be reached until the stock would split almost two years later: $38.50. Citron almost had their "back to $20" moment.

Almost.

At a price of approximately $38.70 per share, u/DeepFuckingValue doubled down, as he shared in his February 19th post, and his first post in over two weeks, "GME YOLO update — Feb 19 2021," which showed his position of 50,000 shares had grown to 100,000.

u/namonite: "You were literally the only person at the hearing who could: / 1. Speak in complete sentences / 2. Use technology / 3. Not need a lawyer present / 4. Buy the dip."

u/timeintheocean: "5. Sleep with my wife."

DFV would only update his positions seven more times after this. At 4:20 p.m. on Friday, April 16th, 2021, u/Deepfuckingvalue would submit Reddit's most awarded post of all time, "GME YOLO update — Apr 16 2021 — final update."

After exercising his call options, DFV used his winnings to exercise and purchase a combined 100,000 shares, bringing his GME share total to 200,000 and effectively doubling down one more time.

Then, Gill's social media accounts went dark for good.

22: If They're Still In, I'm Still In

February 24th, 2021 | GME: $44.70

With trading open for the first time since DFV's first time doubling down, the truly faithful returned to the still blood-soaked battlefield on Monday, Feb. 19th, nearly pushing the stock price back to $50 again.

The stock's daily decline over the span of two weeks had bottomed out and would remain steady for the first three days of that week. But Wednesday, February 24th, brought unexpected results. GameStop's stock price began a steady climb as it had a month prior. I bought my second share at $70, doubling my own position in the process, albeit to less fanfare than DFV.

Largely unnoticed by the news media, trading on GME was halted twice before the day's end, and in after-hours trading, the price reached a whopping $180. There was no doubt this was the MOASS, at long last. Additionally, there was no news to motivate the event besides an announcement that GameStop's CFO was stepping down.

The next day, February 25th, brought even more extreme volatility on even less information, as the stock whipped wildly between $184.68 and $101.00. On that day alone, Yahoo reported a trade volume of over 150 million.

Something was unresolved, but no one knew what. Almost no one.

GameStop chairman Ryan Cohen (AKA Papa Cohen, Book King, et al.) tweeted just before things got hectic on Feb. 24th. The tweet was simply a frog emoji with the image of a McDonald's ice cream cone attached.

The cryptic tweet would be Cohen's third and his first since the events of January 2021. His almost weekly posts would become the players' newest obsession in DFV's impending departure, as The Street would report more than a year later:

"GameStop investors are trying to decipher the meaning behind Ryan Cohen's potentially 'coded' tweets."

"While all of this speculation could well be wide of the mark, we do have to, at the very least, acknowledge the amazing ability of some Redditors to develop creative interpretations of Cohen's puzzling tweets. Meme investors are willing to look for needles in a haystack."

But some of Reddit's best guesses were anything but stabs in the dark, especially compared to what Jakab and Mezrich surmised in their two immediate publishings about the event. Some Cohen tweets took days to make educated guesses, while others couldn't be deciphered for weeks or months. Some tweets were theorized to be sequential in nature to spell out hidden messages, while others were just simple tributes to Cohen's family and company, nothing more.

The erratic guessing merited a mention in 2023's *Making of the Meme King*, an hour-long made-for-TV special from CNBC. Unfortunately, the documentary failed to shed light on some of Redditors' best guesses. Luckily, this isn't CNBC, so here goes...

On June 13th, 2021, more than three months after Cohen's ice cream tweet, an insane guess was posted by u/SamRandomFox, one which redditors didn't have the groupthink to figure out when it originally happened: "I think the frog emoji was not random at all, as he was hinting the T+21 and T+35 cycles!"

The post isn't some long theory. Instead, it's a Google search result for "life cycle of a frog, [in] days," which brings up a brief explanation provided by Google: "It takes about 21 days for tadpoles to form…. It takes about 5 weeks [35 days] for this change to begin."

Now, measuring specific parts of a frog's life cycle can be pretty obscure, and there are plenty of other possibilities; however, the post was met with great acclaim to the tune of over 12,000 upvotes. Moreover, this theory had some meat to it because the stock surge of February 24th might be explained by what are known as Failures To Deliver (FTDs), which were briefly theorized about during the most cataclysmic sneeze moments.

An FTD occurs when a tradeable asset is considered past due and must be delivered. For example, if naked shorting has occurred, and entities are owed assets that weren't first located, one ends up with a failure to deliver. FTDs take forms including T+21 and T+35, referring to trading days. The FTD cycle runs repeatedly, and Redditors would try to match it to major moves in GameStop's stock price, which for much of 2021 did have a bizarrely correlating pattern.

If February 24th and the price run-up of the 25th truly did correspond to the height of the sneeze twenty-one trading days prior (i.e., calendar days minus weekends and holidays), then there were entities that had deliveries that couldn't be reconciled. At long last, shorts were forced to buy.

u/JBeezy1214 cheered, "Ya know, this might not have anything to do with anything but god damn the shit you guys find never ceases to amaze me. I had never been on Reddit in my life until this whole thing started. I love this place."

Other Redditors suggested that McDonald's ice cream machines are broken so often that tweet could also be a reference to a failure to deliver. Coincidentally, in September 2021, McDonalds' ice cream woes had made the company the source of an FTC probe, which remains unresolved at the time of publication.

A since-deleted user, who we'll refer to as T21 Guy, posted the day before the tadpole post, "An analysis of tweet activity and corporate announcements," where they compared Cohen tweets, price spikes, and the T+21 cycle dates to prove the hypothesis that price spikes are connected to the cycles, and not to Cohen's tweets or company announcements.

Regarding Cohen's tweet on February 24th, 2021, T21 guy says, "Ryan Cohen tweets the famous ice cream cone on Feb 24, lining up perfectly with the T+21 net capital requirement date. The price rockets that day."

On March 25th, 2021, Cohen tweets a gif of sentient movie teddy bear Ted coughing up a bong hit, lining up with the next T+21 date. On over 50 million shares in volume, the price that day soared from $123.49 to as high as $187.50.

On April 21st, 2021, Cohen tweets a gif from an episode of South Park, where characters are scared of an oncoming train. "This is one day before the T+21 or 75% Net capital cycle," T21 Guy says.

And finally, on May 25th, 2021, just after midnight, Cohen tweets "Don't try this at home," accompanied by a gif from the show American Dad. The share price leaps that day from $181 to as high as $217.11, on a far higher volume (15 million) than had been seen since the month prior.

T21 Guy's final post in the series went live the evening of June 23rd, an hour after Cohen's tweet that night: "Hi All, It's Ryan Cohen T+21 tweet Guy. I'm losing my shit."

"With the introduction of this 5th tweet, he has now placed tweets on 5/6 T+21 days (missing only the first one, when he might have not even known about the trend). Including his father's day tweet and also this most recent one, The probability that these tweets are random is… 0.00707%," a figure that T21 Guy attributes to a calculation using hypergeometric law.

u/nostbp1: "I'd love for them to take him to court. / Judge: Mr. Cohen, explain the charges against you / RC: Your honor, it was a gif of a fart. I thought it was funny."

Another since-deleted user took the top comment with the revelation, "The clip, from South Park Season 5 Episode 5, 'Terrace and Philip: Behind the Blow,' features the boys watching their favorite show. [They say,] 'Aw man this is another rerun.' …. T+21 rerun anybody?"

By T21 Guy's logic, there was a 99.993% chance that Cohen was tweeting to point attention to one or many things that Cohen couldn't say outright. At least, not until a transition period had passed after his election to the board, though that didn't end the cryptography when it did occur.

Some of Cohen's other tweets, which didn't land on FTD dates, were also the subject of intense speculation. As I saw each one, it felt like I was watching the Seinfeld episode "The Betrayal," season nine's infamous backward episode. As the episode continues, the entire story makes more and more sense. The writer's room had it all figured out the whole time, and it was for the viewers to piece together over the course of 23 minutes.

On May 28th, 2021, Cohen tweeted a photo of a tombstone with the text:

RYAN COHEN

R.I.P. DUMB ASS

www.tombstonebuilder.com

u/ammonitions had the best of immediate replies on this one, to the tune of 8.5K upvotes, noting, "If you look at the site itself, there are 4 slot spaces where you can enter text into the tombstone. / 1. SOME NAME / 2. 1957-2007 / 3. YOUR MESSAGE APPEARS / 4. ON THE TOMBSTONE…. The name Ryan Cohen is entered into the DATE slot space. / and then in the 3rd (or 4th) slot space, you enter YOUR MESSAGE. RC is saying that he is (or he controls) the date when the HF's get liquidated. die. cease to exist."

u/Suspicious-Tip-8199: "Tombstone has a meaning in stocks as well / [Investopedia Citation] / 'A tombstone is a written advertisement that gives investors basic details about an upcoming public offering.'"

Cohen's tweets about bowel movements and male genitalia remained numerous, even after the T+21 speculation had gone by the wayside. South Park themed tweets erupted, including a gif from an episode where, in a wider shot, "Oh my god, they killed Kenny! Bastards!" is spelled out in Spanish above the teacher, which Redditors thought could be attributed to a certain potential short seller. Cohen posed in front of video games arranged to match the magic number, 741, another easter egg repeatedly debated by users, perhaps a hint at a 7-for-1 stock split or a reference to the percentage float that remained after famous short buster Carl Icahn squeezed Herbalife with 25.9% of available shares.

While 741 remained a mystery: a 4-for-1 split in the seventh month of the year, July, did occur in 2022. The split record date (July 18th, 2022) would occur almost exactly a year after another of Cohen's most cryptic tweets, posted on July

19th, 2021, which shows Cohen sticking chopsticks up his nose with the caption "PG-13."

Cohen's 2022 tweet, "Short sellers are the dumb stormtroopers of the investing galaxy," remains one of the most simple yet elusive to figure out. And one of Cohen's most famous tweets, which seemed to be about poop, will be discussed shortly.

For all of Cohen's potentially cryptic tweets of 2021, the two years that followed would deliver crystal clarity. Cohen strongly advocated for better commitment throughout, at one point pinning his tweet, "Work hard or please leave" at the top of his profile. His hands-on approach to improving the company at a fundamental level furthered social media's approval of him.

u/Terrible-Sugar-5582 had one of the best instances of Cohen dedication, announcing, "I'm swapping pictures of Ryan Cohen into frames in our house. Let's see how many I can do before my wife notices."

The Cohen fandom only surged as u/DeepFuckingValue made his final update. It was the perfect time for GameStop's true leader to take the reins (according to Redditors).

Whether or not there would be an online community to hear his words was yet to be determined.

23: The New Frontier

March 15th, 2021 | GME: $159.92

In the wake of the sneeze and after the initial GME price slide, r/WallStreetBets was in shambles.

It was obvious that bad players had infiltrated the community with bots, which could steer sentiment in any number of directions or simply bury posts that were actually interesting. Suddenly, as material discussion of GameStop faded, actual pump-and-dump schemes became more common.

Articles about the most popular tickers on WSB started to show up and would never stop. To the outside investor, it seemed WSB was the new kingmaker of value stock picks, though the truth was anything but.

Conversation about GameStop was also growing less useful with each passing day. I would comment on u/cfiznuts' February 21st, 2021, post about upcoming catalysts with the question, "Is this the best DD on what's happening right now? Or have you seen something more current, OP? I need some DD and stat." u/cfiznuts replied, "We don't know. None of these things line up."

Even worse, and to the constant complaints by long-term members, WSB itself had slid badly. From its heights the month prior, the online casino was so over-crowded with newbies that the real gamblers had lost interest.

When a forum "slides," the most dedicated members of that group typically splinter into their own forum. Much like forming new religious sects, this effect is at the root of many of Reddit's most diverse and intriguing subs, WSB included.

The Diamond Hands made their way to r/GME, a subreddit formed years prior. There, the first AMAs were hosted with market reform experts like Dennis Kelleher and Alexis Goldstein, the first days of the new group's self-education.

No longer would it be YOLOs on the tails of individual DFV-types making their informed pitches for different tickers. Instead, this was a collective consciousness built on the power of true algorithmic democracy and higher education, just as Huffman and his colleagues intended.

The journey from WSB to r/GME and what followed is best told by following u/rensole, a GME mascot in desperate search of a stadium sideline.

u/rensole's update history careens between a series of subreddits like r/Wallstreetbets, r/GME, r/WallStreetBetsNew, and r/DeepFuckingValue (a subreddit named after DFV, not the user himself) in February and March 2021. At that time, u/rensole's daily updates grew in readership, bringing legitimacy to the venues where he broadcast them.

It was in the latter part of March that u/rensole's posts crystallized into what drove the r/Superstonk community in its earliest days.

As u/rensole had done in days prior to — and would continue to do for months after — landing with r/Superstonk, they opened every post with an image of Stonks Man, which the Surreal Memes Wiki describes as "a meme of disputed surreality featuring Meme Man in a business suit with a background representing the stock market.... a sarcastic reaction image mocking instances of people showing poor financial knowledge or having stupid finance-related ideas."

"Good morning San Diego," u/rensole would open, a reference to 2004's *Anchorman: The Legend of Ron Burgundy*. "I am Rensole, / Do you smell that?" which I can only assume is a reference to *The Big Short*'s mortgage bonds scene. (In that scene, the answer is money).

After a detailed analysis of the previous day's events, intermixing their own thoughts and opinions, Rensole would end every post with a *Bill and Ted* meme with the caption: BE EXCELLENT TO EACH OTHER, and a reminder that "Ape no fight ape."

After three subreddits, it became increasingly clear that internal strife was the easiest way to disrupt the inner workings of a hedge-fund-liquidating internet hive-mind — far more so than bots and mainstream media articles, though those continued in full force.

Redditors quickly realized "mod drama" was by far the most deadly FUD campaign, but only if they allowed it to propagate. In that spirit, I don't feel it's worth delving into here with regard to Rensole or tales of runic glory.

On July 18th, 2021, u/rensole would end his nearly unbroken string of Daily Stonk updates with the post, "Fuck it I'm done with this shit." Luckily, the good work had been done, and r/Superstonk was the new GameStop subreddit. As was the case with most other Redditors, you either die a hero or live long enough to see yourself become the FUD.

With a few hundred thousand members, Superstonk was a legitimate force, albeit a smaller one, in comparison to WSB's 10 million-plus. When the Rensole drama reached its peak, and other mods were removed in mid-2021, users stayed put rather than splintering again. There were two camps: those who participated in the community and those who bought shares and held them silently. When drama erupted amongst the former, the latter was always there to remark, "So anyways, I bought and held more," a reference to Marvel's series *Loki*.

The community aspect of Superstonk did keep its users returning more often than a casual HODLer might check on their crypto portfolio. The political incorrectness softened, and any imbalances of gender were ameliorated. Superstonk was founded on teamwork and goodwill rather than cynicism and a penchant for gambling. The sub belonged to the apes, and the ape quickly became the sub's mascot.

Above all, Superstonk remained absolutely anonymous to reporters, who continued to focus on WSB. The mods committed to not speaking to the press throughout their tenure, especially after polling the group on the subject. With figures like Rogozinski continuing to talk to the media months and even years later on behalf of a reluctant WSB, Superstonk was almost purposefully squirreled away, afraid of similar consequences. As u/Anonplox would post over a year later with almost 8,000 upvotes, "'They Who Will Not Be Named.' — The fact that MSM will not recognize Superstonk by name is EXTREMELY BULLISH."

With the intense fluctuations of March 2021 in the rearview mirror, the subreddit quickly found itself in a holding period as they continued their HODLing. It was time for the golden era of DDs.

Thanks to Reddit's algorithm, when a groundbreaking DD with subreddit-wide acclaim hit the feed, its amount of upvotes could catapult such material to r/all, where non-GME fans would see it, read it, and join in the movement.

Superstonk would quickly become what WSB had previously been: a dominating hitmaker on r/all, over and over again.

Memes, DDs, and even NFTs are welcome on Superstonk. Apes shall not fight ape, and apes shall never speak of non-GME tickers or content. Karma restrictions allow the mods to have precise control over posters and commenters, which vastly improves the subreddit's overall quality and weeds out bots.

A year after mod expulsions, stock drops, and more, r/Superstonk stood nearly a million members strong, still deciphering each and every Ryan Cohen tweet with alacrity.

u/Anonplox added, "If the stock was really a joke, they would be linking to this sub and naming SuperStonk at every chance they could. They could ridicule us, call us every name under the sun, etc. / But they don't. They continue to act as if this sub doesn't exist. / They are afraid of people learning about the years of research that retail investors have completed about GME…. They are afraid of Superstonk and refuse to acknowledge its existence."

But not everyone was ignoring Superstonk. I was there every day, as were many others. We radiated the silent energy of Truman's *Good morning, and in case I don't see ya, good afternoon, good evening, and good night!* There was always something worth reading, learning, or talking about.

And that squeeze was not squoze.

24: First Time?

March 10th, 2021 and March 29th, 2022

Viciously beaten by market forces on multiple occasions after the sneeze, apes were big fans of the meme from the Coen brothers' 2018 film, *The Ballad of Buster Scruggs*. In the oft-meme'd scene, James Franco's character stands on the gallows next to a fellow criminal and, having survived a prior hanging, asks him, "First time?" as the noose is strung around their necks.

Only the darkest of humor could lift spirits after the events of March 10th, 2021 and March 29th, 2022.

These two days, though a year apart, were moments that apes in February 2021 thought they might never see again: a true MOASS ignition and one all too similar to what they saw during the sneeze.

In the days leading up to March 10th, I was preparing to make good on my commitment to accept a new puppy into my family. But first, I had to get my initial Pfizer COVID shot. There are a lot of COVID events that people have done their best to forget, including the waiting period required after one took their shot, just in case of side effects.

In those early days of March 2021, exactly a year after I had watched the stock market plummet while that infected cruise ship pulled into harbor, I found myself forced to kill fifteen minutes of post-vaccine observation time at a CVS in Stephenville, Texas. Today, markets weren't crashing. GameStop's share price was exploding.

While the price volatility during the sneeze is legendary, GME price dips of our present are compared to what happened on March 10th, not January 28th. On March 10th, there weren't millions of Robinhood users flooding to the stock for the first time. GME had almost been forgotten about by anyone but the diamond-handed apes.

Between February 24th and March 9th, 2021, GameStop stock had run up from $44.70 to $208.41. Those who had bought at unreal heights without paper handing were suddenly hopeful again for MOASS, or at least a less shameful cost basis. Many users had now migrated from Robinhood to more reliable brokers. And now, maybe a $1,000 share price would really happen.

As Rensole stated that morning in "Synopsis for 03-10-2021 what we need to know before the market opens DD," "If this break[s] $xxx dollars I'll do ....nothing! / Because I'll be holding to 100k minimum. / if I look at the graph it tells me the last spike was $347 (163asdaq) just to give you an idea[,] we are just a 100 bucks or so away from that RIGHT NOW. / folding at a $1000 is still paperhanding in my book[,] but that's just me, I'll be holding for 100 times that."

And thus, the seeds were planted for five, six, seven, and even nine digit target prices as one thousand dollars disappeared in the rearview mirror.

If historians are looking back on what occurred at this stage, just remember that there were times when apes would have sold at $420.69 or $1,000. And that chance has passed.

If anything, cryptocurrency had taught Redditors that prices in the tens of thousands were possible, and that was even considering that bitcoin hadn't been nakedly shorted when it was the price of a Happy Meal, like Redditors believed was the case for GME. A self-admittedly satirical website was set up to track GME's ever-increasing floor price. (At the time of publishing, the floor stood above $200 billion per share.)

For posterity's sake, Rensole adds, "Ok so I heard a lot of talk about 'if it go's [sic] to 100k it will ruin the economy'.... first of all 'ruin the economy' is, and always has been, a dogwhistle [sic] for rich people losing their superyachts, how many times was the 'economy' ruined and the people on wall-street [sic] went on with business as usual?"

But in the current moment, Rensole's conclusion would be the most prescient: "I believe that they [GME shorts] have one last ditch effort, they're going to let it rise... and then drop it down. just in an effort to get most of us to paperhand."

The ticker opened on March 10th at $269.43 after another $20+ of gains in extended-hours trading. In a livestream from Youtuber Tametheark, where traders were following the stock's movements live, there was a clear 2-4% rise in the stock price as the morning progressed.

But just after 11:00 am EST, the stock broke through the 4% ceiling, at the same time that DFV's Twitter account @TheRoaringKitty posted a video of the game *Mortal Kombat* spliced together with an episode of *Spongebob Squarepants*, making it look like the character Liu Kang was unleashing a never-ending bicycle kick finisher on their foe.

Over the course of a half hour, GME would climb another 14% to heights around $330 before slowing again. The stock was (unbelievably) back to Musk tweet levels.

u/Corno4825 had summarized each trading day with some level of accuracy and did so this day to the tune of 5K upvotes. As the ticker neared its daily high, they observed, "They used 50,000 shorts [to lower the price], but Apes don't care. GME is nearly $100 ahead of where it ended yesterday and it's showing no signs of slowing down. GME might break 400 [dollars] before EOD."

What may have been incorrect here was the assumption that short shares had been "used" by their purchasers after being bought, i.e., short buyers selling shares into the marketplace to lower the price. At the start of the trading day, u/Corno4825 observed that IBorrowDesk's shares available to short count had decreased from 850,000 to 350,000, meaning entities had likely bought up half a million shortable shares. The user said, "Don't be surprised if there is a dip at the start."

But the predicted dip wouldn't come at the start. It would arrive just after 12:15 p.m.

In the span of mere seconds, GME plummeted from around $329 to $302.68 before being halted. On the youtube stream, viewers reacted in real-time with a variety of jaw-dropping sounds, chief among them a shouted "Jesus Christ!"

At 12:27 p.m., after a five-minute halt, trading would resume. Within another 25 seconds, the stock would drop another $40 before stabilizing again. The price now stood near $250. But that wasn't the end. As the GME comment post locked for exceeding the 100,000 comment limit, users migrated as they had done during the sneeze, where u/Corno4825 continued, documenting halts at 12:31 p.m., 12:36 p.m. and 12:41 p.m., as the stock price dropped under $200.

By their count, GME would halt seven times in this period, apologizing, "Y'all, my lunch ends in 10 minutes. I'm going to try to keep y'all updated after lunch at the risk of getting fired. This shit is absolutely insane right now."

While the historic plummet was gobsmacking, it uncovered one of the still most dearly held ape conspiracy theories, an overwhelmingly antagonistic media. The media was eager to pounce when it came to GME's doldrums.

CNBC reported, "GameStop drops by 40% in 25 minutes: *The GameStop story added another wild chapter on Wednesday as the retailer's stock popped 40% before quickly falling back to earth. The move appeared to be on no new headlines.*"

The headline was wicked fast. So fast that Redditors took notice, especially Rensole, editing his daily post: "Apparently CNBC is so fast they wrote this in less then [sic] 50 seconds."[8]

But it was MarketWatch who would also suffer that afternoon. Their article was published two minutes later, at 12:43 p.m.: "The meme-stock roller coaster just reached new heights of volatility." But users claimed, "Google says the Market Watch Article was indexed...before the price plummeted."

---

[8] The rest of the CNBC article is full of fluff, so it could have been mostly written well in advance of the day's expected crash.

On top of that, a Twitter user claimed that the article itself had posted almost twenty minutes before the plummet began. And finally, users even shared unconfirmable screenshots of Google indexing said article almost a full day prior to its posting.

While any number of tech glitches can explain these sorts of things away, the coincidences were too much for Redditors to simply shrug off. To them, it was all coordinated.

As the stock price stabilized in the mid-200s, Rensole would add, "Seriously chill, I just got me some tendies on sale." And again the next morning added, "I told you to expect fuckery now didn't I?"

@RoaringKitty on Twitter would add a gif from *Fleabag*, where Fleabag laughs before laughing a little too hard and starting to frown.

Theories emerged about what could have caused the "flash crash" of March 10th, and while those theories would be debunked or ignored, the event only crystallized existing diamond hands. Like some kind of horrid exposure therapy, penny-stock-tier volatility brought these apes no fear.

But "hedgie fuckery" would outlive Rensole. Long after their departure from r/GME, r/Superstonk, the Evergrande tumble, and the inflationary explosion of 2022, there came yet another candidate for MOASS in March of 2022.

I wasn't chasing a puppy around my apartment or recovering from a COVID shot one year later. I was working at my desk with a one-year-old dog sleeping at my feet, watching GME's price climb ever closer to $200.

A week before, on March 22nd, 2022, CEO Ryan Cohen purchased 100,000 additional GME shares, and according to Reuters, "Shares of GameStop closed up 30.7% at $123.14, registering their biggest one-day percentage gain since March 25 last year." This climb would continue over the week to come as more buyers piled on, taking the stock up to its $188.24 open on March 29th.

Within sixty seconds, at 9:37 a.m., both GME and AMC were halted due to volatility, the first time that the two tickers had halted together since the sneeze.

Per The Street, "Meme stock favorites GameStop and AMC Entertainment were briefly halted from trading on the NYSE Tuesday as shares snapped one of the longest rallies on record for the video game retailer." And that's when things started to get really interesting. Though the stock price wouldn't officially exceed $199.41 that day, Robinhood users would begin receiving notifications to the contrary.

u/wacoked earned 3,000 upvotes with their post "RH Calls ITM Alert $240-$490 3/29/22," which showed a series of app notifications from Robinhood including, "Your GME $240 4/14 Calls are now in the money." and "Your GME $490 4/14 Calls are in the money."

u/p00pdicked replied, "File a regulatory complaint with SEC and FINRA plz" to which u/wacoked agreed, "1000% will…. This is just another day at the GME carnival."

Other users suggested what was likely the most correct answer: Robinhood had glitched due to what's known as the buy/ask spread. But Robinhood wasn't the entity in charge of those buy/ask numbers. And what appeared there was even more enticing.

Until this point, the Bloomberg terminal had remained immune to apes' attempts to poke holes, most famously with a controversy surrounding Brazilian put options.[9] However, with a subscription priced at over $20,000 per year, the Bloomberg terminal remains a stalwart of trading information and accuracy. According to the company, "Sitting on the desks of 325,000 of the world's most influential decision-makers, the Bloomberg Terminal is a modern icon of financial markets."

---

[9] Much thanks to u/keyser squoze for pointing me to u/TuaTurnsdaballova's July 2021 post, "Can anyone explain the over ONE MILLION PUT OPTIONS that showed up in today's Bloomberg terminal snapshots?" u/Itsmeitsyouitus would reply with comment, "Two completely random ass investment firms in fucking Brazil now own the most [GME] puts…… And we're supposed to assume that's completely legitimate and they're not a front for anything?" The Brazilian puts remain a source of controversy and debate.

A Bloomberg terminal screenshot showed an alleged ask price of $448,950.00, as reflected in u/WhatDidIDoNow's post with 13,000 upvotes, "Straight from BOOMERBERG, I can't fucking wait to fucking leave this place. LET'S GET READY TO FUCK!!!!!!!! $448,950.00 FUCK BLOOMBERG!"

The image in the post shows a string of ask prices against no bids, which had been cleared due to the halting of the stock. At no point that morning was the stock primed to sell for any amount higher than $200, yet for the first time, genuinely staggering numbers were beginning to appear.

The stock price closed on March 29th at $179.90, ending the rally. Having felt robbed of a third MOASS, users stormed to Reddit with their discontent.

u/CexySatan claimed, "Hedgies suppressed the price right before our eyes during the halt" to 3,000 upvotes and a chorus of agreement from users like u/pspiddy: "I get everyone's pissed but holy shit if today isn't conformation we're knocking on moass' door idk what is," and u/SnapOnSnapOff: "There is not a person alive that can convince me that the MOASS wasn't starting."

To the tune of 16,000 upvotes, u/BarberTricky171 posted, "Possibly the BIGGEST piece of information we learned from today… Hedgies are so FUCKED / All the gaslighting and bullshit media articles since Jan 2021, telling us it's over, shorts closed, meme mania is over and move on! / Yet here we are, March 2022 where the hedgies SHIT THEMSELVES at 200$. Where multiple glitches showing astronomical Asks and prices are showing up, where we have to get halted to stop the MOASS."

First time?

Probably the third.[10]

---

[10] Maybe the fourth, if you include the four trading halts that would occur on May 12, 2022, when the price would leap again on little to no news.

It was obvious that simply buying and holding weren't going to win the fight against the powers that be, assuming those nefarious powers were pulling strings faster than a harp factory worker on methamphetamines.

Equally inspired by the magic of the blockchain, Superstonk realized that what they needed was something real. But, like Watto refusing Qui-Gon Jinn's republic credits in *The Phantom Menace*, there was a growing consensus that something about, well, all of it, just wasn't.

Further down the comment stream on u/CexySatan's post, u/notacop_for_real asked, "What. Do. We. Do?" to which u/valtani responded, "DRS the entire float."

After weeks and months of treading water, r/Superstonk had discovered the nuclear option: a Direct Registration of Shares, known to the sub as DRS.

These apes had discovered fire.

25: Get Out the Vote

June 9th, 2021 | GME: $138.79

"Let's suppose that there is a bomb underneath this table between us…. The public is aware the bomb is going to explode at one o'clock and there is a clock in the decor. The public can see that it is a quarter to one. In these conditions, [an] innocuous conversation becomes fascinating because the public is participating in the scene."

This famous hypothetical by Alfred Hitchcock is one that I think most apes would identify strongly with, watching their peers invest in global markets with faith in regulatory agencies, market makers, and overall fairness while they believed there could be immense criminality and/or instability underneath the whole system.

Such theories surfaced on Superstonk during 2023's banking crisis and SVB bank run, especially during UBS's taking on the embattled Credit Suisse accounts, which were once suspected of holding what Redditors believed to be a high number of "swapped" GME shorts. In the late March press conference, the Swiss banking executives danced around discussions of idiosyncratic risks present on the balance sheets they were now taking over. Superstonk read between the lines and drew their own conclusions: if a bank was holding the hot potato of GME shorts, the crisis might only have been getting started. At time of publication, these theories could not be confirmed or denied.

The master of suspense concludes his theory, "The audience is longing to warn the characters on the screen: 'You shouldn't be talking about such trivial matters. There is a bomb beneath you and it is about to explode!'"

While there's no way to shout through the screen, should you wish to warn a Hitchcock hero or heroine of their impending doom, Superstonk users could warn the general public of the market's weakness.

But they needed a smoking gun to do it.

In April 2021, GameStop released their proxy materials for the annual report two months later, meaning shareholders could vote on board elections and re-elections without having to attend the annual meeting in person. Understandably, when a company wishes to poll shareholders, it would rather they do so ahead of time and online rather than crowd into a single boardroom or convention center.

In Rensole's "Synopsis for 04-23-2021 what we need to know before the market opens DD" post, they cheered, "YOU GET A PROXY, AND YOU GET A PROXY EVERYONE GETS A PROXY."

The get-out-the-vote campaign was on and only furthered by a popular late April post by u/TheFFAdvocate:

"Voting is now just as important as buying and holding. [Ryan Cohen] would need to prove that there are naked shorts and synthetic shares, the ONLY way he can PROVE this is more votes than that actual float. If 100 million votes come in with a float of only 22 million, he can use this as ammunition as it PROVES there are naked shorts and synthetic shares. Why else would GamsStop want us to cast our votes AS SOON AS POSSIBLE[?] Never before have they included this statement in the proxy."

As is the case for most, if not all, publicly traded companies, proxy votes are tallied by the number of shares held by the voter. Usually, these elections occur at lower numbers of votes because proxy voting isn't always of great interest to most shareholders. Though the apes of Superstonk were not average shareholders, they were determined to change that low turnout for GameStop's 2021 annual meeting. And that wouldn't be easy for everyone.

To the glorious tune of 23.7K upvotes, u/Nauaf101 posted on May 26th, "Your Votes Are IMPORTANT. The Time To Vote Is NOW." The post included a comprehensive list of brokerages and their voting instructions.

Some programs like Fidelity, TD Ameritrade, and even Robinhood — as some users still hadn't yet migrated from the maligned app — had straightforward instructions. But other brokers, like WealthSimple, required phone calls, proxy numbers, and more. And even some international brokers, like those in Sweden, struggled to even register non-votes when asked by their users.

One of the perks of voting was to receive a custom flair next to one's username, APE VOTED. As months passed, users' custom flairs would change, yet the o.g. APE VOTErs can still be found in the wild.

Excitement built throughout May 2021 as more and more users voted and received their flares from every corner of the world. The share float at the time of the vote was either around 55 million (shares available) or 65 million (total shares outstanding). Complex analysis of the shares outstanding wouldn't be as closely examined in this phase because Redditors assumed that the vote count would either fall well short of this number or blow this number out of the water.

At 5:00 p.m. on June 9th, the Q1 earnings call kicked off with an operator announcing, "Greetings and welcome to the GameStop first-quarter fiscal 2021 earnings conference call." George Sherman, the CEO who would depart two weeks later, went on to discuss positive developments in e-commerce recruitment, paying off company debt, and some positive words regarding incoming CEO Matt Furlong.

Sherman ended the eleven-minute call with, "I also want to take this opportunity to thank… an amazing group of shareholders who have so demonstrably exhibited their support for us."

These shareholders would have mixed feelings about the proxy vote results. The 8-K filing would be posted around the same time as the earnings call, showing 55.5 million total votes, unfortunately, a lower number than the hundreds of millions that apes had hoped for and a number strangely similar to the available share float.

Confusion and disappointment were rampant the evening of June 9th, 2021, on Superstonk, but calmer heads prevailed. Rensole would sum things up the most accurately the next morning, with "The Daily Stonk 06-10-2021," leading off by appreciating the proximity of votes to the available float number, both near 55 million and suggesting what others had said to less fanfare: accountants might not allow an over-vote to be publicized.

Rensole and many others suspected the vote count had been trimmed, not with malicious intent, but rather as a rule. It could still be considered a W ("dub").

Rensole cites a social media post from eToro, sharing that "63% of eligible GME shares held on eToro were voted" as a sign that even if 99.9% of the float (or 85%, if the target was indeed 65 million) had been voted, there were numerous shares that hadn't been voted, and the thesis would be proven at that point. It was this line of thought that encouraged those who had been irked the day prior and one that permeated the subreddit as the hours dragged into the early dawn of June 10th.

Rensole cites one of the most popular posts from June 9th in the next day's Daily Stonk, written by u/stronkape89: "YOU CANT REPORT AN OVER-VOTE ON AN 8-K. PASS IT ON. STOP THE UNINTENTIONAL FUD!!!" to which u/Sioned-Song adds a brilliant piece of insight: the 2020 8-K makes a statement regarding vote totals that the 2021 form omits:

"According to the Inspector's final tabulation of voting, stockholders representing 42,886,817 shares, or 66.4% of the Company's common stock outstanding as of the record date for the Annual Meeting, were present in person or were represented by proxy at the Annual Meeting."

These documents are so meticulously worded that omitting text can speak volumes. Could vote totals have been omitted because it would be a lie in the case that totals had been trimmed?

It would take another year until the next proxy vote before apes would have more data to incorporate. Or so they thought.

Rensole ended the Daily Stonk with, "Buy and hold, and now we can add 'buckle up,'" because Ryan Cohen, in some of his first words spoken as the chairman the day prior, ended the shareholders' meeting by saying, "As my dad would say, 'buckle up.' Meeting is adjourned."

"Buckle up" would become the apes' next great rallying cry.

And what came next would be one of the most fascinating developments in the history of the stock market.

26: A House of Cards

April 21st, 2021 | GME: $158.40

In 1978, transfer agent and investor services company Computershare launched in Melbourne and would rapidly grow into a global company worth billions of dollars, officially entering the United States in 2000.

As one of Melbourne's earliest start-ups, Computershare claims that the company "remains a unique Australian success story. We built on our share registry business by successfully expanding into employee equity plans, stakeholder communications, corporate governance, [and more]." The company now boasts offices in numerous countries and remains a share registrar for a large share of the marketplace, GameStop included.

The ape interest in Computershare didn't happen overnight, nor was it a direct result of the proxy voting campaign. Instead, it came from the ongoing series of DDs dropping from informed crayon eaters with time, dedication, and wrinkled brains.

Within a year of Superstonk's start, the Superstonk DD Library amassed over 200 posts, theses, and other documents, all having to do with GameStop due diligence. The library's "Diamond Handbook," which contains the most popular DDs is no less than 800 pages.

When someone asks me about GameStop, I tell them about the DD Library, and while I suggest saving its contents for their next moment of downtime, most of it's just too engrossing not to tackle immediately. But it's not for the faint of heart.

Anyone who reads a Superstonk DD will recognize some blend of mad science and frustration in a lack of market transparency, no matter the author. What goes into the Diamond Handbook must be speculative, radical, and open to debunking. More than anything, Diamond-Handbook-tier DD must make for an engaging read, especially if the author wants it to have success when their work moves beyond Superstonk into r/all, should it be so highly regarded.

The earliest and most well-known DDs are authored by users u/atobitt, u/Criand, and u/peruvian_bull, though there are many, many more DD authors out there, and listing any more of them would do injustice to the rest. DD writing is tedious, leads to no merit in scholarly circles, and leaves its writers open to ridicule should they be debunked or accused of FUD.

u/atobitt's DDs were some of the first to make a splash in Superstonk and his most well-known include:

Citadel Has No Clothes — An in-depth look at Citadel Securities' balance sheet and allocation of funds, which atobitt claims reveal high levels of risk.

The Everything Short — An investigation of Citadel entities, one of which has, by atobitt's estimate, holds large short positions.

Walking Like a Duck Talking Like a Duck — Atobitt proposes that Citadel has knowledge of practices that regulators have fined the company for, yet Citadel maintains that any such practices were accidental or unintentional.

It's the *A House of Cards* series (in three parts) which apes clamored the most to read over the many months of 2021. This DD series made apes question if they were really targeting the right foe in brokers, hedge funds, and/or even their trading apps. That war on multiple fronts was about to consolidate into one.

In *House of Cards Part 1*, u/atobitt shines a light on the Depository Trust Company (DTC), which was established in the early 1970s to handle clearance between counterparties on a quicker basis due to the surge in trading volume taking the market by storm.

Besides the 1987 crash, the DTC functioned without complaint for two decades, that is, until a flurry of complaints emerged in 2003 about naked short selling occurring within the regulator's ranks.

Despite the complaints, u/atobitt shows that the DTC was allowed to continue with business as usual. This includes their entity Cede & Co., which acts as a depository, holding physical share certificates in "street" name. That way, instead of mailing share certificates back and forth during a transaction, a trader can make a phone call or a simple keystroke.

The drawback is, Cede & Co. holds onto your shares. As u/atobitt's cited headline from American Banker confirms, "You Don't Really Own Your Securities."

He ends the DD with a defiant "DIAMOND.F*CKING.HANDS" and a threat to further investigate the parties with their hands in the DTC, as he would do in *House of Cards* parts 2 and 3.

House of Cards led to the subreddit's acknowledgment that the once obscure DTC (and its clearinghouse, the Depository Trust and Clearing Corporation) plays in the GameStop saga, leading users to come up with creative acronyms for these entities, many of which surreptitiously substitute "counterfeit" for one of the C's.

At the time of *House of Cards Pt. 1*, though, the notion that a massive entity like the DTC could be involved wasn't in the mainstream of Superstonk. Soon, it would be.

One of Michael Burry's since-deleted tweets may have hinted at this fact, and well in advance of *House of Cards*: "May 2020, relatively sane times for $GME, I called in my lent-out GME shares. It took my brokers WEEKS to find my shares. I cannot even imagine the sh*tstorm in settlement now. They may have to extend delivery timelines.... #nakedshorts."

As users debated *cash* accounts versus *book* accounts versus margin accounts under their respective brokerages, they all slowly began to suspect that underneath each hydra head was the same beastly body. This realization came not as the result of another app outage or international broker glitch; instead, it was arguably the king of retail brokerages, Fidelity, who would put an end to lingering trust in the 'boomer' brokers.

Thanks to Fidelity's industry-leading customer service, user interface, and security confidence, the broker had become the unofficial favorite of apes in the wake of the Robinhood exodus. Yet, on a day in late November 2021, Fidelity made a mistake, as reported by Business/Markets Insider: "Reddit traders fume as Fidelity incorrectly lists millions of shares of GameStop available to short."

The visible number of short shares available was 13 million when in reality, Fidelity only had 2 million available. The company's explanation also added to customers' sour feelings, saying it was simply an "overestimation."

An overestimation? Does rounding up lead to an overcount of eleven million?

While the general public and Superstonk were forced to accept that explanation, the tinfoil types leaped to conclusions like tadpoles with newly sprouted legs. They postulated a dire calculus: if Fidelity held millions of GME shares for its users, yet those users had deactivated share lending, where did these shares come from? If the number indeed was over ten million, which Fidelity has denied, it meant that Fidelity had an immense number of GME shares and seemed willing to lend out each and every one.

In that scenario (which again, Fidelity firmly denies), the squeeze could never truly ignite because short sellers could always deflate prices. Liquidity would theoretically be infinite so long as retail shares were held by Fidelity.

With that fudged keystroke, Fidelity would be the final domino to fall in the quest to lock the float and ignite MOASS by brokerage. If the best couldn't be trusted, no one could be.

Except the Australians, of course.

The Computershare movement's ignition DD belonged to u/Criand, the other aforementioned DD author, whose avatar is an unmistakable pomeranian. On September 16th, 2021, he posted, "Direct Registering Shares (DRS) is the MOASS key handed on a golden platter…. ComputerShare is not some shady company. They are the designated transfer agent for 37.4% of the market."

"As long as the majority of the float remains 'Street Name' Registered rather than 'Direct' Registered, [shorts] can continue producing phantom shares and resetting fails. Essentially nullifying all buy pressure from retail.... The good news is that Direct Registering of Shares is a process that is provided through 'transfer agents' for companies. So, it's possible for retail to register the shares in their name and chunk down the float."

"ComputerShare provides transfer agent services for many companies of all sizes.... Check out who also uses ComputerShare: [images include Microsoft, Apple, and Amazon].... In my opinion? DRS is the killshot."

u/Doom_Douche followed up a week later with "Computershare and Direct Registration," which brought in nearly 30K upvotes. With this being one of the highest upvoted posts in some time, the game was back on after a slow summer of licking our proxy vote wounds.

As more DDs emerged, r/Superstonk was about to see more purple circles than a grape-flavored condom factory.

27: Wall Street's Ticking Time Bomb

December 8th, 2021 | GME: $176.60

It was early October when the @Computershare Twitter account would post, "Shares held directly on the books of US companies through a transfer agent are not held at DTCC. As such, shares are not available to be loaned for any means within the security markets. Computershare is a registered transfer agent & therefore does not lend shares in any capacity."

This calmed the holdouts inside Superstonk, knowing Computershare wouldn't sell them out to the shorts.

Like any movement, the Computershare march would have its peaks and valleys. But at its start, share registration was a wild rush to Cede&Co.'s exits.

For each Computershare account, a purple donut chart appeared on Superstonk, showing the percentage of held stock in a user's online account. In the case of almost every user, this circle would be 100% purple unless they chose to register other shares of other companies too. The iconography of purple circles on Superstonk quickly overtook that of crayons and chimpanzees.

On October 1st, u/sorehamstring scored 9,000 upvotes with their image, "Actual photo inside computershare as the apes arrive for the final battle," which was the wide shot from *Avengers: Endgame*, with Wong's teleportation circles recolored to Computershare purple, deploying all of Earth's soldiers to the final battle.

Computershare direct registrations would range in number from one share to over ten thousand. It was quickly apparent that the subreddit needed a tracker for their efforts.

u/QuestionAll was the first to leap into the void with "Be the change you want to see in the world," a post that cited their earlier comment, "We need a guy to track... the float vs # of CS accounts."

Quite simply, QuestionAll charted three columns: a constant float just under 62 million, increasing numbers of Computershare accounts, and what the average ownership per holder would have to be to lock the float. But this method didn't accomplish much besides sharing updates of account totals, and even the account totals were off by a power of ten due to Computershare's more secure data entry format adding an extra random digit to ascending account numbers.

After QuestionAll came DRS Bot, which proved to be far more effective. Thanks to restrictions on accounts and karma levels, bots had been relatively scant in the ranks of Superstonk, which meant bad actors could be kept to a minimum when tabulating shares.

Reddit bots range from the hilarious to the downright annoying, and bot makers must walk that tightrope deftly. Some of the most useful bots include the aforementioned RemindMe!, a translator, and an image modifier for colorblind users.

u/Roid_Rage_Smurf would make r/Superstonk's latest and greatest bot in the middle of October 2021: "I did a thing... and now I'm going to bed for the first time in...like... days." Their image shows a tally of DRS Bot's early findings, just over 100,000 shares, with the caption "Let the games begin."

A month later, u/Roid_Rage_Smurf would post their own purple circle, announcing, "I'm a Senior Software DEV Manager...who literally Googled 'How to create a Reddit Bot' 30 days ago. Now I'm finally about to eat my own dog food."

u/CaptBiscuits: "THE BOT KING HAS ARRIVED. Thank you for your service u/Roid_Rage_Smurf and to all the witnesses. Its [sic] been one hell of a ride, the best is yet to come."

But the best tracker would arrive on the back of u/jonpro03, providing the visuals that would display the true impact of DRS Bot and other stonk trackers.

u/johnpro03 created a very nice-looking website called computershared.net, which, according to the site's disclaimer, "is not affiliated with ComputerShare or GameStop." Visualizations on the site take many forms, including but not limited to DRS estimates, number of accounts new and old, average distribution of shares per holder (between 16 and 64 shares, as of July 2022), and calculation of available float.

As registered shares climbed, it was this latter statistic that required a reevaluation because, as was apparent during the first proxy vote campaign, the available float can exist in any number of formats.

Due to reporting requirements (and non-requirements), calculating share floats can feel like a game of averages rather than certainty. But for the first time in r/Superstonk history, apes had a truly customizable visualizer.

In mid-2022, just before the share split, the estimate stood as follows:

Out of 75.9 Million Shares Issued,

Almost 14 Million are held by Institutions,

An estimated 8.4 Million are held by mutual funds,

An estimated 6.6 Million are held in ETFs,

And 13.2 Million are held by Insiders.

This leaves 33.8 million shares in the hands of retail investors.

While almost 34 million is an estimate and could be changed by institutions selling or buying their stock, it's a metric with far more data to back it up than apes had access to some six months prior. Should financial markets ever make a full transition to decentralized platforms, share counting difficulty will be a laughable artifact of past times.

By December, DRS accounts surged, but the process wasn't easy for everyone who wanted to join in the fun. In the same way that proxy voting became challenging for small brokers and international brokers alike, so too were DRS transfers held in a degree of uncertainty by many of the same parties.

While purchases of GameStop shares can be performed within a Computershare account, a transfer is the best way to protect one's cost basis for tax purposes. When you're raking in tens of millions of dollars of tendies, it'll be important for Uncle Sam to only tax you on 99.98% of that income.

DRS speedbumps took two forms as the movement picked up speed. First, while brokers like Fidelity were producing wickedly fast turnaround times (e.g., 2-3 days), other sources could take weeks or even months to transfer even a small number of shares. In essence, by removing shares from a broker, you were taking business elsewhere. While legally required to allow you to do so, brokers weren't always chipper to participate. To counteract this, users began to transfer shares from slower brokers to Fidelity and then would DRS from Fidelity. This was a practice that Fidelity likely didn't appreciate, but also did not disallow. Their customer service remains top notch, and I'd wager they've gained new customers in the process.

Brokers occasionally discouraged DRS transfers. Such recommendations like, *your shares will be less liquid in a DRS account* were taken as hedgie-sponsored FUD when in reality, these were likely just employees trying to retain their company's customer base or help customers understand what an online forum had told them.

There were instances where smaller brokers were stalling on share transfers, and larger brokers were putting guardrails around DRS requests. In both cases, apes sought out "corporate compliance officers," essentially Karen-ing the manager.

As u/abbytron shared in early 2022, "Don't Let These Crooks Control Your Shares! If Brokerages are Stalling Request to Speak to their Compliance Officers! Did this myself and it WORKS!" Their post included a screencap of a tweet by economist Dr. Susanne Trimbath, author of apes' favorite book, *Naked, Short, and Greedy: Wall Street's Failure to Deliver*. "It shouldn't take 3-4 weeks [for brokers] to push a button."

For all that apes had accomplished in October and November of 2021, the energy around DRS'ing slowed after its first weeks. With little news from outside sources and no idea as to the accuracy of the figures on the DRS Bot or Computershared.net, the DRS effort risked stalling out.

The only clues that apes could distill in these early days of DRS were revisited Ryan Cohen tweets. u/Onebadmuthajama asked, "Computer+chair = computershare?" to the tune of 2,000 upvotes, in reference to Cohen's July 23rd tweet, which went largely unnoticed at the time.

u/footmashingweirdo speculated on Cohen's tweets from the months prior, starting with the infamous frog ice cream: "McDonald's ice cream cone = cone. Dumb and dumber character on the throne = poo. His face on a chair = chair / Put it all together, and you've got cone-poo-chair…. Still not sure? Dancing turd = poo. Sears sign being torn down = tear. Porcelain Office thrown [sic] = Chair. / Poo-tear-chair."

u/Reeeeaper: "This is the biggest leap I've seen since febuary 29th [sic]. I'll have some of whatever you're smoking."

The armchair computer scientists were about to be totally gratified in their quest for data, though. No longer would DRS'ing be restricted to the early adopters and brave souls. While a great deal of attention had been paid to June's 8-K filing as a result of the vote total, apes were about to discover another seemingly insignificant financial filing: GameStop's Q3 2021 10-Q form, filed on December 8th, 2021.

According to Investopedia, "SEC Form 10-Q is a comprehensive report of financial performance that must be submitted quarterly by all public companies to the Securities and Exchange Commission (SEC). In the 10-Q, firms are required to disclose relevant information regarding their finances as a result of their business operations."

For the first time in GameStop's 10-Q history, the company released a count of directly registered shares: "As of October 30, 2021, 5.2 million shares of our Class A common stock were directly registered with our transfer agent, Computer-Share."

The Superstonk reaction was monumental, as demonstrated by over 30,000 upvotes on the post "5.2 million shares registered through ComputerShare" by u/OgarTheDestroyer.

Moreover, u/ipackandcover chimed in to another 7,500 upvotes: "I searched through all 10K and 10Q forms filed within the last year on SEC's EDGAR database. GameStop's 10Q form from today is the only filing that mentions the number of directly registered shares."

u/Lonan27 shouted from the mountaintops, "IF YOU ARE SOMEHOW STILL ON THE FENCE ABOUT CS, THE MERE MENTION OF HOW MANY SHARES WERE DRS'ED LAST QUARTER—WHICH HAS NEVER ONCE BEEN DISCUSSED IN ANY EARNINGS REPORT—SHOULD GET YOU OFF YOUR ASS IMMEDIATELY." And Twenty thousand apes agreed.

u/cre_guy_3: "Was this in previous quarterly reports?"

u/DeansFrenchOnion1: "Nope!"

u/cre_guy_3: "So we have a scoreboard now."

And that scoreboard would be put to good use, as another variable could now be eliminated from the complex calculus of how many shares existed and how far apes were from locking the float.

DRS Bot had tabulated 10% of the 5.2 million shares as of October 30th, while Computershared's trimmed average was almost twice that. u/jonpro3 would adjust their math that next day and both models would improve as time progressed.

In terms of validation and scoreboard accuracy, the release of Computershare numbers was one of the defining moments of r/Superstonk's first year. The DRS efforts surged to life again, and word began to spread as winter turned to spring.

Without fail, GameStop's first "ten" form of 2022, the annual 10-K, would bring fresh life to the effort again on March 17th, 2022: "As of January 29, 2022, 8.9 million shares of our Class A common stock were directly registered with our transfer agent, ComputerShare."

The second data point also brought more statistical validity to computershared.net, as u/jonpro03 posted the next day, "The 10-K gave us exactly what we needed to know to track DRS progress accurately... maybe start making predictions."

By the third release of data in June 2022, the predictive numbers were starting to get really accurate on u/jonpro03's site. GameStop's June 10-Q revealed 12.7 million shares registered as of April 30th.

Computershared.net estimated just over 16 million shares registered at the time of the stock split in July 2022, representing almost 50% of the 33.8 million share float, which was all accomplished in less than a year, and almost exactly one year since the proxy vote count let down the group's hopes.

And speaking of proxy votes, care to guess what the vote count was on GameStop's June 2022 8-K? Just over 57 million shares, which is only about 2 million more since the hotly contested 2021 vote, and a number that occurred after a year when five million shares were added to the float.

If nothing else changed, including shareholders continuously buying up more stock, one could expect that the mid-fifty million is where that vote count would land and stay for the rest of recorded time. But the vote counts in the 2022 8-K went largely ignored because GameStop used the document to announce a new move, which would be their first major step into the fray, igniting a new wave of DRS FOMO.

So Wall Street's ticking time bomb isn't GME or MOASS. It's truths about the market that the GameStop story has, and still might, reveal. The real ticking time bomb is traders' withdrawal of capital from the very markets that they no longer believe to be free or transparent, whether or not MOASS is as imminent as locking the float.

Unlike Hitchcock's suspenseful bomb, this bomb has already exploded. What remains to be seen is whether the explosion also burns the entire city to the ground.

28: Weapons Free

July 11th, 2022 | GME: $128.56

As weeks turned to months, apes questioned when GameStop might take action. Speculation started as soon as the sneeze that GameStop could strike down naked shorts, market manipulators, and more, but users argued over the best available course of action. Some suggested a share recount, while others proposed removing shares from the DTC entirely.

But both those lines of thought ended with the same result: landing on the shoulders of a regulator to enforce a punishment, if any. And in apes' collective opinion, the SEC, the DTC, and Congress weren't up to the job. If GameStop acted within the regulatory rules and called out the smoking gun, nothing might come of it besides more gnashing of teeth.

On February 12th, 2022, u/lawsondt asked, "Mr. Cohen — Do you see what I see? … The available float of GME is turning over every 5-9 trading days since the beginning of the year."

Whether it was the proxy vote, the daily volume of shares, or something else entirely, Redditors had returned to the MATH, and the math wasn't adding up. Finally, they sought a reason why.

Graphics would show that, compared to other stock tickers, GameStop's float traded at insanely faster levels compared to any FAANG stock, which might trade its entire float over the course of months, at most.

It wouldn't be until July 2022 when GameStop would make not one major move but two, which both increased their future company prospects and, according to apes, put pressure on short sellers. First, the launch of the NFT marketplace was an all-important next step in GameStop's quest to re-establish itself in the gaming space. NFTs had surged in the wake of the sneeze as meme stocks were cast aside by the general public, no thanks to the repeatedly negative stories about GameStop as its stock price returned to immense heights.

Non-Fungible Tokens stored on the blockchain would quickly take the world by storm, presenting yet another item for collectors to get their hands on. The most well-known NFT collections would begin to sell for tens of thousands, hundreds of thousands, and millions of dollars, most of which was transacted by the cryptocurrency Ethereum, whose market cap was second only to that of Bitcoin.

The magic of NFTs is that they're located on a blockchain, so unlike buying physical collectibles, an NFT can be immediately verified, past ownership can be seen, current prices can be compared, and the security of said NFT is protected by one's digital wallet. NFTs originated with collectibles and soon spread into artwork, one-of-a-kind items, and, unavoidably, porn.

Luckily, for NFT collectors not wishing to transact pornography, the world of NFTs crystallized rapidly throughout 2021. The surge of 2-D art plateaued as collectors increased attention in NFT communities, trading cards (i.e., expansions from the NBA into the NFL, MLB, and UFC), and the amorphous metaverse.

As an NFT creator, I became one of the first NFT creators, if not the very first, to create an NFT from a motion picture film reel titled *Kodachrome 1976*. One year later, I had created over a hundred NFTs across three or four collections, and zero have sold at the time of publication. Am I winning yet?

Before nft.gamestop.com, platforms OpenSea, Rarible, Foundation, and Mintable were first on the scene as attention surged in early 2021, with NBA Top Shots as an honorable mention. Each marketplace had its quirks, and as an NFT fan myself, I dabbled in four of the five platforms:

OpenSea — According to their sign-in page, "OpenSea is the world's first and largest NFT marketplace." The site is truly massive in scope, and remains a behemoth in the NFT marketplace space. OpenSea's internal practices have come into question on occasion, for instance, as a result of insider trading charges against an employee.

Rarible — A slightly smaller and more curated platform, Rarible straddled the quantity of OpenSea and the quality of Foundation without being too exclusive. In addition, Rarible allowed for the minting of entire collections (for the low gas fee of nearly $1,000 at one time) and made for a more friendly user interface compared to its counterparts.

Foundation — The most exclusive of early NFT platforms, Foundation was an invite-only and community-focused platform, selling high-value items and maintaining the highest quality.

Mintable — The poor man's NFT platform, Mintable was the first to test "gasless" minting, which other platforms would later follow. This form of minting didn't actually mint anything; instead, it allowed users to post items with the expectation that the buyer would pay their gas fees, which ranged from $20 to $100.

The early days of NFTs were the wild west, but other players would lie in wait to release their own platforms. For instance, the cryptocurrency app Coinbase released an NFT marketplace in May of 2022, and to less than positive results.

Many of the early kinks were being worked out, and corporations were beginning to see the value of NFTs as add-ons to user experiences. And, of course, NFTs also became a fantastic new way for yesterday's B-list actors to keep their nostalgia-powered money printers active.

On July 11th, GameStop's NFT marketplace launched in tandem with an already released NFT wallet, both of which operated beautifully on the Loopring blockchain and existed at what's known as Level 2 (L2). When GameStop entered the NFT market, things changed for some lucky few, especially those involved in r/Superstonk, who were granted early access to minting their own collections.

On L2, the insane gas fees that plagued early creators were now $1-$2 at most. GameStop's NFT marketplace existing on L2 was a brilliant move and was one of the many factors that led to great success in the marketplace's first days.

u/elevenatexi weighed in that evening to the tune of 6.5K upvotes with "My thoughts on the NFT Marketplace launch today, it was a tribute to us!"

"I was initially a bit underwhelmed and disappointed that today[']s launch of the NFT marketplace didn't have any premier partners… but then I started to see what they actually did. / They gave the artists and creators that they recruited right here on Superstonk, the talented among us, the first dibs at the platform, what an honor! And these creators knew exactly what types of NFTs we would find delightful, because they are us. / It's a soft launch for family and friends, and it's a privilege we will all cherish in the years to come when the marketplace has transformed into something much grander as it evolves. / The elite brands will come, the games and ownership of media will come, and yes, the new stock market exchange will come as well, but we were first."

It's true. The launch of the platform was a quiet one but outperformed the likes of Coinbase, for instance. I purchased two NFTs, one by Superstonk mod and fellow TDS author u/Luma44 and another that claimed to be the first TV pilot released in NFT format, *Into the Veil.* In a future round of creator applications, I hoped to release the first feature film to the platform, so the latter was as much product research as it was a part of history. Early transactors were eventually rewarded with an "achievement unlocked" NFT, directly from GameStop.

Trading during the week of July 11th to 15th briefly topped $150 before ending the week just above $140, a rise of nearly 10% since open July 11th. A solid gain, no doubt, but not a short seller's worst nightmare. The nightmares would be reserved for the following week when the "splividend" was set to occur, the second exciting development that would spring from GameStop's busy summer.

In a normal stock split, a company releases shares at a set fraction of their given price in an effort to make more liquidity available. Stock splits are why a single share of Walmart or Coca-Cola at their offering dates, then worth less than $100, can today be worth hundreds of thousands. While stock splits have been a common occurrence for decades, weaponized stock splits were first made popular for retail traders by Elon Musk and Tesla, where lowering share prices made the stock more attractive to long investors and at great expense to frustrated shorts.

When news emerged that GameStop planned to split its stock, the sentiment across r/Superstonk was that the company had finally arrived on the battlefield.

On March 31st, 2022, GameStop filed form 8-K, with the revelation, "GameStop… announced its plan to request stockholder approval at the upcoming 2022 Annual Meeting of Stockholders… for an increase in the number of authorized shares of Class A common stock from 300,000,000 to 1,000,000,000."

By a vote of 53,145,489 to 3,769,297 (with 110,690 abstentions), the option for the split was approved as of the June 3rd, 2022 form 8-K.

But that's not all. As revealed in GameStop's July 6th, 2022 press release, the stock split would be "a four-for-one split of the Company's… stock in the form of a stock dividend."

An explanatory post was rapidly added to the top of r/Superstonk for all to see: "4:1 Stock Split (in the form of a dividend!) | Everything you need to know!" by u/goldielips. As explained in that post and elsewhere, the difference between a standard stock split and a split as a dividend can have significant implications if there are discrepancies in share counts. A typical stock split is simply done as a ratio, whereas a dividend is made with a transfer of actual shares.

u/younonomous speculated with July 7th's "The two-pronged Genius of RC's Dividend Split":

"Attack #1— hit the DTCC hard. By doing a dividend split the DTCC is going to be handed a limited number of shares…. This puts serious pressure on the DTCC because there's going to be a ton of people expecting stocks to show up in their account and the DTCC is going to have to find them…. Attack #2— Forcing price action that will trigger margin calls and liquidations."

u/MoonTendies69420: "self defense is more like it."

But pressuring intermediaries wasn't the only potential result. u/dbzkid999 proposed on July 8th, "SPECULATION ON THE MASTER PLAN BEHIND THE DIVIDEND SPLIT":

"4:1 SPLIT DIVIDEND ALLOWS THEM ROOM TO DO A 3:1 SPLIT AFTERWARDS AS A BACKUP…. IF THEY SAID 7:1 INITIALLY, THERE WOULD BE NO BACKUP AND THEY WOULD HAVE TO VOTE ON AN INCREASE OF MAXIMUM NUMBER OF SHARES AGAIN. BUT SINCE

THEY ARE DOING A 4:1, THEY CAN NOW DO A 3:1 AS ANOTHER DIVIDEND SPLIT IF FCKERY [sic] CONTINUES."

u/dbzkid999 concluded their post with the apology, "I'VE HAD TOO MUCH COFFEE THIS MORNING."

Apology accepted.

One image comparing GameStop's ballooning share price to Tesla's in the early days even made its way back to WSB, where anticipation began to build again that money could be made on GME once more. Attention on WSB had calmed, and the o.g. degenerates were slowly trickling back into the casino.

With the assumption that Computershare users would receive preferential treatment, a new spike in DRS transfers was initiated (with some particularly creative memes to motivate traders, like a Cameo video from the Halo voice actor.)

u/RaiderGlenn-FLA cheered the morning of July 15th, "The [uptick] in DRS is unreal. The FOMO mofo apes are not playing," as the Computershared.net count showed over one million shares had been DRS'd just that week alone, some 2-4% of the projected float. This would be the largest projected surge in direct registrations since tracking began and would be reflected in a momentous DRS count released in GameStop's September 2022 quarterly update, which totaled almost 18 million shares registered.

The newest surge was partially spurred by Fidelity, who, a week earlier, had angered customers again with the news that their direct registrations had been momentarily halted. The uproar fueled a number of calls to Fidelity's corporate compliance department. Whether as a result of their newly realized requirements or because the technical issue had been fixed, Fidelity returned to DRS'ing shares without issue.

Apes with other brokers wouldn't be so fortunate, though. Webull and IBKR would experience trading halts and delays on transferred shares, respectively. Also, several other brokers would experience kinks and delays, according to Redditors. For instance, on the day of the splividend, u/idontdislikeoranges claimed, "My bank SOLD my shares and PURCHASED."

GameStop shares would inch past $160 throughout Wednesday and Thursday.

Like apes on the night before Christmas, the record date Thursday evening was festive. And at 4:40 am (with a post by yours truly), the splividend was effective: "Apes, the time is now 4:04am. Welcome to the splividend."

Within minutes, and even a minute or two early for some users, the stonk count had quadrupled on trading apps and Computershare accounts.

Abracadabra.

Market open on the day of the split was relatively uneventful when it did occur around five hours later. However, the split was overshadowed in mainstream news by a rapid decline of Snapchat shares following bad earnings. GME followed market averages down as morning turned to afternoon and ended its first splividend day at $35.78, equivalent to just over $143, which was a noticeable decline.

Buy the rumor and sell the news, perhaps?

No one was selling though. I didn't even know how to sell from a Computershare account. Apes upvoted a posted red square just as fervently as they might a green square: "6.96% Splividend Day Discount." Still others voiced displeasure.

u/Black_Label_46's evening post, "Can you please all, for the love of stonk, calm the fuck down?" made it to r/all, as Reddit witnessed a minor meltdown over the lack of fireworks that day.

u/Black_Label_46 summed up the overall reactions fairly well, though:

"'I didn't get my shares yet! Crime!'

'The price dropped! Crime!'

'Cramer said something mean about the apes! Crime!'"

"SHUT THE FUCK UP!"

It wasn't all bad. Four days after the splividend, the first of the true HODL'ers appeared, u/StonkMarketbet, who asked from a zen paradise (or a recently ended coma), "I'm super confused... I only had 17 GameStop shares [some time ago].... Now my Webull is saying I own 68 GME shares. My purchase history shows me only purchasing 17 shares also. Can someone please explain what's going on?"

u/Cfcgaz replied, "King of the fucking diamond hands."

29: All Hell Breaks Loose

August 1st, 2022 | GME: $33.80

Some of the chapters in this book I wrote as they occurred, while others, especially those covering over a year of r/Superstonk development, I penned after months of collecting data and seeing where certain threads would go. That's why there's no Evergrande chapter, for instance. It didn't end up mattering enough.

I wrote *Weapons Free* as the dividend occurred in almost real time. For that reason, I didn't think it was worth going into further detail on the splividend process. Before we embark on this chapter, it's now necessary that I correct that mistake, because everything changed after that.

Unlike Margot Robie explaining Michael Burry's gambit in *The Big Short*, I am not sitting naked in a bathtub for this next part, nor do I have a naked actor or actress available to deliver what follows. My deepest apologies.

The "stock split as a dividend" process involves a transfer of shares, rather than typing in *share times four* on an account's existing holding, though that computer entry can occur once the shares are received.

In the case of GameStop, the company allotted 230 million shares for the 4-to-1 split held by their share registrar, Computershare. Computershare then transferred the shares to its holders and the rest to its clearing house, the DTC.

At that time, the DTC passed shares on to their list of brokers and banks — or put shares in their street name — so that each entity had three shares for each existing share on their books. So, the sequence goes Gamestop, Computershare, DTC, Banks/Brokers, and then Retail.

Got it? Good. Here we go.

On the morning of Monday, August 1st, just ten calendar days (six trading days) after the July 22nd splividend, the uneventful splividend shed its calm facade.

While some apes had still failed to receive shares a week after the splividend, an ongoing tally of failures to receive was tracked at the header of Superstonk. But it wasn't the American apes who would be affected by these failures; instead, it was their German brethren, first reported by u/Masterchief_m: "PSA: The german Volksbank just deleted all dividend shares!! Almost with all german banks and brokers[,] the Dividend Shares are gone!... my position just lost 75% of [its] value."

In an update, Masterchief added what the broker had told them, "Subsequently, a stock dividend will be recorded at a ratio of 1:3. You will receive the credit for the new shares from the stock dividend by means of a separate booking. We apologize for any inconvenience caused."

The downhill flow of the Volksbank issue was extreme, affecting apes at numerous other brokers across Germany. For a moment, it seemed all hell truly had broken loose until Volksbank was found to be the only upstream source of the mayhem. No one in Germany had the correct share counts, and Superstonk was aflame with the fireworks they'd previously hoped for.

Volksbank's complete name is Volksbanken Raiffaisenbanken, self-described as "an important pillar of the financial industry, [and] we assume responsibility for helping to shape the transition to a sustainable economy."

It seemed Volksbank had made a mistake in booking the shares as a split. But the error encouraged other shareholders to dig further. u/mtgac posted on August 1st, "Fidelity confirms that they are handling the GME Stock Dividend as a STOCK SPLIT (7 images)."

Mtgac's most fascinating screenshot of his chat with Fidelity customer service reads as follows:

mtgac: "I am not asking for what GameStop has announced. I am asking if the DTCC is asking/telling Fidelity to treat this recent GameStop split/dividend as a regular Stock Split or if the DTCC is asking/telling Fidelity to treat it as a Stock

Dividend?"

Fidelity: "Thank you for your patience. I just received confirmation that the GME, the DTCC, and Fidelity are treating this as a stock split."

mtgac: "Thank you for the clarification."

mtgac: "Please DRS my remaining GME shares immediately."

As a disclaimer, this user's story was anecdotal, and Fidelity's customer service representatives eventually got their story straight. But, the "as a split" rather than a dividend language began to appear in other places too.

Brokers and banks were suddenly in knots as to whether they had issued a dividend or split, sometimes claiming both, likely due to misunderstandings by different customer support agents. As a result, German banks were taking back shares to ensure they were booked as dividends, while the Americans were claiming that the shares were never meant to be anything more than a split.

Economist Dave Lauer, another Superstonk favorite economist, tweeted a thread shortly after, starting with, "Sounds like the GME stock split/dividend has completely destroyed some brokers['] back-office systems — I keep hearing about the nightmare of dealing with TDA[meritrade]. Also sounds like overseas brokers are having serious problems, and German brokers are struggling getting shares to people."

"It's possible that distributing the split as a dividend has exposed a lot more problems in how brokers are booking and holding shares for their customers. FINRA should investigate."

u/ronk99 posted a support forum message screencap with the heading, "German broker Comdirect says that the DTCC told… their despository [sic]…that the splividend should not be treated as a dividend but as a regular stock split."

Something in the supply chain was broken, and Redditors worried that GameStop might have released instructions contrary to the company's announcement. Maybe they were the source of the confusion.

With all the buzz about the dividend-to-split direction events, which seemed to be far more common than the Volksbank split-to-dividend corrections, u/educational_nanner posted just before market close, "Just spoke with the DTCC. They issued the split as a normal stock split not a dividend."

Nanner included the DTCC phone number they used to make the call, and when I called to try to confirm what Nanner had claimed, I was asked, "What is the asset that you're looking for?"

"The asset is GameStop," I replied.

The voice on the other end of the line waited for more. "OK."

"I just wanted to know… if the recent split was issued as a split or as a dividend."

And the line went dead.

This experience echoed another user's, u/pee-reminder-bot, who commented just after 4:00 p.m., "i called earlier today too and they hung up on me," making a new flair for their account: i started drinking after the dtcc hung up on me.

u/RyanMeray suggested that two other similar dividends were issued, very recently, thanks to Google/Alphabet, and there weren't any similar issues with those. Tesla would also issue a dividend in weeks to come, and without issues.

u/Reverse_Drawfour_Uno posted their unconfirmed theory that "DTC Fell Into Cohen's Splivadend Trap" to the tune of almost 4,000 upvotes, with a link to an archived SEC document: GameStop's December 8th, 2020 prospectus.

The document read, "We expect that… upon receipt of any payment of principal, premium, interest, dividend or other amount in respect of a permanent global security representing any of such securities, [intermediaries] will immediately credit its participants' accounts," and, "If a depository for a series of securities is at any time unwilling, unable or ineligible to continue as depository… we will issue individual securities."

u/stephenthetech7 commented in reply, "I feel like a 5 year old watching a magic show every time someone points out a... 5-d (five-dimensional) chess move.... it's glorious."

The next DRS wave had been ignited with more firepower than ever before.

u/Zelttiks shared their DRS request chat with Fidelity customer service, where they were asked, "Is there something going on on Reddit that has everyone doing this today?" To put it simply: yes. u/manbrasucks estimated over a million split shares had been registered based on Computershared.net numbers from August 1st alone.

"We might see the first 'stock run' in history," u/zimmah suggested that evening, wildly speculating without sources: "As there is more and more evidence of... the brokers not having the shares that they are selling us... we are seeing what is essentially a 'stock run'. / In other words, apes taking out their stocks from the brokers, and DRSing [them]. [It's] much like a bank run where after losing trust in the banks, [we are] taking out the money from the accounts and withdrawing it into physical bills. Obviously, once this causes a systemwide crash, they can no longer hide it form [sic] the public, as they have successfully been doing for god knows how long".

No sooner had u/Parsnip neared the end of their daily Diamantenhände post[11] in the early morning of August 2nd that more clarity arrived. This day would be even more damning for the suspected culprits as the pincer closed ever more tightly on each side.

u/Goldjunge_Chriz garnered a Reddit r/all post and over 20,000 upvotes with, "German here, THIS IS HUGE: Bafin (The German SEC) has just confirmed in a publication that GameStop dividend shares are incorrectly booked in Germany."

---

[11] Parsnip diligently tracks the GME price on the German exchange as American exchanges close each night. This is a community gathering place for the night owl North American apes.

Germany's BaFin (The Bundesanstalt für Finanzdienstleistungsaufsicht) is the Federal Financial Supervisory Authority, according to the English version of their website. They result from a May 2002 merger between Germany's regulatory authorities on insurance, securities, and banking.

According to BaFin, their function is simple: "BaFin operates in the public interest. Its primary objective is to ensure the proper functioning, stability, and integrity of the German financial system.... Through its market supervision, BaFin also enforces standards of professional conduct which preserve investors' trust in the financial markets."

Goldjunge translated the BaFin message: "GameStop Corp. resolved a stock split in the form of a stock dividend at the beginning of July. BaFin has — also due to some indications from investors — instructed the custodian banks to ensure the deposit of the new shares. Technically, however, the capital measure has so far been treated by the relevant data providers as a stock split and not as a stock dividend."

BaFin goes on to state that German investors who had their share status reversed (some of whom saw portfolios plummet 75% in value as a result) would be made whole again when the matter was resolved.

A day prior, the authenticity of the dividend was the weakest link. No longer.

This was backed up by messages with Computershare staff as the day progressed, courtesy of a screenshot from u/Blanderson_Snooper: "Confirmation from Computershare that they sent Dividend Shares to the DTC," in which the Computershare representative messages, "Upon checking, the shares will be issued directly from the company to DTC then to brokers. So if you still don't receive the share split in your brokerage account, kindly coordi[n]ate with your broker for them to check with DTC."

u/deadbeatbusman replied, "[Middle men] took the shares and didn't have enough and we all know it."

u/ItsAllJustASickGame illustrated the issue with a great infographic, which won't be shared here for legal reasons. In essence, the graphic posited GameStop shares being split between Computershare and the DTC. When enough banks and brokers in the next stage came knocking for those DTC shares, some were told to multiply by four, while others were allotted said shares. Was that accurate, and was it because the DTC didn't have enough to hand out? No one could know one way or the other.

A dividend had entered the DTC, yet a split had come out the other end, but only for some parties. If the Volksbanks of the world hadn't said anything, apes would have been left with nothing. But Volksbank did say something, and others would follow.

u/dathislayer suggested as much in a post titled "Theory: Brokers realized they're losing the game of hot potato":

"My theory is that brokers saw they were going to get thrown under the bus. There is no way they put in writing that they didn't issue a dividend unless it's for self-benefit."

u/Parsnip greeted the Diamantenhändes just before 2:00 a.m. on August 3rd with, "This level of manipulation is exactly why so many of us are HODLing for market reform. That such crimes are committed so brazenly without SEC intervention like BaFin's statement is inexcusable. It is clear that [someone] is trying to prevent a disaster for their… masters here. Will the SEC allow this to happen?"

While the SEC stayed silent, I messaged my broker that afternoon once I'd bought a recently split share of Alphabet (i.e., Google). With so many identical split-as-dividend processes being processed in the months prior, I wanted to use that to compare Google with GameStop in an A/B Test.

Me: "When Google performed their split last month, did Google send [broker] their new shares for each customer who had shares before the split?"

Broker: "For each share of Alphabet Inc held on July 1st, holders receive 19 shares on July 18 (ex-dividend date)."

Me: "So [broker] received 19 shares from Google for every 1 share that their customers held on the execution date?"

Broker: "Yes, customers who held shares of Google as of the record date of July 1st 2022, would receive 19 shares for every one share they had on record."

Me: "Thank you. Were shares sent during the 4-to-1 GameStop split that happened after this Google split? It seemed like they were doing the same kind of corporate action."

Broker: "Yes…. It goes from the company –> Transfer Agent –> DTCC –> [broker]."

While the shares hadn't been "sent" or "given" to the broker (which I later was informed of during a beatdown in the Superstonk comments section), the broker chat agent was able to say with certainty that my shares at their brokerage had originated from dividend shares, not a split.

Unfortunately, I didn't have a long list of brokerages I could compare this with. I only had my boomer broker and Computershare. But on WSB, traders were continuing to trickle back through the doors, confused by their trading accounts.

u/Fabulous_Cellist_219 earned over 2,000 upvotes with, "Austrian retard here which didnt receive his GME dividend [and is now] 75% down" and u/strongholdtheline with "Heng Seng Bank said not received."

Finally, an ape from Norway, u/Joddodd, posted a document provided to his Norwegian broker by the DTCC with the instruction, "Processed As: Stock Split." While the document was difficult to verify or debunk, if it's legitimate, it supports the Redditors' concerns.

u/Jabarumba made their 75th consecutive post titled "Day 75: The DTCC has their own Twitter account. I choose to politely ask them questions every day until I get a public response." As of August 3rd, Jabarumba was 0 for 75, which they confirmed with me via DM:

"What made me decide to start tweeting was the realization that we, Apes on SuperStonk, are just normal people leading normal lives participating in a once in a lifetime event. One day, I just decided to tweet at the DTCC and put it on the SuperStonk…. I thought, I'm a normal person, I can tweet, why not? That was it. No special moment or DD [inspired it]. I just did it."

u/Jabarumba wasn't some depressed young man on Wall Street Bets whose stock gambles were informed by socioeconomic psychology. Jabarumba just did it. Mad as hell. Not going to take it anymore. Meddling with the primal forces of nature, and all that jazz.

AMC or "popcorn" — named because mention of other tickers on Superstonk had been banned in favor of GameStop-centric content — was in the process of announcing their own less interesting stock split the afternoon of Thursday, August 4th. But u/Alarming-Option-3728 couldn't care less for the $APE split and was asking the question the rest of us wanted to know:

"Is this one of the [pivotal] moments in the GME Saga that has been discussed several times?"

u/TheLevelHeadedGuy alleged, "DTCC [is] in the fuck around and find out stage."

30: Bishop to c7

The stock price ended the week of all hell breaking loose just a smidgen above $40 ($160 pre-split).

Not since December 2021 had GME been worth this much, except for the spike that lasted a week or two in April 2022 when the split was announced.

A combination of market factors seemed to fuel the rise, which started a month earlier during the NFT marketplace launch, through the rally of the overall market from June lows and a resurgent DRS campaign by users to pull shares from sources that could use them for shorting.

GameStop wasn't the only ticker moving in such a direction, and Superstonk wasn't the only subreddit chasing a massive short percentage this month. But something had to first bring the WSB o.g.'s back to roost.

Bloomberg reported on August 4th, "AMTD Became a $470 Billion Meme Stock By Accident." The Register reported the same day, "Obscure Asian fintech AMTD Digital becomes the new GameStop." And USA Today reported August 3rd, "AMTD Digital stock, HKD, is up more than 14,000% since its IPO. Is it a new meme stock?"

To anyone who hadn't visited WSB in a few months or had written it off entirely due to random pump-and-dumps and continuing bot infestations, AMTD's moonshot rise brought active members back to the sub to see what was really going on and to see if they could profit.

In short, they couldn't. At least, not by much more than the tens of thousands of percentage points already reported by major outlets. AMTD Digital was "a three-year-old Hong Kong fintech company with 50 employees," according to

Bloomberg, and only reported "$25 million of revenue" in its most recent statement, despite a momentary valuation of $470 billion, among the top ten companies in the world.

But when those users returned to WSB, they found very little waiting for them. The site subredditstats.com reported a slight uptick in comments and posts in the early days of August compared to the rest of summer 2022.

As a Quiverquant graph demonstrated at the time, the gradual rise in mentions belonging to SPY, GME, and other common stocks remains fairly consistent, but it's AMD (one letter off from AMTD) and HKD that experience surges just after August 1st.

The WSB hivemind determined AMTD was "The perfect wallstreetbets sucker bet." The WSB lost children might have been easy to FOMO into a YOLO or two on a P/E ratio over a hundred, but not when it came to fundamentals they considered to be this piss poor.

Now WSB looked like a bunch of fraternity and sorority members who showed up to an empty house expecting a party. It wasn't like they could just start from scratch. They had to muster whatever booze they had in their trunks and make the best bathtub gin they could. It just so happened there was a sterling candidate waiting in the wings.

Another dandy part of Reddit's algorithm, and another aspect of the site that exceeds the algorithms of Facebook and Twitter, is its ability to refresh users on rising posts for their favorite subreddits, and without showing posts that users have already seen. This likely contributed to users returning to WSB after their initial visits on August 4th because their custom feeds kept them abreast of information valuable to the subreddit.

I first saw mention of Bed Bath that week in the form of the battering ram meme, with police labeled "BBBY" breaking down a door marked "$6.50," i.e., the stock was challenging that price point. That was around the time that Bed, Bath, and Beyond's short interest exceeded something around 30-50% by some counts.

Sound familiar? To WSB, it certainly did.

A few months earlier, in March 2022, I had FOMO'd a small amount of money into shares of BBBY when it was announced that the company had reached an agreement with Cohen, who'd taken a stake in the company similar to that in GameStop.

The board chair, Harriet Edelman, offered the following in the company's press release: "'We are pleased to have reached this constructive agreement with RC Ventures, which we believe to be in the best interest of all our shareholders…. The Board is highly committed to fundamentally reshaping Bed Bath & Beyond for our customers while driving growth and profitability across its banners. We look forward to benefitting [sic] from the contributions and perspectives of our new directors.'"

The stock price would rocket to almost $30 in the days that followed that announcement. But this skyrocket also raised the alarm for short sellers, who arrived en masse, knocking the price down with as much as 30% rises in short interest percentages in two-week reporting periods. Three months later, BBBY had fallen below $5.

Whether the short interest was actually around 40%, as most sources reported, or truly exceeded 100%, as users had found on certain sites, was beside the point. If it looked like a GameStop duck and walked like a GameStop duck, then the answer was, "Don't think about it just throw all your money in," u/CartelFinancial commented on August 5th, as the share price returned to $8.

The week had been a steady climb for "towel" (BBBY) and "popcorn" (AMC). While similarities in price action follow market averages, for a period after the sneeze, everything that GME did, AMC did too, and eventually, BBBY joined.

I would compare the two tickers in my trading apps in bewilderment most days, unsure how this was possible. But there it was, time and time again throughout 2021, noticed as early as February 10th, 2021, by u/kxsshole on r/WallStreetbetsELITE: "It[']s so weird how the GME chart and the AMC chart always move at the same rate. Always lookin like a copy of each other… why is that?"

The 20-30% returns on my portfolio on Friday, August 5th, weren't what would knock my socks off, though. It was what followed.

Like a chess grandmaster making an opening in the most conservative fashion possible, GameStop's messaging until now seemed to resemble what's known as a Hedgehog opening, which uses pawns "as the spines of the hedgehog — short, but dangerous when provoked.... Black is short of space but has plenty of ideas" (The Chess World).

When the black player wishes to break their opening and begin attacking white's position, they typically move their Bishop to the square c7. GameStop was about to initiate the midgame, whether that was the company's intention or not.

Just before 5:00 p.m., GameStop released the following, which garnered over 25,000 upvotes on Superstonk, and was a welcome break from the BBBY madness erupting in WSB:

"GameStop Guidance for International Stockholders with Split-Related Questions"

"GameStop has notified its transfer agent and the Depository Trust Company ('DTC') that some of our valued stockholders in international geographies are still trying to determine if they have received the proper stock dividend associated with the Company's recent 4-for-1 stock split. Please note GameStop has already distributed the shares of common stock required for the stock dividend to its transfer agent, which has confirmed it subsequently distributed the appropriate number of shares of common stock to DTC for allocation to brokerage firms and other participants.... We appreciate your investment and enthusiasm. Although we are not able to engage with individual brokerage firms, we are monitoring this situation and will keep you informed of any relevant updates we obtain through our transfer agent or DTC."

Superstonk was ecstatic. But much like an infomercial, that's not all!

Ryan Cohen's first tweet in over a week dropped moments later: "Ask not what your company can do for you — ask what you can do for your company."

My jaw hit the floor for the first time since Elon Musk tweeted his first *gamestonk*. To avoid standing in the way of the ape community and their collective surge of excitement, I'll leave my own reaction at that.

The one-two punch of the corporate statement combined with the RC tweet was unlike anything the subreddit had seen before from the usually stoic front office. The corporate statement was a smoking gun confirming so many theories about where the splividend had gone awry.

u/theriskguy commented on the statement, "Oh shit. / 'We gave CS shares, they gave DTC the appropriate number of shares' / It's actually happening."

u/UniverseInfinite: "Wow, this is actually notable. / GameStop has never officially commented on any details of the ongoing saga."

u/TallWineGuy: "Monday is MOASS, just in case you didn't know."

Because at Superstonk, tomorrow is always MOASS.

Even WSB was back in the action after a day of pumping towel and popcorn, with u/Expensive-Two-8128 posting, "GameStop wrote the DTC a spicy little love note re: the splividend [kissy emoji]."

u/Sciglide replied, "What a fucking time to be alive."

While WSB and Superstonk were on the same side once more, Superstonk still lacked comments like those between u/dank420memes420 and u/aRawPancake:

"GME lied to all the apes because they think you're trash."

"Sounds like you should gargle my balls."

"As soon as GME squeezes above 40 I will."

"I consent."

u/aRawPancake would post that afternoon to over 3,000 upvotes, "A debt must be paid… u/dank420memes420," leading to the inevitable ban of the latter from WSB.

While it was one of the most notable events in the history of Superstonk, there wasn't a peep from the outside world. u/GoPhotoshopYourself shared, "It's been more than 3 hours since GameStop's announcement about the Splividend's processing and not ONE article has come out about it... the silence is deafening." u/roor1337 replied, "They all must have forgot about GameStop."

Still, others speculated on the meaning of Cohen's tweet. u/iforgotmypasswwoordd postulated, "I think [Ryan Cohen] wants GameStop stockholders to DRS."

Apes hadn't considered the difference between Cohen's tweet and the corpo statement until now. Namely, Cohen's tweet may have implied that more work was required, beyond what the company could do for shareholders. With that move having been made, it might very well be the shareholders' turn to finish the fight.

u/GetThisNick's comment was so popular with 2,000 upvotes, it got its own re-posting as a screenshot with 8,000 more, hypothesizing: "[I believe that Cohen] is YELLING at us to DRS the synthetic shares they've been printing for the dividend. It's so blatantly fucking obvious. He's telling us to stop crying for GameStop to jump in and fight.... Stop bitching about the crime happening with the split/dividend. We KNEW they were going to try to fuck us and sweep it under the rug.... Not financial advice, I kiss my dad on the lips before bed time."

u/miraclebob came clean: "I sat on 7 broker shares for a year."

"I DRSd my 100 shares and kept 7 at Fidelity; I had convinced myself it's [no big deal] and doesn't make a difference, especially when I saw whale posts for X,XXX DRSd. / Well I just DRSd the 28 I had in Fidelity."

An even greater wave of purple circles was on the horizon, and the public would finally take notice.

As u/segr1801 posted to 1,500 upvotes, "Check Mate."

Part 4: Endgame

"It's gravely concerning that retail participants, literally just regular everyday people, were able to figure out that something was wrong... before... regulators took appropriate action....

When people on Reddit and Twitter can spot... mismanagement before the regulators, something is terribly wrong."

— Sen. Kyrsten Sinema, March 2023 SVB Congressional Hearing

31: Where There's Smoke, There's Fire

Something rotten in the state of Sweden

In a world where astronomers warn us of cataclysmic asteroids with a 1-in-100,000 chance of destroying the planet, seismologists foretold 1-in-10,000 odds of devastating earthquakes, and DraftKings gives the Houston Texans a 250-to-1 pre-season payout for winning Super Bowl LVII, isn't it worth discussing a crisis with 1-in-100 odds, if not 1-in-10, or fifty-fifty?

What if a crisis wasn't a matter of odds but was instead only a matter of time?

Like some kind of ticking nuclear bomb that Jack Bauer doesn't locate and defuse within twenty-four hours, such an event would be unprecedented. But such a suggestion also deserves a healthy serving of skepticism.

So let's start with the basics.

Remember when we saw that image of the black hole for the first time in 2021, thanks to the Event Horizon Telescope? Seeing that image didn't invent black holes for scientists. Physicists had known of black holes for decades, thanks to researching the warped space around the star-swallowers. It was those physicists who pointed astronomers to warped sections of deep space and begged them to develop the tools to confirm such theories. And so they did.

In the same way, there are a handful of data points in the GameStop story that have been "black hole" moments for me and many others, where apes can't see the black hole, but space-time warps and buckles so violently that there must be something causing it.

Put simply: where there's smoke, there may be fire.

Or a black hole.

Example 1: The Consumer Survey (June 2021)

Homegrown experiments are my favorite, especially when there's no one else to do the dirty work. Growing up, I spent my weekends pouring baking soda over plastic volcanoes, testing the flight patterns of model rockets, and watching pendulums shift ever so slightly at the Fort Worth Museum of Science and History.

Homegrown science experiments don't exist to learn anything new. Instead, they're there to introduce young people to the laws of physics and chemistry. You might say, "See? The world does rotate on an axis, based on how we've watched this pendulum rotate for the past thirty minutes. Now, for the love of God, let's proceed to the gift shop."

But it was always worth watching just a moment longer, just in case the world stopped rotating like it was supposed to. Just in case you caught a glitch in the matrix.

Data experiments can reveal unforeseen results, i.e., glitches in the matrix of public opinion.

On June 17th, 2021, it was u/Get-It-Got who had been eyeing the pendulum, waiting for an aberration. To 4,000 upvotes, they posted, "Using Randomized, Representative Surveying Data to Model $GME Ownership Among the U.S. Adult Population."

"Representative sampling allows researchers to understand the behaviors and/or characteristics of a population by identifying the behaviors and/or characteristics of a subset of the population. In the case of this research, this was done through a randomized, internet-based survey that asked a very simple question about the status of $GME share ownership."

The goal: take an informal census of shares held by retail, trim that study to its lowest possible margin for error, and extrapolate. If the results land within even twice the publicly available float, then the publicly stated numbers would be correct.

u/Get-It-Got used Google Consumer Reports[12] for the survey to avoid the biases that might accompany a less expensive platform and/or a platform that would slant too heavily toward Superstonk users, as previous Reddit-based polls had done.

Between June 9th and 17th, according to the results, 300 consumers were polled, out of which only 19 revealed they held GameStop stock. That means 281 of 300 surveyed consumers, or almost 94%, did not hold GME shares. It seems disappointing, but it proves the mettle of the survey method: escaping the Reddit echo chamber to reach people in the real world.

Out of the 19 surveyed individuals who admitted to owning GameStop stock, half owned around five or ten shares on average, a few owned GME but had sold it, two owned between 20 and 100 shares, and four owned over 100 shares.

If you extrapolate that to the size of the U.S. adult population, you can imagine the results might far exceed the stated float of GME at 75 million shares, especially the retail float that's around half of that amount. But the issue then becomes using five or ten people instead of five or ten million, providing an atrocious margin of error.

u/Get-It-Got realized as much, and upon concluding that the poll's U.S. GameStop ownership was in the hundreds of millions of shares, they resolved to survey a higher sample size.

u/Get-It-Got returned in July with the help of an anonymous donor who added more users to the sample size: "At LEAST 164MM $GME Shares in Hands of U.S. Retail… [and] My Best Guesstimate For Total Shares Owned Globally [is] 531MM."

---

[12] This process also assumes Google can build a reliable consumer reporting platform. As Google itself notes, "Real people answer your questions as they browse the internet… Leading marketers trust data over gut. Google Surveys will help you integrate real consumer insights into important business decisions."

Using the original 300 survey members, adding another 300 to re-check the initial results, tacking on 1,500 provided by the anonymous contributor, and then wrapping all of that together with the knowledge that Google won't re-survey the same person, the sample size could now be a more reliable 2,200, albeit spread over a couple of weeks.

The 2,200 sample size isn't insignificant by comparison. The political polls that determine seismic matters like presidential approval ratings typically use half this sample size. As u/anthro28 noted, "if he's wrong by a margin of 75% we still own the float."

With the 2,200 surveyed, the percentage of GME ownership remained steady at 5%.

Sources of error were taken into account, such as couples with joint ownership, so u/Get-It-Got added a penalty, shifting the U.S. adult ownership under 4%. To avoid share averaging errors, u/Get-It-Got assumed the lower bound of each survey response amount, e.g., someone who said they owned between 5 and 20 shares was given a value of 5. This method gave share-owning U.S. adults a rough lower bound estimate of 34 shares on average.

So at 34 shares per 4% of U.S. adult couples, the conservative guess comes out to somewhere around 200 million shares. If U.S. adults in July 2021 truly owned 200,000,000 shares of GameStop, the results would be cataclysmic because the United States is only one part of the puzzle (a puzzle that's supposed to have only tens of millions of publicly available pieces). Assuming that these surveys only returned the lower bounds of 150 million U.S. shares, that number would still remain three to six times the expected retail float of 25-40 million, once one subtracted for non-retail buyers.

u/Get-It-Got told me a year after their surveys, "I can't help but feel the story is just getting started. It's... sad... that the surveys are even necessary to try and get a glimpse of what might be really going on.... But as apes have shown... we'll do it ourselves."

Their most recent poll, which attempted to focus on DRS counts, showed almost 15% of respondents in a pool of four hundred said they owned GME, and nearly all of those surveyed said some or all of their shares had been directly registered.

The Google Survey certainly was intriguing, but on its own, it's neither smoke nor a smoking gun. If there were hundreds of millions of shares where there were only supposed to be tens of millions, there would be other signs of trouble.

With as fragmented and multi-tiered as our financial markets are, it would take a powerful conspiracy to maintain a lie about something like share overcounts. But just like a magnet can be held at the south pole of a compass, it's not outside the realm of possibility.

And when you do hold a magnet to a compass, the pointer might occasionally jump to true north, if only for a moment. Unless it stays there for an entire weekend.

Example 2: The Yahoo Finance Glitch (September 2021)

While share and float counts glitched on more than one occasion — and across multiple trading platforms — one particular "glitch" roiled r/Superstonk over a September weekend in 2021.

On September 11th, u/sweatysuits posted, "Anomaly No More! GME float keeps going up. It's not an anomaly or a glitch."

u/sweatysuits and other users that Saturday morning had found a data point on Yahoo Finance that had been raising eyebrows since the preceding day: a float reported at 249.51 million shares, three to four times the usual stated float of around 70 million:

"I began writing this DD when the declared float was 248.48m. I went to get a screenshot for this DD and it fucking changed. Now it's 249.51m. / A glitch that continues to glitch and somehow not unglitched for almost 2 days? Nah."

u/flaming_pope would follow up on Sept. 14th with an image titled, "Peaking [sic] behind Yahoo Curtain … Found a footprint/artifact indicating they changed algo/number manually."

Analyzing data from the Wayback Machine (archive.org), which preserves changes in websites over time, u/flaming_pope alleged, "When you have data from 6-different sources, it's highly abnormal for the numbers to line up perfectly. Especially with harmonic data updates such as Yahoo's sources. So when I noticed the numbers lined up TOO perfectly, I checked Yahoo-GME's history and noticed that there's a steady ~5M footprint (a phase offset) in the past data, which was removed in the 'Fixed' float, indicative of potential fuckery in the new data."

The moment ended almost as quickly as it began, and it would take a computer science degree to get to the bottom of FlamingPope's unconfirmed allegations that Yahoo changed its share count manually.

The best possible explanation to the contrary was commented by u/arikah: "One theory is that the CAT [FINRA's Consolidated Audit Trail] system is active now since Sept 1…. Since CAT is fairly new, it's possible yahoo (and other finance data scrapers) are picking up on data they 'aren't supposed to see,' because CAT is designed to be more transparent. / I think the real questions are why did it happen twice today, and the number went up even more?…. Why has this only happened to GME, and none of the other memestonks or normal stocks so far?"

Example 3: The Swedish Brokers (January 2022)

In the same way that a mathematician can begin to solve a multi-variable problem when one variable is revealed, so too, Redditors were hungry for any concrete share count information to spaghettify inside their statistical accretion disc. Until now, they had been working with variables that were only defined by other variables and guesses.

Swedish broker Avanza provided that concrete figure in January of 2022 with the tweet: "For now there are 511,178 [GME] stocks owned by around 20,902 users on our platform."

A similarly sized Swedish broker, Nordnet, released their share numbers of GME as well, pressured to do so by their Swedish customers after Avanza's tweet. As a result, Nordnet revealed another 300,000+ shares across their user base, which provides just under one million known shares in Sweden, accounting for as much as 2-3% of the retail float (pre-splidividend).

Considering Gamestop is so prevalent in the United States, ownership nearing seven digits in a medium-sized European country is shocking. Sweden ranks fifteenth in population for European countries, and Avanza and Nordnet are only two of its many brokers.

u/irishdud1 posted, "We are all Swedish today: 245M shares exist extrapolating Avanza's data" above a chart applying percentages of banked citizens and per capita GDP to potential GME shares by country.

u/bowls4noles: "Linear extrapolation doesn't really work here... but it[']s still good info!"

The Avanza/Nordnet episode is significant not due to its trimming of one variable off the float's calculus but instead because of its simple transparency. In a very short time, not one but two brokers chose to release their internal counts of Gamestop shares. This hadn't happened previously (nor in the following year), and that silence was louder than any number short of seventy million.

u/TheRecycledMale noted just as much: "Just to state what has become obvious to me (based upon Avanza's tweet), ALL Retail Brokers have the ability (assumed) to report how many shares are held by their customer (in their brokerage account), and how many accounts hold those specific equities (stocks).... Every single Broker could provide that report. If it was provided (not just for GME but for any listed stock), it would become extremely obvious... that Wall Street is really just a house of cards."

u/daimondhendz would post updates from Avanza in weeks and months to come, where their app continually showed how many users continued their HODL'ing of GME, a feature not yet available in any app I've used or seen outside of the blockchain.

Is this ~~a pigeon~~ a sign of fire?

Superstonk members have tried for two years to find concrete evidence of a reasonable float based on reliable data and have discovered something else entirely, also including but not limited to daily volumes in the hundreds of millions, higher-than-average failures to deliver, and glitch after glitch after glitch after (you guessed it) glitch.

Glitches have become so common in the GME saga that the standard response is *glitch better have my money.*

As u/icupanopticon would gripe, "How the fuck have we gotten to a point where no one has a clue how many total shares really exist? Shouldn't this just be primary investment data for everyone to see when making investment decisions?"

Popcorn CEO Adam Aron tweeted in June 2022, "Inbound tweets ask over and over for a 'share count.' AMC has done a share count 6 times in the past year. We know of 516.8 million AMC shares. Some of you believe the count is much higher. As I've said before, we've seen no reliable info on so-called synthetic or fake shares."

Look up any trading site, ask any CEO, and they'll tell you plainly how many shares exist. But that's not what ICUPanopticon is suggesting.

The suspected fraud went further beneath the surface than even Aron's sources of information might reveal. The sources that those sources cited weren't even the culprits. Either there was something rotten at the core, and everyone else was an intermediary, or the DD was wrong, and everything was just fine.

The Event Horizon Telescope, which caught the first image of a black hole, didn't just build a large telescope and capture a photo. Instead, the "telescope" isn't a telescope at all but a collection of data scientists positioned at observatories around the globe. Their collective information is processed with powerful computers to turn zeroes and ones into pixels.

After more than a year of groundbreaking DDs, unprecedented glitches, regulatory reports, and a stock splividend gone wrong, apes were hungry for a statistical kill shot.

32: Suckers at the Poker Game

Unlike O.J. Simpson's book *If I Did It*, where the "if" is in tiny text to drum up buzz, controversy, and book sales, what you're about to read should come with a massive, unmissable "if."

IF

Like most members of Superstonk, I fully realize this coming summation of DDs, theories, and ideas could all be wrong. Moreover, I hope it is.

I hope that our financial markets function with total fairness and transparency. I hope that corruption doesn't allow greedy giants to hamstring regulators. When I chat with people in finance who shrug and explain that the system runs really well despite what the tinfoil hats say, I sincerely hope they're right. And I hope that self-regulatory entities act with the utmost ethical code despite their bottom line.

But just in case any of that isn't true 100% of the time, let's consider the alternative as Superstonk currently believes it. For educational purposes, future generations, and frankly, the fun of it.

Know When to HODL 'em

Do you know what staplers and donuts have in common? Both have been used to describe complex facets of astrophysics and finance in cute ways that smooth-brained readers and audiences can digest. Respectively, they appear in the film adaptation of *The Martian* and the book version of *The Antisocial Network*.

I hate staplers and donuts. Most of the time, these descriptors aren't necessary, even for the smooth brains. They're added because writers, filmmakers, and authors like me want everyone to feel like they're wrinkle-brained. Participation trophies all around.

Until now, I've resisted such analogies out of respect for your intelligence. But just like any short seller is a future buyer, so too, I must now close my short against donuts, staplers, and every cute little analogy out there. (And yes, I'll phone Andrew Ross Sorkin with the news first thing tomorrow morning during *Squawk Box*.)

My donut/stapler is an imaginary casino, El Casino Del Stock Exchange, where the only game played is Texas Hold'em poker. In Texas Hold'em, there's always a percentage chance that you're a winner or a loser based on the fact that there are only 52 cards in play at a time. The cards are non-fungible, as it were.

For this reason, the game of blackjack is so rarely offered with one to two decks in play. While counting cards in blackjack will get you kicked out of a casino, counting cards is a prerequisite in playing Hold'em.

For example, we can view the sneeze as if it played out at Casino Del Stock Exchange. Let's say retail trader ButtFarm timidly entered the poker hall carrying a (legal) cheat sheet that ranked the value of Hold'em hands, ranging from high card to a pair to a full house and all the way up to the mythical Royal Flush.

ButtFarm is a newbie that can be spotted from a mile away, and most of the deep-pocketed analysts, money managers, and bankers that play at the Casino Del don't pay him a mind. His pennies aren't worth their time.

When ButtFarm does find a table he can sit down at (a visually appealing, somewhat rickety table named *Silicon Valley Trading app*), the next gambler over, biting into a small orange, sees a new sucker. So he bets big on the next hand without considering the cards in play. The citrus-eating gambler ignores the fact that ButtFarm's hand turns out to be excellent, and when ButtFarm invites friends (in this hypothetical casino, mind you) to bet on his pot, his friends see the value in his cards, so they agree.

Before reaching the dealer's final community cards, the "turn" or "river," ButtFarm's wager is so large that citrus can no longer bet against it without going all-in, and folds. But now, with the pot this large, an even deeper-pocketed player named Hedgie had to ask for money from world series poker champ, Biggie.

As gamblers from all sides of the casino saw the stakes mounting and realized ButtFarm had a winnable hand against Hedgie, they piled their chips into ButtFarm's coffers. When all seemed lost for Hedgie and Biggie, drowning under the squeeze, the trading app poker table shattered under the weight of the chips, and the game had to be forfeited.

Straightforward enough?

Our poker game has everything that a normal game of Hold 'em might, but with twists representing the quirks of Superstonk's market theses — some real and others purely speculative — and all of which we'll dive into before the end of this penultimate chapter.

Rehypothecation and Naked Shorts

There's been an elephant in the room, and one that had bothered me to no end, even as I read the DDs, the Diamond Handbook, and watched the video AMAs: the numbers still didn't add up.

On the Wednesday of the sneeze, January 27th, 2021, u/SnooCauliflowers4003 commented what the rest of WSB supposed: "FRIDAY is the reckoning for GME… that's when shorts have to cover. But if there's no shares left.... hehehehe."

Instead, it seemed like there was slippage, which prevented the concrete math that market experts claimed was at the core of our world. The shares never went to zero despite massive buy pressure as the week began. Thanks to that slippage, an unstoppable force and an immovable object had found common ground, to the great disadvantage of Reddit's tendies.

At the time of the Volkswagen MOASS, the short interest was only 12.8%. During the sneeze, GME short interest went over 100%, and even in mid-2022, stood at double the Volkswagen numbers. So why did 12.8% equal MOASS, but over 100% didn't?

Percentages are fractions, numerators over denominators, and users had always assumed the denominator was the public float of seventy-ish million shares (before the splividend). But what if the denominator wasn't seventy million?

If there were extra shares, as Redditors postulated in all three instances in the previous chapter and plenty of other times, then short interest could have been far less than that famous hundred-plus percent. When that's the case, it means there are more shares available to exit a short than previously thought. And, there becomes less chance at MOASS.

At the allegorical casino, ButtFarm discovers something just like this. As he scrapes together his chips from the sticky floors after the table collapses, his friend PotatoInAss rushes to help.

"Stay away from my chips, Potato," ButtFarm grumbles.

Potato grins and hands ButtFarm the chips she's picked up. "I'm trying to help! You have to do this again. There's a sturdier table over there with lots of structural fidelity, and a seat just opened up… Here."

She hands ButtFarm his original stack of chips plus citrus guy's losses. ButtFarm traces her line of sight toward a larger table, where a poorly upholstered stool is avoided by players wanting more comfortable places to sit.

He approaches this seat, where there's wording sewn into the seat: *brick-and-mortar* retailer.

"You don't want to sit there, kid," mutters a banker, sitting the next chair over.

Not having a choice, ButtFarm takes the seat and puts down his chips, ready to replicate the game where he was robbed of his big win.

ButtFarm finds himself in excellent spirits when he gets his first hand and compares it to the community cards the dealer has put at the center of the table: there's a three-of-a-kind of kings on the table, and he holds the fourth king card in his hand.

Even more to his delight, ButtFarm watches as the other players at the table make big bets, each of them bluffing that they are the holders of that elusive fourth king, the only winning hand. Using every penny he's got, plus some margin, Butt-Farm matches their wagers, ready for a massive payday in the likely event he's won the hand.

But then, the cards are revealed: everyone has the same card as ButtFarm, a king. In a deck that was only supposed to have four identical values across four suits, there are no less than eight of those values in all of these players' hands.

Because there's an ace in the community hand alongside the three kings, everyone is left with equivalent hands, and the result is a push. All the players get to keep what they put in.

ButtFarm is mystified and asks the dealer, "Is this a normal deck?"

The other players chuckle amongst themselves as the dealer nods and shows ButtFarm all 52 cards of the next deck before shuffling. In that deck, there is the correct number of values, four of each.

The next hand starts just as well for ButtFarm. Another three-of-a-kind lands in the community hand (a statistical improbability, but helpful for this analogy). ButtFarm again holds the fourth in his hand. This time, ButtFarm (and Potato watching over his shoulder) focus on the deck intently to ensure the dealer hasn't messed with its contents or added extra cards.

When this hand ends, the result is the same: every player at the table has the same card in their hands to complete the four-of-a-kind. And worse, every player except ButtFarm has an ace in their hand, too, meaning the others split the pot, and ButtFarm loses his wager, divided amongst them.

ButtFarm is as frustrated as he is beside himself. This is going to be harder than he thought.

There are a few hands where ButtFarm doesn't get good cards or doesn't get a hand that he thinks is playable, but it's not long until his luck returns. Again, ButtFarm opens a hand with the cards for something special, and that's when he notices the issue: the other players step away from the table throughout this hand, or worse, chat with players passing by their seats.

ButtFarm realizes his problem isn't the deck or the dealer. His problem isn't even the decks at the other tables — it's that every deck at every table is in play because the other players are actively trading their cards between tables.

When ButtFarm is closing in on the next round-winning wager, holding a fourth-of-a-kind king again, someone at his own table even walks up to PotatoInAss and asks her, "Got a king?"

When Potato shakes her head no, the player grumbles and returns to the table, where he scribbles "KING" on a cocktail napkin. When the hand ends, every player inevitably has the needed king, resulting in another tie.[13]

ButtFarm asks the dealer, "Why can he use the napkin? These other cards aren't from our deck, but his napkin isn't even a card at all!"

The dealer says, "The napkin is a nakedly borrowed king. He'll get a real king after this hand is over unless you all want to wait for him to go find one?"

The immediate grumbling from the players, ready for another hand, strikes down that idea. Liquidity and pace of play must be preserved at all costs at the casino.

ButtFarm tries one last time. "But if anyone can make cards out of anything, then there can't be a squeeze!" The dealer shrugs. "Not my problem."

The dealer turns to the player with the napkin king, pushing a mountain of chips back to his coffers as he does to the others. Flustered, Potato points out to the pit boss, Sally Erricson Charles (initials S.E.C.), and complains, "That guy just counterfeited a card and cost ButtFarm a win."

---

[13] Self-ascribed "Wall Street Bank Veteran" Tobin Mulshine gives a great interview in HBO's documentary series Gaming Wall Street, where he reveals his own experience of naked shorting: "You appreciate the order, and if that involves shorting a stock naked, you do it anyway. Because management essentially tells you, 'just create the business.'..... All the prime lenders, they all do it," he alleges.

SEC informs ButtFarm, "Napkin did that to increase liquidity, which we think is important, so long as he doesn't do it too much! Besides, he could have lost a lot of money, and that could have caused a contagion."

Whether it was extra kings floating around the poker hall when there were only supposed to be four in the deck or because when push came to shove, players could invent extra kings when Sally didn't watch closely, ButtFarm's struggle to score a big win was being hampered by what seemed like infinite card liquidity.

ButtFarm furrowed his brow. Even if he went table-to-table and took every king in the room, would the rest of these guys be able to draw more cards on napkins?

This section of the analogy doesn't do a perfect job of describing how apes believe the deck is stacked against them but instead echoes the emotion at the center of it all. When MOASS is dependent on a lack of liquidity, then liquidity as a result of naked practices feels doubly unfair.

But unfairness is only the beginning.

Phantom Shares and Failures to Deliver

The seemingly high share count of GME continues to be the source of debate, whether hypothetically 100 to 500 million shares (pre-splividend) or legitimately somewhere in the tens of millions. If the float does exceed the number of shares GameStop initially offered, it's a result of either shares being rehypothecated, nakedly shorted, or both.

In *The Revolution That Wasn't*, Spencer Jakab claims, "Another major misunderstanding about short selling… was the notion that short sellers illegally sell shares out of thin air…. So called 'naked shorting,' once common, is almost always the result of innocent clerical errors these days. The fact that more than one hundred percent of the available shares of GameStop were sold short by early 2021 looked suspicious, but happened because people who bought shares from short sellers lent them out again, a legitimate process called 'rehypothecation.'"

You have to appreciate Jakab's statement for its blissful ignorance: naked short-ing exists but only if there's innocent clerical errors. If you actually believe that, I have a bridge to sell you, Mr. Jakab.

Mark Cuban reiterates this same idea in his AMA: "There can be more shares shorted than there are [in the] original float. That is by design. If i borrow a stock from you to short, and when I short it and your buddy buys it, then they can loan it to someone else to short, etc. All of those people who borrowed the stock paid to do so, and they realize that if enough people buy the stock and ask for the shares, they will get called in. So the chain of custody is there. The system… is doing what it[']s designed to do."[14]

The SEC report on GameStop includes a single mention of naked shorting on page 29: "The unusually high amount of short selling raised the question of whether some of the short sales were 'naked' — namely, made without arranging to borrow the underlying security. When a naked short sale occurs, the seller fails to deliver the securities to the buyer, and staff did observe spikes in fails to deliver in GME. However, fails to deliver can occur either with short or long sales, making them an imperfect measure of naked short selling."

So paraphrasing our regulators, *we only have one metric of naked short selling, and it's imperfect but good enough for us to go with it.*

I also have a bridge to sell you, SEC.

The measure of rehypothecation versus naked shorting at the core of the sneeze may never be known. Unfortunately, no one has a tally of the true extent of naked shorting before, during, or since, either. On top of that, a continuously rehypoth-ecated chain of custody can leave just as many "napkin poker cards" (in IOU form) floating around our allegorical poker room.

---

[14] Back in the days of paper shares, when a share was sold short it could actually be marked as such on the share. Unfortunately, this made the share hard to sell once it had been shorted, and so traders tried to avoid it. Now, such a practice might be laughed out of the room or simply impossible.

The SEC, on their own website, actually encourages naked shorting if done for the sake of market functionality: "'Naked' short selling is not necessarily a violation of the federal securities laws or the Commission's rules. Indeed, in certain circumstances, 'naked' short selling contributes to market liquidity."

If you feel the need to yell into a pillow after reading that last sentence, you're not alone. Consider taking up a martial art if you're already hoarse.

There is academic research as recent as 2021 on naked shorting, thanks to The Journal of Corporation Law: "Naked short sales are not illegal; moreover, failures to deliver are also not necessarily violations of Regulation[s].... When market participants use short selling and naked short selling to perpetuate intentional wrongdoing, then the SEC may investigate. However, enforcement actions for violations of Regulation[s]...are rare; successful private litigation by issuers against short sellers is even rarer."[15]

In the Spring 2008 issue of Regulation, John W. Welborn writes an article with one of my favorite titles, *The Phantom Shares Menace*, wherein he argues, "The SEC and the DTCC defend occasional naked short selling and delivery failures on the grounds that they foster 'liquidity.' Such arguments reveal that these regulators and professionals have forgotten that a price is a mixture of scarcity, risk, and value; unlimited liquidity obliterates scarcity and undermines the price system. As William Donaldson, Pitt's successor as chairman of the SEC, once remarked, 'How much fraud are you willing to tolerate for liquidity? I think the answer is zero.'"[16]

---

[15] Hurt, Christine, and Paul Standi. "Short Sellers, Short Squeezes, and Securities Fraud." The Journal of Corporation Law, vol. 47, no. 1, fall 2021, pp. 105+. Gale Academic OneFile, link.gale.com/apps/doc/A694379456/AONE?u=scottsdale hq&sid=bookmark-AONE&xid=89d10675. Accessed 11 Aug. 2022.

[16] Welborn, John W. "The 'phantom shares' menace: naked short selling distorts shareholder control." Regulation, vol. 31, no. 1, spring 2008, pp. 52+. Gale Academic OneFile, link.gale.com/apps/doc/A178080800/AONE?u=scottsdale hq&sid=bookmark-AONE&xid=18a9ea7. Accessed 11 Aug. 2022.

In the same way, at the casino ButtFarm was helpless, as there were always fake or borrowed cards available to prevent actual scarcity and kneecap his victory. Not to mention in the real world, such buys could occur outside of markets, referred to as "dark pools," and then more sales could happen on "lit" exchanges, further burying true price discovery.

Welborn, in his article, and (ape favorite) Dr. Trimbath, in her AMA with the subreddit, both reference a Bloomberg Markets article by Bob Drummond from April of 2006 called *The Corporate Voting Charade*. The article's header teases, "One share does not always equal one vote in the crazy math of proxy [voting] contests. When short sellers borrow stock, investor democracy can be a sham."

"Wall Street securities firms such as Goldman Sachs Group Inc., Merrill Lynch & Co. and Morgan Stanley lend shares from a central pool, and the brokerages don't attribute loans to the accounts of particular clients. While the small print in a typical brokerage contract says a customer's voting rights may be affected if the firm loans out stock, most brokerage customers likely don't even notice when short sellers borrow stock because their accounts typically list the same number of shares as before."

It's precisely what apes encountered during their proxy vote campaigns in both 2021 and 2022. They maxed out the vote count with ease.

There's a more timely blog from The American Prospect released shortly after the Game Stopped hearing, which criticizes these results:

"[Kenneth] Griffin noted, 'Institutional investors earn substantial returns from lending out shares, 25 or 30 percent.' He didn't point out that a gain for those investors is a loss for the borrowers, often big hedge funds. So their brokers commonly wink and do a 'locate,' not a borrow,[17] effectively saying, 'Yes, I know where the share is and can buy it when the time comes to deliver.' Except it doesn't work quite that way.

---

[17] The opinions of this author are theirs, and theirs alone.

The problem is worsened by off-exchange trading, including secret internal trading systems called 'dark pools' and ex-clearing trades inside or between cooperating brokers that evade DTCC clearing. Dark pools handle more than half of all trading, with most dark pools owned by the big prime brokers…. Beyond that, the SEC… is so weak, traders can roll over naked shorts and stay naked indefinitely."[18]

Back at the poker table, ButtFarm waited intently for napkin guy's time to expire, who had yet to draw a true king or even locate one. Yet, when finally pressed for the king by the dealer, the napkin guy mutters, "Uh. I'll fail to deliver."

Sally takes a few seconds to finish her coffee break before casually walking over to the table and slapping the napkin guy on the wrist. "Don't do that."

As a fine, SEC takes away napkin guy's smallest poker chip, a small price to pay for not losing his entire wager only a few hands ago. So now, napkin guy doesn't even need to find the king and already has a new stack of napkins at the ready.

He's not stupid, though. Napkin guy hands the dealer a $5 chip and asks for a few more singles in case he's fined again. Napkin guy sees ButtFarm furrow his brow and shouts over to him, "Nothing personal. It's just the cost of doing business."

Potato whispers, "There are cocktail napkins all over the place. This is nuts." The real issue is that the napkin guy isn't alone. Every table is trading with napkins by now. So long as the deck lacks its 52-card legitimacy, ButtFarm won't ever make a big win.

And that's when the poker games began to slow down, thanks to a handful of dealers being forced to accept napkins rather than actual cards into their decks.

---

[18] "The GameStop Mess Exposes the Naked Short Selling Scam." The American Prospect Blogs, 25 Feb. 2021, p. NA. Gale Academic OneFile, link.gale.com/apps/doc/A652986999/AONE?u=scottsdale_hq&sid=bookmark-AONE&xid=ece 7f46a. Accessed 11 Aug. 2022.

This impacts the casino, because they make money based on how many hands of poker get played every day. It turns out the Casino Del Stock Exchange isn't motivated by fairness so much as it is the pace of play.

In the modern-day broker's infamous payment for order flow system or PFOF, volume of transactions, rather than a dollar amount per transaction, is a money maker. The more transactions a broker can pass on to a market-making partner, for instance, the more it can charge that partner for those sales. Market makers and brokers made tons of money during the sneeze for this reason: volume.

Wanting to increase the rate of play, the analogous casino issues a new rule: cards will now exclusively be in napkin form, and the dealers will hold one actual card per napkin in their secure safe.

Now, the Casino Del can make even more money from increased plays, just like real-world brokers using computer entries over physical shares. The dealers in charge of the safe are instructed to maintain that flow rate by any means necessary. While the dealers are there out of fairness to the players, they're on the casino's payroll and are considered self-regulatory by Sally.

ButtFarm's odds of getting an exclusive hand of any card are totally out the window now as he looks down at his hand of comparably worthless napkins. He asks the dealer, "Is there any way I could have real cards, just so I know what I have is the real thing?"

The dealer shakes their head. "Sorry, we don't do that anymore." They begin the next hand.

Now, players who dash around to look for borrows are at a disadvantage to those who more quickly scribble napkin cards into existence. It becomes a game of dollars and sense as players are suddenly incentivized to take the napkin approach, even with the casino's wink and nod.

The spice must flow.

Of course, Sally does her best to penalize naked borrowers, but who can even tell who's acting nakedly? As long as there aren't too many fails to deliver, Sally will continue sipping her coffee and wait for more easily prosecutable crimes.

Cellar Boxing and Total Return Swapping

During the September weekend, when the Yahoo share count glitch was in its heyday, u/thabat managed to dig into the Wayback machine regarding a phenomenon called "cellar boxing."

On Sept. 11th, 2021, u/thabat garnered over 60k upvotes on the post, "I found the entire naked shorting game plan playbook posted on a forum in 2004."

The forum writer, Blurring, makes the following argument: as markets transitioned from prices at 1/8th's of a dollar to a decimal system, the lowest possible price for a share went from around sixteen cents to $0.0001, which Blurring refers to as the "cellar." Blurring suggests that market makers can use the cellar as a starting point for manipulation, especially when the difference between hundredths of a penny can result in spreads of 200% or more in profit, which would be harder to do between the previous eighths of a dollar.

Even more, Blurring posits that market makers could nakedly short companies into a cellar box and hold them hostage there to induce bankruptcy and delisting from the exchange, freeing the shorts of capital gains tax.

"A lot of management teams become overwhelmed with grief and guilt in regards to the huge increase in the number of shares issued and outstanding that have accumulated during their 'watch'.... [but] a huge number of resultant shares issued and outstanding is unavoidable[,] and often indicative of an astronomically high naked short position[,] and is nothing to be ashamed of."

u/missing_the_point_ adds on Sept. 12th, to another 20k upvotes: "A letter on the SEC's WEBSITE begg[ed] them to do their job in 2008, calling out naked shorting, FTDs, cellar boxing, and even suggesting the Secret Service get involved since it constitutes counterfeiting. We aren't the first to uncover any of it."

In the unearthed SEC comment, written by a John Drombosky, there are some eerie similarities to the postings of apes almost fifteen years later, including the allegation, "The way naked short selling is done, it constitutes counterfeiting of securities, since the broker/dealers who participate in this practice assure the victim-buyer that [']yes, the share exists,['] even if it's just an electronic marker in the buyer's account. It's a fake share that was created out of thin air. And the result when done en mass [sic], is to drive the price per share of the target company into the cellar."

Unlike naked shorting, which has been sparingly acknowledged by academic papers (and Melissa Lee during a June 2021 episode of Fast Money), cellar boxing is even more theoretical. And as u/derfmongol suggested during Superstonk's cellar boxing discovery period, "[it] only happens to penny stocks that are being traded at the lowest possible price of $0.0001. This will never happen with $GME."

But this retort highlights the biggest issue with naked shorting and cellar boxing. If this was a practice so sinister that blog posters and SEC commenters knew about it in 2004 and 2008, how popular might the practice have become two decades later, now that digital transaction volumes have ballooned, and computers or algorithms could induce a stock price freefall with newfound alacrity?

If cellar boxing was the goal for GameStop, it would mean the saga and company turnaround were even more unprecedented than anyone could have imagined. Never before had a company destined for the cellar box been turned around, much less into a billion-dollar entity.

For once, ButtFarm had a reason to hope after so many letdowns at his poker table. What had started as a simple hope to win some pocket change had unfurled into all-out combat against everyone to his right, left, and center, except for PotatoInAss, still rooting him on from a safe distance.

The next development in ButtFarm's story, and our allegory with cellar boxing, reverts to what ButtFarm remembered his neighbor muttering as he sat on top of the ragged brick-and-mortar stool. He politely taps that neighbor on his shoulder as the man busily draws a queen on the back of a wallet-sized photo of his grandson.

"Hey dude, why did you tell me not to sit here?"

The banker shrugs and turns to ButtFarm. "That chair's on its way out. Look at it. 'Brick-and-mortar retailer?' As soon as COVID hit, we knew it was done for."

ButtFarm looks down between his legs. "But it's not done for. I'm sitting on it."

The banker shrugs. "For now, but that doesn't change jack shit. Everyone else here knows it's as good as gone. We all have a side bet that they're going to toss out this chair!" He chuckles. "We're all so certain that that chair is on its way to the dumpster, everybody couldn't help chipping in, ya know? It's free money! I think the whole room's got a piece of the action."

ButtFarm studies his chair, which despite its poor outward appearance, has received some excellent upgrades thanks to a bit of quiet maintenance. For instance, it now has a comfortable kickstand built by the Cohen computer chair company, it's pivoted to a more forward-leaning angle, and even has a comfortable cushion of available cash under the seat.

ButtFarm meekly asks, "What if I like the chair?"

The banker rolls his eyes. "Oh, you'll exit the chair eventually. Your kind never sticks around."

ButtFarm looks over at a locked cabinet behind the cashier, where stacks upon stacks of poker chips are sitting in a container. It's not just little bets here and there but entire pensions, retirement accounts, and mutual funds from hard-working people outside the casino.

ButtFarm checks his remaining chips. If he sits in this chair for enough time, so many poker players will lose the side bet money that they'll be forced out of the casino. If that happens, fewer poker players might mean fewer cards his rivals could use during the next four-of-a-kind.

ButtFarm decides to long his ragged stool and commits to playing on it as long as his antes are affordable. In the PFOF casino, that could last forever.

Back here in the real world, if the cellar box did exist for GameStop, would all that money wagered against GameStop be known about? Probably not. Of all the hidden informational black holes that Superstonk's Horizon Telescope would hope to image, this remains one of the most elusive.

A public revelation of a short position got Melvin bludgeoned, and Citron, too, for that matter. If a position contains lots of risk or results from naked shorting, that's two additional reasons that a firm wouldn't want the public or their clients to be aware of it.

u/Criand released what came to be known as "The Theory of Everything," to the tune of over 30k upvotes and inclusion in the DD Library.[19] It was in this post that the Pomeranian offered the possibility that "Hedge Funds can enter into... swaps and get short exposure to the stock without directly shorting it. They can enter into tons of these swaps and create tons of synthetic shares without ever worrying about the short interest being reported."

Investopedia defines a total return swap as "a swap agreement in which one party makes payments based on a set rate.... The underlying asset, referred to as the reference asset, is usually an equity index, a basket of loans, or bonds. The asset is owned by the party receiving the set rate payment."

Swaps brought down Bill Hwang's Archegos Capital only months after the sneeze. As stated by the WSJ, "Using total return swaps instead of simply buying shares of companies provided two main benefits for Archegos. The use of these types of derivatives helped enable the firm to increase its leverage, in essence owning more of an asset or assets than its cash would have otherwise allowed it to. In addition, these swaps allow investors like Mr. Hwang to maintain their anonymity."

At the time of publication, Hwang has been arrested for the alleged practices at his hedge fund. If he was using the same tools as his colleagues at any tier of the

---

[19] In all fairness, the DD's full title is The Puzzle Pieces of Quarterly Movements, Equity Total Return Swaps, DOOMPs, IT CALLs, Short Interest, and Futures Roll Periods. Or, "The Theory of Everything."

financial food chain, could there be more weakness in the system? And who was on the other side of those swaps?

Essentially, if GameStop was the beginning of the end for Archegos, but Archegos didn't hold the GME short positions, who did? It was only problematic if the GameStop shorts hadn't closed. Apes were all but certain they hadn't.[20]

Shorts Never Closed (according to Superstonk)

Back inside the casino, ButtFarm wasn't the only gambler eyeing the cellar box after a few more hands had been dealt. The longer he sat on the brick-and-mortar stool, gamblers around the room began to glare at or outright ridicule him.

One gambler in particular eventually called over a cocktail waitress named Millicent Sarah Montez and handed her a big tip before pointing at ButtFarm.

Moments later, MSM was standing over ButtFarm, but she wasn't offering him a drink. Instead, she was sneering, "Hey kid, that chair's a bad bet. Better get out while you've still got some of that cash."

ButtFarm responded as he had before, "I like this chair, and it's the only one available."

MSM shrugs. "Guess that's why they call you the dumb money."

The verbal assaults from bribed cocktail servers and bots only increased as Butt-Farm held his position. Why did they all care so much where ButtFarm sat? They hadn't cared about ButtFarm's poker chips during 2008 when they all told Butt-Farm to hold while they all sold. They didn't care about ButtFarm's savings in

---

[20] Another theorized aspect of shorts not closing exists in what are referred to as DOOMPs, which according to Criand, are "deep out of the money PUTs. Like, bankruptcy-low bets. It's impossible that the stock would go this low. So rather, these were used as bankruptcy credit bets for the credit hedging." DOOMPs are a favorite of the wrinkliest of brained apes on Superstonk, and continue to reveal more about how shorts may have kicked the can over the course of 2021 especially. I include it here to fulfill the ape requests to do so.

2020 when they told ButtFarm times were hard while printing money into the inflationary stratosphere.

This was the media blitz that the GameStop HODL'ers suffered in 2021 and 2022, even as the stock price failed to drop anywhere close to $0.0001, or even Citron's promised $20. The question then was the same as it is now. Why was the media so wholly antagonistic toward GME?

Every week there seemed to be a new financial news segment that got cut short as soon as someone said something positive about the stock, only for fumbling explanations to show up the next day. Why did CNBC promote that Melvin had closed its position in a sponsored post on Twitter during the sneeze? Why would Entrepreneur re-post a Stock News article from September 2022, a full twenty months after the sneeze, with the headline, "The Worst Stock to Buy on Wall Street Right Now"?

Maybe they just disliked the stock. Maybe there were other motives. We'll never know.

Mark Cuban suggested in his AMA, "[The short's] goal is to never cover their short. But that would take the company going out of business or being delisted."

And according to the SEC, Cuban was right. Shorts didn't cover, at least during the sneeze: "Whether driven by a desire to squeeze short sellers and thus to profit from the resultant rise in price, or by belief in the fundamentals of GameStop, it was the positive [retail] sentiment, not [shorts] buying-to-cover, that sustained the weeks-long price appreciation of GameStop stock."

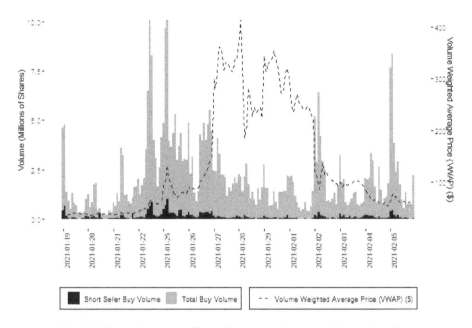

The SEC figure showing retail buy volumes pitted against miniature short buys.

The SEC's revelation that shorts never covered was a massive piece of news when the report debuted in October 2021, around the time of the DRS rise.

You would expect that with an even higher stock price, the buying-to-cover ratios would climb like they had on the 21st, 22nd, and 25th as the ticker ran up further and further. But instead, the ratio plummeted to nearly zero, potentially because positions were so untenable for shorts to close.

The next day, the buy button got turned off.

If there were hidden shorts, who had target prices of $0.0001 and had created mounds of nakedly borrowed shares, and then all of these shorts were deeply underwater as the price failed to dip below $80 after two years, might that still be a problem?

The short answer in the long history of the stock market is *actually not*. There would always be more cocktail napkins to continue selling against buy pressure (using our casino allegory), and the price would return to the fundamentals that inspired the massive short campaign with infinite time on hand.

It's this same calculus that ButtFarm began to realize as day turned to night inside the casino. If there was some way he could get real cards back into circulation, it would mean an end to napkin madness. He could avoid the market's reliance on the passage of time.

A neutral party up to this point, ButtFarm looked to the dealer for help. "I realize I can't have my cards from the safe, but I'd just like to see that they're there."

The dealer squinted at him, confused.

The Intermediaries

I think this is where I must offer (former young Bulgarian boy) Vlad Tenev an apology, words I never thought I'd say after yanking my hair out during the Game Stopped hearing back in February 2021.

Mr. Tenev, I apologize for personally blaming you for the buy button incident. While I personally believe you deserve blame for your app's many troubles, regulatory concerns, and capital requirement shortcomings, it is no longer my opinion that you were a villain at the center of the events of January 28th.

The drama surrounding capital requirements that day won't see the light of day, most likely. Thanks to the congressional report (and other forms of media, including a narrativized chapter of *The Antisocial Network*), we do know a few things about how it went down:

"The NSCC assessed a $3.7 billion collateral charge to Robinhood on January 28, 2021.... This charge, which ultimately prompted Robinhood's trading restrictions, had several components. The two largest components were the Value-at-Risk charge, which totaled $1.3 billion, and the Excess Capital Premium charge, which totaled $2.2 billion.... Robinhood had no visibility into the possibility of, much less the precise level of, Excess Premium Capital charges that it could be required to pay during the Meme Stock Market Event."

len

"Robinhood received a waiver of the largest component of its deposit requirement from the DTCC. Without this waiver, which Robinhood had no control over, the company would have defaulted."

The billions of dollars in capital requirements were a shock to many people with knowledge of the situation, especially inside Robinhood. When Robinhood was granted the fee waiver, saving the company, their fate was sealed, and the buy button had to be turned off against what was likely their PR team's better judgment.

The DTC wasn't only at the center of the buy button controversy, though. As apes learned more about the DTCC and their control over physical shares, they found the DTC and its subsidiaries appearing in more than one curious situation.

In steps the splividend and GameStop's statement.

PotatoInAss nudged ButtFarm, just as Casino management wheeled their secure cart across the room. Luckily, there were still people in charge who cared about legitimacy. The locked cage contained dice, cards, and more, which were routinely rotated to avoid cheaters with loaded dice or marked cards.

Potato tells ButtFarm, "They're going to replace the cards on a four-to-one basis. So if the players made too many napkin cards, they'll have to go get real cards again. There's no way out of it for the cheaters." ButtFarm nods and waits excitedly for the dealer to retrieve the decks from the safe.

Slowly but surely, ButtFarm receives his replacement cards, as does the banker to his left and the man to his left. But then, because cards had to be handed out to the rest of the room, the dealer inevitably runs out.

ButtFarm gets excited, realizing the infinite card liquidity is now at an end, and he can finally win a hand. But his excitement is quashed as the dealer frowns, turning to the other players. "Well, split your napkin cards into four pieces if you didn't receive the dividend."

The players smile and do so willingly, wiping sweat from their brows. ButtFarm is shocked and looks at the dealer. "The casino gave you the cards to hand out. You have to stick with the new cards."

The dealer looks at the casino worker, still pushing around his cart, and explains, "The system wouldn't work if we did that." To which the casino worker adds, "We don't want that to happen!"

ButtFarm's jaw drops again. What kind of system was this, where the fairness of the game came second to the survival of a broken system? Something had to change, but what could ButtFarm do about it in addition to what he'd already done?

Dr. Susanne Trimbath's book *Naked, Short, and Greedy* is a favorite amongst apes. A full year before the sneeze, Dr. Trimbath detailed the struggles of companies, both large and small, throughout the early 21st century as they're bombarded by alleged naked short-selling, allegedly fraudulent proxy voting, and alleged share counterfeiting.

While the book itself is a fascinating read, its eighteenth chapter offers a possible solution against alleged complicity by intermediaries, summarized by Trimbath's publisher, Spiramus Press: "A diamond mining firm, CMKM, orders a 'cert pull' to get all the company's shares out of the DTC. It reveals how many phantom shares are in circulation as a multitude of investors — dubbed the UnShareholders — are left holding the empty bag.... But the evidence is there: brokers assigned phantom shares to their most vulnerable customers while getting real certificated shares for themselves and favored clients."

In the case of CMKM, the lack of action by the market's regulators, whether the DTC, SEC or someone else, leads not to the downfall of regulators or naked short sellers but a massive segment of the shareholders, who are thrown under the bus. "Before it shuts down, the UnShareholder project reveals the same [CMKM] circumstances applied to over 100 investors for 21 more companies across 15 brokerage firms."

In the splividend, GameStop confirmed it had handed the dealer all of the playing cards necessary, but the dealer appeared to do what would preserve the system's present functionality rather than addressing deeper risks, hence the splits across various brokers.

Again, that's just how it appeared. After months of petitioning regulatory agencies and pressing brokers on split versus dividend, apes could only groan allegations and continue buying, holding, and DRS'ing.

ButtFarm, sitting at the poker table, had one final option. He asked the casino employee, "If I'm not allowed to hold the physical cards held in the safe, can I at least have them transferred to another safe instead?"

The casino employee radioed the question to a manager, and after a short discussion over his earpiece, and a lack of protest by the dealer, he nodded. "Sure. But you won't be able to play your cards as easily when you do that."

ButtFarm accepts, despite that caveat. Every time a hand is dealt, ButtFarm folds but retains any aces he receives. He watches the safe behind the dealer, where his cards are removed and moved into a separate safe next door.

When ButtFarm draws enough aces and folds enough times, he watches confusion break out at the first safe. The casino employee returns to the table, admitting, "There aren't any aces left in the room's safe."

ButtFarm looks at the ace in his hand and then at the napkin aces in the hands of his fellow players, as well as the stacks of aces lined up around the poker hall. On the table, there are even three aces in their community hand.

ButtFarm announces, "I'd like to use one of my aces in the second safe on this hand, if you don't mind."

The casino employee shrugs and walks over to the casino safe. He hands the ace to ButtFarm, who plays it to make a four-of-a-kind.

When the other players attempt to play their aces to force another push, Butt-Farm protests. "Those aren't real aces." To which the men collectively reply, "Sure they are!"

ButtFarm holds firm. "No, they're not because I own all the real aces that your napkin aces were based on." The men fume as their aces can't be accepted by the dealer, who, at long last, pushes a pile of chips toward ButtFarm.

The men protest to the dealer, "This is unfair! You're not playing by our rules!" To which the dealer whispers, "I can't anymore. If I did, the other gamblers would lose faith in our casino and stop playing here."

The banker beside ButtFarm growls, "You really should get off that stool now that you've won so much. Take the win and go home."

ButtFarm looks toward the cellar box full of tendies and grins. "No. I don't think I will."

Like a party on the deck of the Titanic after the iceberg struck, but before the ship began to sink, ButtFarm glances around the room at the other gamblers holding aces, not realizing the music was about to stop. Whether their napkin cards were nakedly created or connected back and forth through the poker room's chain of custody spider web, a non-fungible threat was finally fissile.

The game finally belonged to ButtFarm. And it was now the "experts" who were the suckers.

Conclusion

Maybe Alfred Hitchcock's already-exploded time bomb started a fire, and maybe that fire did burn half the city. You might still wonder, so what? A generation removing itself from the stock market isn't threatening to the rest of the public, especially when their combined net worths scrape the bottom of the barrel.

But what would happen if every legitimate GameStop share was accounted for, and neither brokerages nor nakedly short borrowers could undo the damage without being forced to buy from apes? Smells like MOASS to me, or at least some far more expensive share prices in the short term.

Either the hypothesized shorts in search of the cellar box will lose big, or their survival will bring doubt to a market system with seemingly infinite liquidity.

More than anything, I hope the poker allegory shows how desperate retail investors are for transparency to avoid all this guesswork and speculation. Why won't the intermediary just stay on the phone with me, ya know?

For those who say this is only a GME or meme stock problem, I'll return to Bob Drummond's article one last time: "The… Securities Transfer Association, a trade group for stock transfer agents, reviewed 341 shareholder votes in corporate contests in 2005. It found evidence of overvoting — the submission of too many ballots — in all 341 cases."

If that's still the case, could counterfeits, naked borrows, or something worse stand underneath the entire house of cards?

Just like during the sneeze and our financial crises, when something bad happens, the culprits will tell us:

This was a one-in-a-million event that we couldn't have planned for!

Everyone else was doing it, so we had to join or lose our jobs!

We just don't like the stock!

However, Reddit didn't nakedly short shares, gamble money on guaranteed winnings, or lie to their clients about share legitimacy.

Apes just bought, held, and DRS'd.

33: Final Update (For Now)

Like an arcade game asking DO YOU WISH TO CONTINUE, apes were madly scrambling for their cup of tokens, desperate to keep the game going.

2021 and 2022 were roller-coasters of emotion, full of peaks and valleys. 2023 started off relatively quiet, in comparison. Sometime shortly after the splividend, it was clear to the apes that they'd entered the endgame. What remained was a war of attrition.

It's for this reason that this volume comes to its conclusion here. The Superstonk roller-coaster period was one of discovery, survival, and debate. At some point, the sub traded that frenetic growth for quiet determination. No longer were FUD campaigns blossoming with each passing week, and no longer were new DD's landing on r/all. It was minor corrections here and there as the hive-mind prepared for final battle.

Superstonk has entered their endgame.

For u/OfficialRedditMan, their journey here had taken thirteen years, starting back in 2008. Their post on August 9th drew a thousand upvotes and reflected just how wide the Superstonk movement had grown in the year since the sneeze.

"This ape marched, fought, and protested during occupy Wallstreet after '08 in 2011 and [ape] need to tell you something… / It[']s a whole lot easier to DRS in the A/C."

As RedditMan shared with me, "I feel [Occupy] was proactively snuffed out[,] but once an idea is born it isn't easy to kill. The same spirit certainly goes on with DRS but in a much more effective way. This time instead of rage, the 99% came with smarts. Playing Wallstreet's own game as opposed to shouting at clouds…. DRS is going back to the core of investing before all the side bets got thrown in."

And the DRS numbers would only continue to climb. The march to lock the float, an afterthought only a year prior when the DRS campaign launched, was no longer out of reach. And users endlessly speculated what might happen when the cards were down.

The answer? No one knew. But they did try to warn us.

u/onceuponanutt would post, "Hey r/all, don't say we didn't warn you" with a series of GameStop's most promising fundamentals.

And it wasn't just the general public that Redditors attempted to warn either. Reddit prolonged their love/hate relationship with regulators, both their only hope for salvation and their most frustrating "frenemy."

Jon Stewart, a lurker on the subreddit, hosted an interview with SEC Chair Gary Gensler in October 2022, the podcast component of Jon's show, *The Problem With Jon Stewart*.

Jon had made his foray into the Reddit world with an AMA in March of 2022. "Starting an AMA. Was gonna do it in WSB and cross post SuperStonks… but apparently that is heresy. This is why we can't have nice things. See ya on Reddit!!!"

In the post, Jon opined on several relevant topics and some not-so-relevant ones as well.

"By the way, to no particular question: Yes, I have done it on weed."

The Redditors loved Jon, not only because he drew a spotlight to their causes but also because he had the insider's view of the situation. At one time, Jon's brother was the COO of the New York Stock Exchange.

So when Jon's show featured Gary Gensler, who Jon had previously interviewed, Superstonk leaped at the opportunity to get the SEC's opinion on direct registration, and they got their foot in the door.

Stewart: "I think that direct registration is trying to find a way to address maybe these larger naked shorting, or you know, what they perceive as the lack of transparency. Wouldn't that bring some order or transparency?"

Gensler: ".... I think that the companies... the GameStop's and the others, are already registered. So the nature of your question I'd have to better understand..."

Stewart: "I think what they're saying is that it's a movement, and it is a question that came from the Reddit community, that the movement is to directly register shares that are bought under the name of the person who buys them, the individual. Not the broker."

Gensler: "... The majority of shares in the US are held in what's called street name.... And I don't know if [direct registration] would help.... And I'm going to ask staff about this, whether it would help with regard to short selling."

u/lovely-day-outside posted to over 10,000 upvotes, "Gary Gensler completely dodges the DRS question on Jon Stewart podcast — goes immediately to just talking about 'Street Name' only." The thread quickly became Superstonk's arena to bash Gensler.

u/1017GildedFingerTips: "Jon actually asked it, what a saint. Fuckin crickets from Gary when he said it too. Somehow he doesn't know the effect but instantly knew Reddit was the one that proposed the question? That fuckin right Gare Bear?"

u/PermitNo1490: "Jon, this is your question now: Reddit wants to direct register all the shares of GameStop because they believe counterfeit shares have been created through naked shorting. What happens when all the shares are removed from [intermediaries] and there is still volume of trades?"

Almost a full year later, Gary Gensler himself would Tweet, "As an individual investor, you typically have several ways to hold the securities that you buy or own, including: Street Name, Physical Certificate, [or] Direct Registration" alongside a link to an SEC Investor Bulletin on "Holding Your Securities."

Back on January 25th, 2021, u/Creative_alternative asked in a GME thread, "Do we collectively have 2.75 billion dollars floating around if they (shorts) do double down?" The answer in October 2022 was a resounding yes.

u/SiffKopp posted to almost 7,000 upvotes, "Individual investors are currently at ~83.3 million GME shares DRSed. / Current price is ~$27.6 / That[']s

$2,299,080,000. / 2.3 Billion Dollars worth of shares are currently DRSed. / Do you even realize how amazing that is?"

Direct registration — and our financial regulators finding out about it well ahead of a potential financial crisis — wasn't the only source of momentum for GameStop in late 2022, nor was it arguably the most important. Superstonk's investors believed in fundamentals. GameStop was putting the "fun" back in fundamentals, finally making good on Burry's years-old criticisms that the company was falling behind in the gaming world.

It was rather late at night in late September when I found myself on Discord. Weeks prior, just after the release of the GMErica NFT collection — GameStop's first release on their own marketplace — I had ventured over to the Cyber Crew NFT page and finally made my first Cyber Crew purchase. I'd heard about Cyber Crew a few months prior to September 2022, back when the splividend and BBBY had everyone's attention. Luckily, the collection prices had fallen a bit since then.

In late July, u/BuzzMonkey asked, "Holy shit, what's going on with Cyber Crew prices on the marketplace? They blew up!!" Six Cyber Crew NFTs were in their post image, and almost 3,000 upvotes were added to their hype.

u/onceuponanutt added the next day to another 2,500 upvotes: "In case anyone missed the most tit-jacking news since the beta marketplace dropped, here it is again — we have offical [sic] confirmation of an immersive, high-quality, blockchain-based metaverse utilizing crypto and NFTs within multiple economies. Here are some stills from just one group — Cyber Crew."

The initial attention around Cyber Crew gathered when it was revealed that the group had designed GameStop's astronauts that occupied the NFT marketplace's home screen for so long. But that wasn't enough to catapult the Crew above the early winners of the marketplace, namely Metaboy. That came with their utility.

Built with 3-D rendering programs used by the largest gaming companies, Cyber Crew assets quickly gained hype as the existing NFTs surged past $1,000 each in the following weeks. Throughout October 2022, the collection would transact over a million dollars, quickly becoming routine for them, and at a time when non-GME marketplaces had crashed from 2021 peaks.

When I looked into Cyber Crew, I found something I had never seen before in the NFT space: utility and potentially unlimited future value. At a time when film studios were deleting digital "purchases" of movies and gaming add-ons were non-transferrable, here was a platform being constructed around truly owning one's digital assets across multiple platforms.

As Cyber Crew would repeatedly post and tweet, #OwnYourAssets.

Cyber Crew wouldn't be the foundational player, just the first to the starting line. That late September evening, I was on the Kiraverse Discord server, where the dev team had organized a playtest for thirty or forty of us. I watched with awe as avatars in skinsuits leaped and bounded around a test map that resembled *Call of Duty's* Shipment. A poorly-blurred GameStop logo on their website hinted at the partnership that would emerge in early October between the two.

When I tuned in to another surprise playtest the next night, it was even more intriguing. The devs took the viewers to their battle royale map, a beautiful and sprawling environment with lighting and design that rivaled the best of *Fortnite* and *Apex Legends*, two similar games I had played in the past but then lost interest in. And a Cyber Crew Clone popped into the avatar slot, rather than the avatars they'd shown the previous night.

"Whoops," the dev muttered, quickly swapping the skin back out. "You guys weren't supposed to see that." But the damage had been done, or whatever the opposite of damage would be in that scenario, because it led to more hype, the fuel of the NFT universe.

The Cyber Crew Discord channel cheered the accidental reveal, which they'd also suspected for some time. Suddenly, it all became clear: in tandem with GameStop, Kiraverse could be one of the first large games built in the metaverse, and assets from the GME NFT marketplace would be usable in it, a fact which was later confirmed.

In tandem, Cyber Crew, Kiraverse, and other groups like Betty Boop and Metaboy began their own releases of new avatars, airdrops, and more, some of which included accessories like weapons and vehicles, 3-D files built for a gaming environment.

The Kiraverse devs explained that week in another stream, "(We wanted to create a gaming world where you own the assets you win, and if you want to assign those a value and trade them, we'll let you do it in the marketplace using our currency)."

This play style is known as play-to-earn and had precedent in games like *Gods Unchained*, also built on the Immutable Exchange, which later connected to the GameStop marketplace. But play-to-earn was only starting its rise at this moment, and even the top P2E games like *Tamadoge* and *Axie* didn't yet rival the *Fortnite*'s of the world.

Kiraverse teased exciting vehicles, crazy movement mechanics, and all the makings of a hit game. Matches allowed for wagering on one's own or in a team, but not in a way that a player might be gambling anything more than in-game currency to do so, or violating present securities laws for that matter. Owners of Kira NFTs would be able to rent their avatars to players to use in-game as well, according to the devs, adding to the NFT's overall value.

Experts studying the addictiveness of gaming have never seen such a combination of excitement, community, and high-stakes wagering. GameStop's Web3 experiment will either crash and burn or deserve a surgeon general's warning. And there won't be an in-between.

The fundamentals finally hit home in March 2023, when GameStop reported a quarterly profit of $50 million, its first time in years.

u/DailyShawarma: "GameStop has become profitable. Shorts are fucked."

We conclude not with financially ruined investors or young people bathing in tendies. Rather, this is a cliffhanger. And if GameStop hasn't conquered our world at the moment you're reading this, you still have time to join r/Superstonk.

Didn't you know? The best time to be alive in human history is now.

Afterword

Indubitably, in an online forum with daily updates, ongoing storylines, and real-life character arcs, there is not only a handful but an infinitely continuous series of deserving stories that I didn't get into here.

Whether for reasons of brevity, story flow, or because said threads had been debunked, determined to be FUD, or hadn't yet reached their true potential at the time of publishing, I take full responsibility for missing any of apes' favorite moments. And, I apologize to apes who feel that these topics deserved chapters — or entire volumes, in the case of the DD library — devoted to such notoriety. I sincerely hope I'll have the opportunity to revisit crucial threads that I missed in this book's sequel.

Nevertheless, there are a handful of topics I can't leave out before we part ways:

EVER EVERGRANDE

For the majority of 2021, and even into 2022, the Chinese real estate giant Evergrande found itself in freefall, thanks in part to its "ghost cities" that were left uninhabited. Being one of China's largest entities while also having investors of all sizes from all across the globe, Redditors chomped at the bit, waiting for the day when Evergrande would default, declare bankruptcy, and leave their international shareholders holding the bag.

Those days came and went, and very little came of it.

TOMORROW, AND TOMORROW, AND TOMORROW

First, a joke due to excitement building each day of 2021, and then a prescription as excitement turned to patience at the end of that year; it soon became the widely accepted result that MOASS is tomorrow. Always.

Starting in June 2021 with less than a hundred upvotes, u/Pharago began posting the meme of starfish Peach from 2003's *Finding Nemo*, as she sticks to the wall of the fishbowl shouting, "Today's the day!"

As Pharago shared with me, "MOASS is inevitable, and I've got some wrinkles, and it means that every day is the day…. There is even the chance that some idiot is gonna trip on some cables at [some hedge fund] and launch the rocket."

But there's more to it than that, especially in the wake of a dissociated subreddit identity replaced by a colorful ensemble. "There is the occassional [sic] comment somedays from someone that goes along the lines of 'I needed this today,' [which] is why I keep doing it."

u/Parsnip is another evergreen user, posting for the Diamantenhände "sub subreddit," where they share the daily price of GME on the German exchange, starting in the very early morning or even late at night, in American time zones.

Users join from all over the world to toast the gathering with a series of good morning's all around, covering all seven continents of the globe, tenuously watching the price action to get their fill and to, of course, watch for MOASS.

Then there's u/Raven5150, who daily posts a meme from an old Bernie Sanders fundraiser with the caption, "I am once again asking for GME to moon so I can stop waking up at 2:45 AM everyday." To many of the early risers fresh off viewing the Diamantenhände feed, Raven is another constant.

Raven's personal take on the GME saga? "We never chose where we cast our first shadow, but our reflections are always our choice."

BUILDINGS WITH LIGHTS ON

There were some slow weeks in this saga, especially prior to the accusations of international securities fraud, purple circle campaigns, and NFT eruptions. What filled those gaps included buildings with lights on.

Almost every week, if there was a downtown building that housed a major bank or hedge fund, and that building had more lights on than those around it, users assumed that it was due to their employees being forced to work around the clock to try to escape the mortal wound that had been dealt the company.

Eventually, bank buildings and hedge fund headquarters alike went dark at the appropriate time each evening, but Superstonk still suggested that the employees may just be working in the dark to evade suspicion.

If only there was a way to see through those windows! And yeah, that happened too. Just once.

In a since-removed post, jokingly re-enacted in a gif, u/_MonkeeInTheSky peeked into the windows of Citadel's (then Chicago-based) headquarters with a drone, where they caught an employee pacing the office in the middle of the night.

That video immediately went viral, almost as immediately as it was removed for violating the Reddit terms of service, in addition to several other regulations and laws. According to the response that Drone Guy received, it wasn't just the mods who had taken notice of the video.

In April of 2022, Drone Guy returned with this post: "Drone ape here — Saw a post today and several comments asking about what happened to me and where I went. I was forced into retirement by a three-letter federal agency back in Jan[uary]. I'll eventually write more about that whole experience, but for now I'm lying low. See you apes on the moon."

RICK OF SPADES

The abbreviation IYKYK (if you know, you know) is one I've always thought was a mouthful and never expected it to hit the mainstream.

When it comes to u/Rick_of_Spades, IYKYK.

If you don't, then know that Rick's inclusion in this book is by popular demand. Extremely popular demand. And the video that Rick posted to Superstonk is not safe for work. Or life in general, by some users' accounts.

u/Walruzuma asked, "Anyone else choose not to watch u/Rick_of_Spades… ?"

u/ButtFarm69 answered, "Don't worry, I watched it multiple times for you all."

IT'S NOT A MEME ANYMORE

Twice throughout 2022, coming up on nearly two years since the sneeze, the term meme stock was stubbornly rampant in not only the mainstream media but also two parties that were supposed to give retail traders slightly more respect. Both instances led to overwhelming scorn from Redditors.

First, the SEC produced a series of videos and quizzes as a part of their June 2022 announcement, "SEC Launches Game Show-Themed Public Service Campaign."

In the SEC's main video, three retail traders compete in a *Press Your Luck* style game show, where each makes poor decisions on trades ranging from "Celebrity Endorsements" to "Tips from your Uncle." When a trader selects the square "Meme Stocks," his cash disappears through a hole in the counter, and he's slammed with a pie in the face to great ridicule.

u/Onebadmuthajama responded to over 4,000 upvotes, "The SEC calls us meme investors, and our stocks meme stocks. I think it's time we call them meme regulators, and meme politicians."

Twitter user @etaleibovitz18 added fuel to the fire with their Freedom of Information Act request to the SEC, discovering the agency had allegedly spent no less than $300,000 (of taxpayer money, most likely) on the ad and the advertising campaign.

But our regulators wouldn't be the only target of rage from the increasingly knowledgeable and financially lethal retail cohort. Fidelity, once more, chose to step into the line of fire.

On LinkedIn the morning of October 26th, 2022, Fidelity posted the since-deleted "Halloween's Hottest Investor Costumes" to their social media pages, ripping on 2022's social media trend of making costume packaging to resemble real-life people.

One of these costumes was called "Meme Stock Guy" and featured a basement dweller type with spilled popcorn and a gamer headset, likely representing AMC and GME, respectively. On its own, the image was everything that Redditors had despised for so long, but that wasn't all.

Unbelievably, Fidelity chose to include a purple circle on the character's phone screen. The post was gone by nightfall.

FIGURE 6 OF THE GAMESTOP REPORT

Figure 6 from the SEC's GameStop report appears not once but twice over the course of this book, and for a good reason. It's the most transparent look behind the scenes that we have on what happened the week of the sneeze.

The bar chart is referred to as Figure 6 in the agency report and has been the source of much challenge as I researched this book. I filed my first Freedom of Information Act request as early as September 2022 for more information on the data in the chart, which is pixelated and difficult to read.

That first request was blocked on the following grounds:

"We have determined to withhold records that may be responsive to your request under 5 U.S.C. § 552(b)(4) and (8), for the following reasons:

— Exemption 4 protects confidential commercial or financial information that (a) is customarily treated as private by the submitter and (b) was provided to the Commission under an assurance of confidentiality; and

— Exemption 8 protects from disclosure, records contained in or related to examination, operating, or condition reports prepared by, on behalf of, or for the use of an agency responsible for the regulation or supervision of financial institutions.

Please be advised that we have considered the foreseeable harm standard in preparing this response."

u/jhw528 was nice enough to share their calculations with me, wherein they used the imperfect method of counting pixel-by-pixel of each graph section. JHW estimated a "shitty count" of around 30 million shares represented by orange bars.

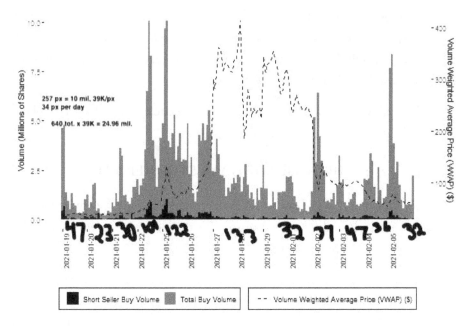

With a new request in hand, some eight weeks after my first attempt, the SEC was able to provide me with a higher resolution version of Figure 6, and that was it.

I struggled to count pixel-by-pixel again, but my count was rough at best, and I ended up with an estimate near 25 million, well short of the shares necessary to escape short interest of over a hundred percent.

T-MINUS TO LIFTOFF

Redditors continue to wonder how long it might take to lock the entire GameStop float. While various theories have been put forth, from one to many years, the slow march toward a float lock continues to find support in updates from GameStop quarterly earnings reports.

GameStop announced in their 2023 10-K more detail than ever before.

"As of March 22, 2023, there were 197,058 record holders of our Class A Common Stock. Excluding the approximately 228.7 million shares of our Class A Common Stock held by Cede&Co on behalf of the Depository Trust & Clearing Corporation (or approximately 75% of our outstanding shares), approximately

76.0 million shares of our Class A Common Stock were held by record holders as of March 22, 2023 (or approximately 25% of our outstanding shares)."

For the first time in months, this added language spurred Redditors to reconsider the value of "book" shares versus "plan" shares within their own Computershare accounts, no less. The game was far from over.

Acknowledgments

Many, many people have been an immense help to me in this book. First, I'd like to thank the many members of Reddit for speaking their minds time and time again, and I would like to ask that they improve their grammar before the next volume in the series.

Back when my own stock was valued at a couple dollars, and my writing career was being cellar boxed by the effects of COVID, there were still people who supported me, including but not limited to my wife, my family, and many of my friends too. Kate, Laurie, David, Michael, James, Joey, Alex, Dallas, Jim, Chelsea, Kevin, and Thomas, thank you all!

A big thank you to my agent, Kimberly, and the Rudy Agency, for their persistence in bringing this book to Histria Books.

I, of course, have to thank Luma44 and the ape historian for their advice as I wrote. Anyone quoted here took the time to chat with me and trusted that I wouldn't warp their words for this production. I hope I got that right.

Additional thanks to Malcolm Gladwell, whose many books and podcasts, alongside those of Michael Lewis, gave me the confidence to write a book about social movements.

Much gratitude is due to the band DragonForce because I jammed out to them during the sleepless nights writing this volume, especially during the sneeze.

And much thanks to u/Introcade for sending Citron's video to me after it had been removed.

To the members of Superstonk and WSB, may you have infinite tendies in Valhalla.

You are highly regarded.

References

"Historical Price Lookup." GameStop, news.gamestop.com/stock-information/historical-price-lookup. Accessed 1 Jan. 2021.

Jakab, Spencer. *The Revolution That Wasn't: GameStop, Reddit, and the Fleecing of Small Investors*. Penguin Business, 2022.

Mezrich, Ben. *The Antisocial Network: The True Story of a Ragtag of Amateur Investors, Gamers, and Internet Trolls Who Brought Wall Street to Its Knees*. Grand Central Publishing, 2021.

Our Story. www.computershare.com/us/our-history. Accessed 1 Sept. 2022.

Rogozinski, Jaime. *WallStreetBets: How Boomers Made the World's Biggest Casino for Millennials*, 2020. Kindle file.

Yahoo GME Price History. finance.yahoo.com/quote/GME/history?p=GME. Accessed 1 July 2022.

Author Bio

In addition to his work as an author, Rob Smat is a writer and director of feature films. His work includes *The Last Whistle* (2019) and *Walkout* (2024), and upcoming books include *The Wedding March* and the action/sci-fi novel, *Backfill*. Under his Reddit moniker u/MadSmatter, Rob has made the site's esteemed front page a handful of times, thanks to posts about independent filmmaking, green bean casserole, and of course, GameStop.

Rob was the keynote speaker for the American Heart Association's Go Red convention, a finalist for the Writer Guild of America's Collyer fellowship, and one of the youngest filmmakers to license a film to Netflix. He grew up near GameStop's Grapevine headquarters in North Texas and now lives in the Southwest with his wife, Kate, and their labradoodle, Chewbacca.

On the GameStop NFT Marketplace, he can be found at <nft.gamestop.com/user/smatfilms>.

HISTRIA BOOKS

GAUDIUM PUBLISHING
BOOKS TO CHALLENGE AND ENLIGHTEN

OLIVIA GOODREAU

BUT SHE LOOKS FINE

FROM ILLNESS TO ACTIVISM

NETWORKS RISING

THINKING TOGETHER IN A FLATTER WORLD

CHRISTOPHER BURNS

DOUG GRECO

TO FIND A KILLER.
THE HOMOPHOBIC MURDERS OF NORMA AND MARIA HURDATO

Firas Jumaah and Charlotta Turner

RESCUED FROM ISIS
TERROR

How a University Professor organized a Commando mission to Rescue Her Doctoral Student from Isis-Controlled Iraq

MACRON Unveiled
THE PROTOTYPE FOR A NEW GENERATION OF WORLD LEADERS
ALAIN LEFEBVRE

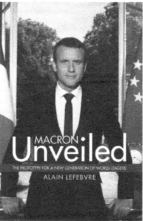

NIKLAS HAGEBACK

THE DOWNFALL
OF CHINA OR CCP 3.0

FOR THESE AND OTHER GREAT BOOKS VISIT
HISTRIABOOKS.COM